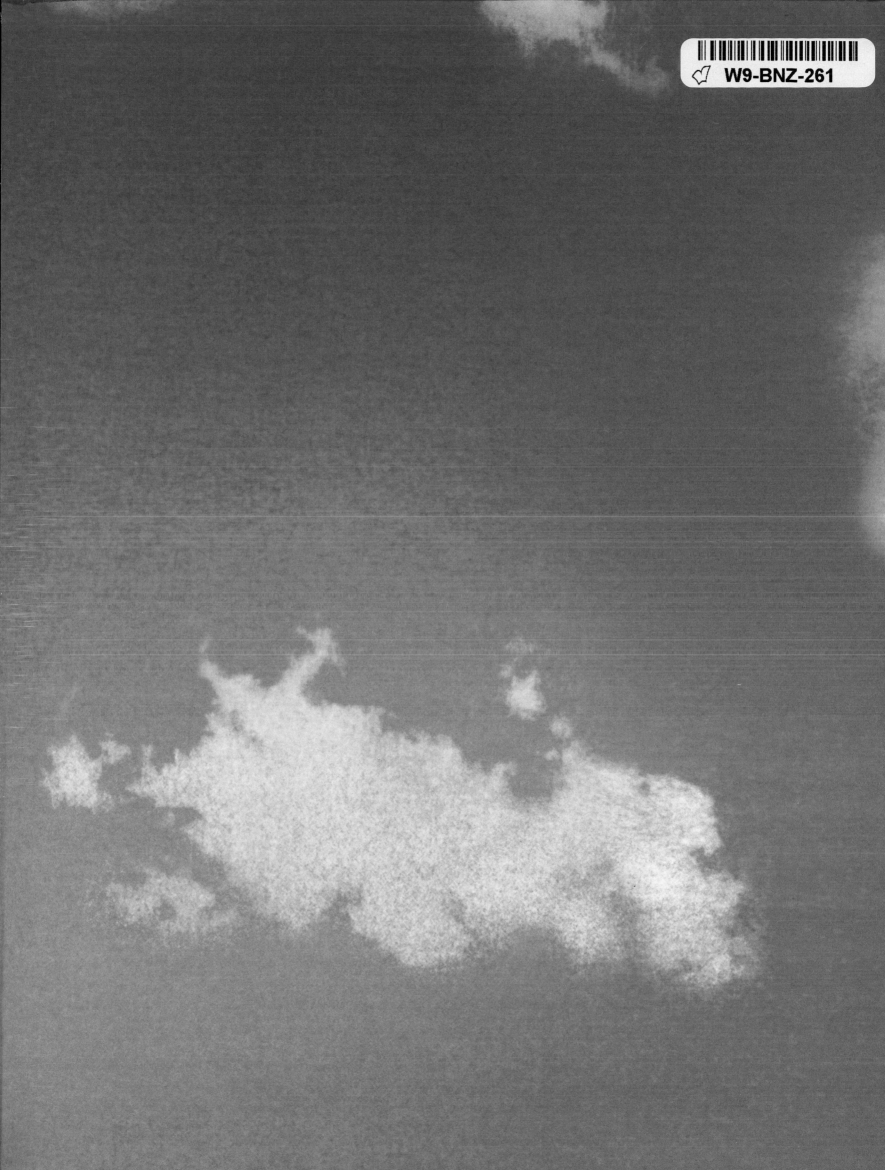

Edited by Simon Hilton
Publishing Coordinator: Tristan de Lancey

Grand Central Publishing
Hachette Book Group
1290 Avenue of the Americas, New York, NY 10104
grandcentralpublishing.com
twitter.com/grandcentralpub

Published by arrangement with Thames & Hudson, Ltd., London

First Edition: October 2018

Grand Central Publishing is a division of Hachette Book Group, Inc. The Grand
Central Publishing name and logo is a trademark of Hachette Book Group, Inc.

The publisher is not responsible for websites (or their content) that are not
owned by the publisher.

Library of Congress Cataloging-in-Publication Data has been applied for.

ISBN: 978-1-5387-4715-5

Printed and bound in China by C&C Offset Printing Co. Ltd.

imagine
john
yoko

by John Lennon & Yoko Ono

with contributions from
the people who were there

GRAND
CENTRAL
PUBLISHING

contents

8-track, 1-inch, studio master tape boxes for the *Imagine* album,
compiled at Record Plant, New York, 4 July 1971.

Previous pages:

1   *Imagine* album cover; polaroid by Yoko. St Regis hotel, New York, July 1971.

4–5   Filming *Imagine* – John & Yoko sitting at one of five plinths of George Adamy's plexiglas artwork *Month of June*, 1970, at 77 Water St on the corner of Front St and Old Slip, New York, 4 September 1971.

6–7   Filming *Imagine*, 'Don't Count The Waves'; Tittenhurst, 21 July 1971.

8–9   Filming *Imagine*, 'I Don't Wanna Be A Soldier Mama I Don't Wanna Die'; East Coast Memorial, Battery Park, New York, 4 September 1971.

10–11   Filming *Imagine* – John & Yoko on the Staten Island Ferry with the World Trade Center (left) and the Statue of Liberty (right) in the background, 10 September 1971.

preface
by yoko ono

This world is separated into two industries: one being the War Industry and the other being the Peace Industry. People who are in the War Industry are totally unified by their ideas. They want to make war, kill, and make money. There is no argument there. They just get on with their objectives. Therefore, in that sense, they are a tremendously powerful force.

But the people in the Peace Industry are like me: they are idealists and perfectionists. So they cannot agree with each other. They're always arguing in the pursuit of the 'perfect idea'. They are asking themselves and each other 'What is the best way to get peace?

Of course, it's MY way. What's wrong with YOUR way is that....'

But instead of doing that, if we can only try to accept each other, forgive the differences and appreciate each other...because the fact is that all of us are in the Peace Industry.

There are some things about the War Industry that we can get some help from. And we should remember that.

If one billion people in the world think peace, we'll get peace. You may think: 'Well, how are we going to get one billion people in the world to think PEACE?'

Remember, each one of us has the power to change the world. Power works in mysterious ways. We don't have to do much. Visualize the domino effect and just start thinking PEACE.

It's time for action. The action is PEACE.

The people who all worked on IMAGINE were Peace People and it was so enlightening and exciting all the way through to be one of them.

Thank you, thank you, thank you.

We are family.

Imagine...

I love you!

Yoko Ono Lennon
New York City
18 February 2018

Yoko at her white Steinway 'O' grand piano on her 85th birthday. The Dakota building, New York, 18 February 2018.

Wonsaponatime there was two Balloons called Jock and Yono. They were strictly in love-bound to happen in a million years. They were together man. Unfortunatimetable they both seemed to have previous experience – which kept calling them one way oranother (you know howitis). But they battled on against overwhelming oddities, includo some of there beast friends. Being in love they cloong even the more together man – but some of the poisonessmonster of outrated buslodedshithrowers did stick slightly and they occasionally had to resort to the drycleaners. Luckily this did not kill them and they werent banned from the olympic games. They lived hopefully ever after, and who could blame them.

John Lennon (1968), *Skywriting by Word of Mouth* (1986)

Two Virgins drawing by John Lennon, 1968.

indica

John: There was a sort of underground clique in London. John Dunbar had an art gallery in London called Indica. I got the word that this amazing woman was putting on a show and there was going to be something about people in black bags, and it was going to be a bit of a happening. So I went down to a preview, the night before it opened. I went in and I was looking at it and I was astounded. I thought it was fantastic. I got the humour in her work immediately. There was a fresh apple on a stand – this was before Apple – and it was 200 quid to watch the apple decompose.

Near the door when you went in, there was a ladder which led to a painting which was hung on the ceiling – a blank canvas with a chain with a spyglass hanging on the end of it. I climbed the ladder. You look through the spyglass and in tiny little letters it says 'YES'. So it was positive. I felt relieved. It's a great relief when you get up the ladder and you look through the spyglass and it doesn't say 'no' or 'fuck you' or something. It said 'YES'.

Yoko: It was almost like a Zen meeting. My idea was for people to climb up a long, long ladder and just go on climbing up and then finally reach the ceiling and you look at the painting with the magnifying glass, and it says 'YES' in tiny little letters. That 'YES' was like an answer to him.

John: Because it was positive, it said 'YES'; I thought, okay, it's the first show I've been to that's said something warm to me. So then I decided to see the rest of the show, and that's when we met. If it had said 'no' I would have walked out.

Yoko: I was an outcast in the avant-garde because the rest of the avant-garde was trying to alienate the audience, trying to play mean and spiteful games in the world. But I was trying to say 'YES'. I was trying to communicate. I was trying to say 'love' and 'peace' and 'yes'. And that's how we met, you see? It was almost like I was saying 'YES' to John, you know?

John: That's to me...it was like a personal – well I guess whoever reads it would feel that, but I really felt it was a personal 'YES' to me from the artist.

Yoko: He came downstairs. I was there and the gallery owner told me, 'This man wants to hammer a nail in your "Hammer A Nail In" piece.' I didn't want him to do it because it was so white and so beautiful and it was still a virgin painting. Nobody had hammered a nail in yet, so I said, 'No I don't want him to do that – after the opening maybe, but not now.' And the gallery owner said, 'Oh no, let him do it.' So I said, 'All right, if he pays five shillings, it's okay,' because I decided that my painting will never sell anyway.

John: So I said, 'Listen, I'll give you an imaginary five shillings and hammer an imaginary nail in, is that okay?' And her whole trip is this: 'Imagine this, Imagine that.'

Yoko: Imagine, Imagine. So I was thinking, 'Oh, here's a guy who's playing the same game I'm playing.' And I was really shocked you know, I thought, 'Who is it?' Every day I was doing an event there, sort of like a 'happening', but my happenings are very quiet, like a Fluxus-type thing. The gallery owner was saying, 'Oh, Yoko Ono is going to do her "Cut Piece",' so everybody expected some fantastic happening

where the girl would become nude or something. But whenever they asked me what is the event today, I just produced a little card and in the middle of it just a tiny little sign saying 'Breathe'.

John: So she just takes a card out and gives it to me and it just says, 'Breathe'. So I said, 'Like that?' [breathing] She said, 'You got it!' I said, 'Uh-huh, all right.' I'm beginning to catch on here. And there was a sense of humour in her work, you know? It was funny. Her work really made me laugh, some of it. So that's when I got interested in art again, just through her work.

Yoko: I heard about the Beatles and I knew the name Ringo, and nobody's going to believe me but still that's exactly how it was. Ringo hit me because Ringo is 'Apple' in Japanese. Yes, I knew the Beatles as a social phenomenon, but rock 'n' roll had passed me by. But I met him and I felt he was an incredibly interesting man without knowing so much about pop and rock and all that. As a guy I thought he was a very interesting guy, immediately. Love at first sight? Sort of, yes. The first meeting was a very intense one.

John: I didn't see her again for a few weeks. It was eighteen months or a year before we got near to each other physically. When I met Yoko (before I realized that I was going to live with her and become that involved) I was interested in her as an artist. And Apple originally was set up to allow artistic expression to people besides ourselves. She was singing a cappella into a little tape recorder in those days and straight, kind of 'song' songs and also her crying, you know, the weird stuff. And I was interested in producing that.

Yoko: In person, John was a much more attractive man than the one you saw in photos and films. He had very fair, delicate skin and soft, sandy hair with a touch of red in it when the light hit a certain way. I would kid him and say, 'You're a redhead!' He would say, 'Never!' But the way he laughed, I knew that had been suggested before. When he grew his beard, it was very definitely predominantly red.

He had three small but distinct moles straight down the centre of his broad forehead, ending where the third eye was. Buddha was supposed to have had one mole in the centre of his forehead, and that was considered in the Oriental physiognomy as a sign of a very wise man. I always thought John's oval and well chiselled classic face looked very much like a Kabuki mask or a face you'd expect to see in a Shakespearean play. And he carried his body with a certain lightness that gave grace to his movements. He was in his twenties when I met him. I was eight years older. But I never thought of him as somebody younger than me. When you were near him, the strong mental vibe he sent out was too heavy for a young person. Some people are born old. That was John. His slumming, clowning and acting the entertainer was just a kind of play-acting he enjoyed. But it was obvious to anybody around him that he was actually a very heavy dude; not a prince but a king.

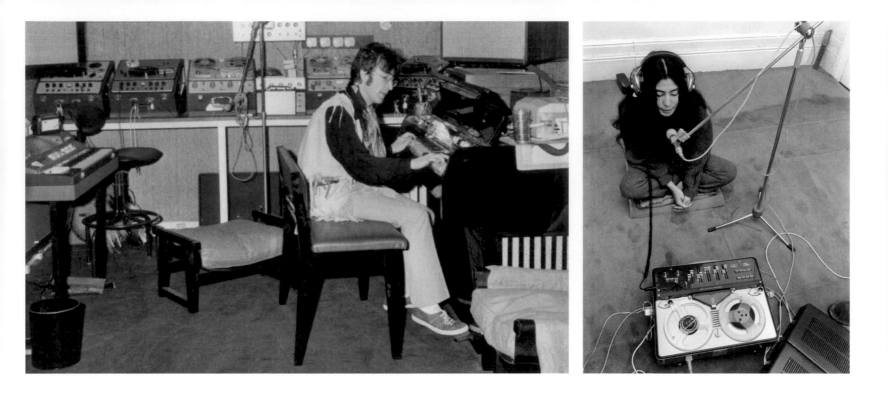

John: I was thinking about her all the time in India. She wrote me these letters – 'I'm a cloud. Watch for me in the sky.' I'd get so excited about her letters. I could see this album cover of her being naked because her work was so pure. I couldn't think of any other way of presenting her. Then when I came home from India, I realized that I'd been thinking about her because I was in love with her.

Yoko came to visit me and we took acid. And I was always shy with her and she was shy. And so instead of making love, we went upstairs and I had this room full of different tapes where I would write and make strange loops and things like that for Beatles stuff. And we made a tape all night and she was doing her funny voices and I was pushing all different buttons on my tape recorder and getting sound effects. And then as the sun rose we made love and that was it. And that was *Two Virgins*. So then I just transposed the idea of her purity through art of her being naked that it seemed natural that both of us should be naked on the cover. And so our picture was taken and presented in a way that was non-sexual. It was just two virgins.

Imagine two cars of the same make heading towards each other and they're gonna crash, head-on. Well, it's like one of those scenes from a film – they're doing 100 miles an hour, they both slam their brakes on and there's smoke everywhere on the floor and they stop just in the nick of time with their bumpers almost touching but not quite. That's what it was like from the first time I got to know her. Yoko and I were on the same wavelength right from the start, from that first night. I had to drop everything. I had no doubt I'd met 'The One'. That first night convinced me

I'd have to end my marriage to Cyn. There was nothing basically wrong with my marriage to Cyn. It was just like an amber light. It wasn't on go and it wasn't on stop. I suppose that me being away so much during the early years of our marriage, I never did feel like the average married man.

I always had this dream of meeting an artist woman I would fall in love with. Even from art school. And when we met and were talking I just realized that she knew everything I knew. And more, probably. And it was coming out of a woman's head. It just sort of bowled me over. It was like finding gold or something. To have exactly the same relationship with any male you'd ever had, but also you could go to bed with it, and it could stroke your head when you felt tired or sick or depressed. Could also be Mother. And all of the intellect is there; well, it's just like winning the pools. So that's why when people ask me for a precis of my story, I put, 'Born, lived, met Yoko.' Because that's what it's been about.

As she was talking to me, I would get high and the discussion would get to such a level that I would be going higher and higher and when she'd leave, I'd go back into this sort of suburbia. Then I'd meet her again and my head would go off like I was on an acid trip. I'd be going over what she'd said and it was incredible – some of the ideas and the way she was saying them. And then once I got a sniff of it, I was hooked. Then I couldn't leave her alone. We couldn't be apart for a minute from then on.

The Beatles had turned me into a puppet. It was OK, but once we'd made it so big, the fun had gone and so had my

own strength. But when I met her, I had to drop everything. It was 'Goodbye to the boys in the band!' I've had two partners in my life – Paul McCartney and Yoko. That's not a bad record, is it?

Yoko: London then was a gathering place of the new aristocrats in music, art and films. They exuded new energy with a certain elegance of self-made people who would change the class structure in England, and would go on to change the world in a big way.

John and I got together in that atmosphere. So we were very surprised that the so-called hip society of the times, to which we both belonged, turned against us as soon as we announced our unity. It seemed as though they had a separate standard for John, or shall we say that their hipness ended at the point where John, their ringleader, chose an Oriental woman as his partner. This was in the Sixties in 'Swinging London'! It made us feel as though, suddenly, the wind of the Middle Ages was blowing around us.

I come from the East. He comes from the West. A meeting of East and West. And to communicate with people is almost a responsibility. We are living proof of East and West getting along together. High water falls low. And if our cup is full, it's going to flow. It's natural for us to give, because we have a lot.

John: I get truly affected by letters from Brazil or Poland or Austria – places I'm not conscious of all the time – just to know somebody is there, listening. One kid living up in Yorkshire wrote this heartfelt letter about being both

Oriental and English and identifying with John & Yoko; the odd kid in the class. There are a lot of those kids who identify with us. They don't need the history of rock 'n' roll. They identify with us as a couple, a biracial couple, who stand for love, peace, feminism and the positive things of the world. You know, give peace a chance, not shoot people for peace, all we need is love. I believe it. It's damn hard, but I absolutely believe it.

Yoko: I think it was a big lesson for the world that we were together and it was a lesson for us too. We didn't realize there was so much racism. And I think it might have helped for people to understand what it means to confront an interracial couple. And we all had to grow and experience that. I would not say it was easy, but it was an education for us. A good experience. We always tried to deal with a lot of difficult situations, John and I, with a bit of a sense of humour and sense of fun.

From left to right: John playing his black Mellotron Mk II in his home recording studio, where *Two Virgins* was later recorded; Kenwood, Weybridge, UK, 29 June 1967; Yoko recording her songs to quarter-inch tape; London, 1966; John Lennon & Yoko Ono *Unfinished Music No.1: Two Virgins* – album cover photo by John Lennon; 34 Montagu Square, London, 15 September 1968; *Bed-In for Peace*, Montreal, Canada, 27 May – 1 June 1969.

Previous pages: attending Cannes Film Festival, France, 15 May 1971, where their films *Apotheosis* and *FLY* were shown.

THE NEW YORK HILTON
at Rockefeller Center

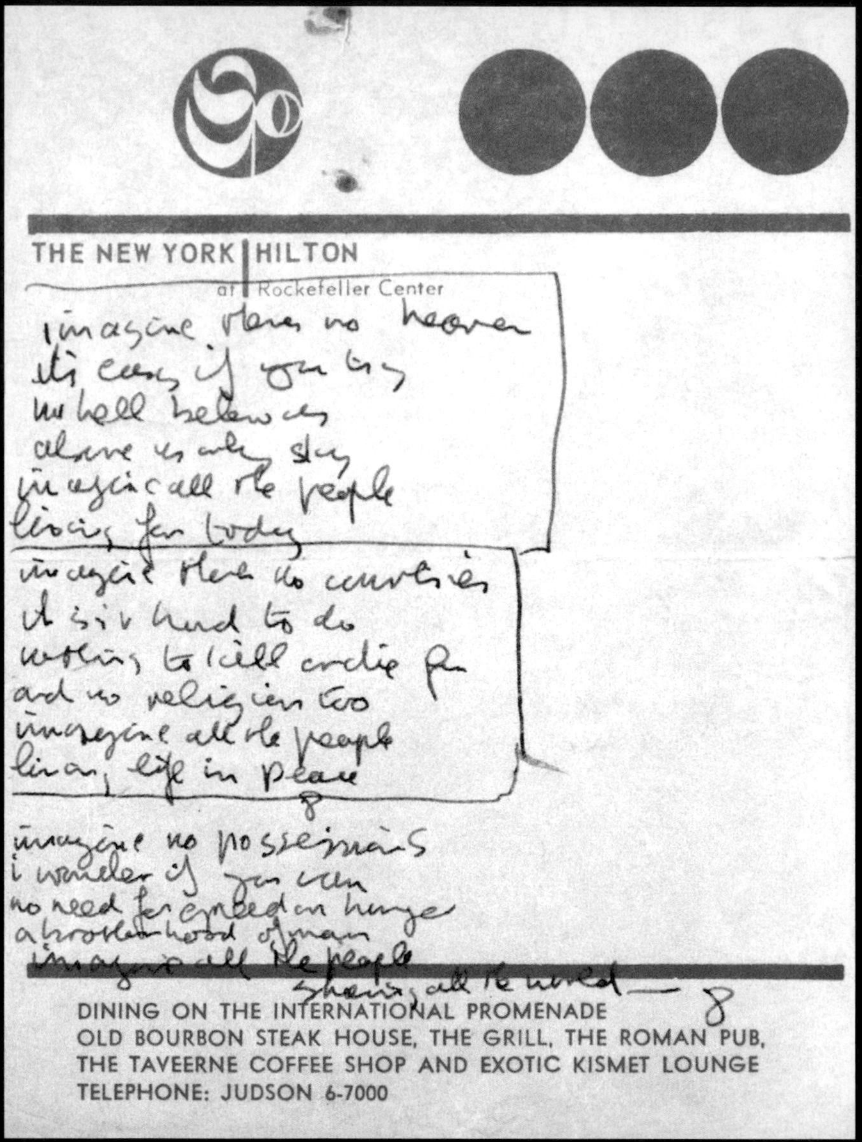

imagine theres no heaven
its easy if you try
no hell below us
above us only sky
imagine all the people
living for today

imagine there's no countries
it isn't hard to do
nothing to kill or die for
and no religion too
imagine all the people
living life in peace
8

imagine no possessions
i wonder if you can
no need for greed or hunger
a brotherhood of man
imagine all the people
sharing all the world — 8

DINING ON THE INTERNATIONAL PROMENADE
OLD BOURBON STEAK HOUSE, THE GRILL, THE ROMAN PUB,
THE TAVEERNE COFFEE SHOP AND EXOTIC KISMET LOUNGE
TELEPHONE: JUDSON 6-7000

imagine

Imagine there's no heaven
It's easy if you try
No hell below us
Above us only sky
Imagine all the people living for today

Imagine there's no countries
It isn't hard to do
Nothing to kill or die for
And no religion too
Imagine all the people living life in peace

You may say I'm a dreamer
But I'm not the only one
I hope someday you'll join us
And the world will be as one

Imagine no possessions
I wonder if you can
No need for greed or hunger
A brotherhood of man
Imagine all the people sharing all the world

You may say I'm a dreamer
But I'm not the only one
I hope someday you'll join us
And the world will live as one

John: 'Imagine' is a song conceived in my head without melody. The first verse came to me very quickly in the form of a childlike street chant 'da da da da da dee dee da dee da ee a eeeh'. The piano intro I've had hanging around in my head for a few years – the chords and melody followed naturally from this. The middle eight was 'conceived' to finish off the song. I think it works as a song. Of course, there is always room for improvement – otherwise I wouldn't make any more. The third verse came to me in an eight-seater plane. It's a song for children.

Yoko: 'Cloud Piece': 'Imagine the clouds dripping, dig a hole in your garden to put them in.' This is not a piece of poetry. Poetry to me is nouns or adjectives. This is verbs. And you have to do them. These are all instructions and when you just do it, then you start to understand it.

John: 'Imagine' was inspired by Yoko's *Grapefruit*. There's a lot of pieces in it saying like 'Imagine this' or 'Imagine that'. If you get a copy of *Grapefruit* and look through, you'll see where I was influenced by her. 'Imagine' could never have been written without her. And I know she helped on a lot of the lyrics but I wasn't man enough to let her have credit for it. So that song was actually written by John & Yoko, but I was still selfish enough and unaware enough to take her contribution without acknowledging it. The song itself expresses what I'd learned through being with Yoko and my own feelings on it. It should really have said 'Lennon/Ono' on that song, because she contributed a lot of that song.

Yoko: John and I were both artists and we were living together, so we inspired each other. And the song 'Imagine' embodied what we believed together at the time. John and I met – he comes from the West and I come from the East – and still we are together. We have this oneness and 'the whole world would eventually become one' is the sense that we will all be café-au-lait colour and we will all be very happy together. All these instructions are for people for how to spend eternity, because we have lots of time.

John: If you can imagine a world of peace, if you can imagine a world with no denominations of religion – not without religion, whatever religion is – but without this divisive 'My god is bigger than your god' business…. Then, if you can imagine the possibility, then it can be true.

Yoko: John was a very religious person belonging to no denomination. He was almost like the idea of a very astute priest in his thinking – a priest who believed in goodness, justice and freedom for all, with plenty of humour as well. You must have seen him – wink, wink. But he took our relationship seriously. I was very lucky to have been with a guy like him.

John: I'm a Pagan – a Zen Pagan to be precise – but that's another story! I was brought up a Christian – Sunday School and all that. It's OK, I have nothing against it except that it organizes itself as a business, the Church. What I do like about it is that Christians talk about being perfect. So was Christ. And I was taught that as a child. Christ is the one who most people in the West refer to, when they speak of good people. If I could do what Christ did, be as Christ was, that's what being a Christian is all about. I try to live as Christ lived. It's tough, I can tell you. I don't know that anyone like me, who questions everything down to the colour of his socks, can believe in an old man in the sky. I believe in something, definitely. I believe there is a force at work that you can't physically account for.

I'm not claiming divinity, I've never claimed purity of soul, I've never claimed to have the answers to life. I only put out songs and answer questions as honestly as I can, but only as honestly as I can – no more, no less. I cannot live up to other people's expectations of me because they're illusionary. We can have figureheads and god, we can have people that we admire and like to have standing up and we can follow examples, but 'leaders' is what we don't need.

So-called Christians are so busy condemning themselves and others, or preaching at people, or worse still, killing for Christ. None of them understanding, or trying in the least, to behave like a Christ. It seems to me that the only true Christians are the Gnostics, who believe in self-knowledge, i.e., becoming Christ themselves, reaching the Christ within. Christ, after all, is Greek for light.

Yoko: We all recognize that the accepted translation of Christ is 'the anointed one'. We, however, were told that in the original Dead Sea Scrolls it is revealed that the true translation of Christ is 'light', which to us made more sense.

John: The Light is the Truth. All any of us are trying to do is precisely that: turn on the light. All the better to see you with, my dear. Christ, Buddha, Muhammad, Moses, Milarepa, and other great ones spent their time in fasting, praying, meditation, and left 'maps' of the territory of 'God' for all to see and follow in our own way.

First edition of *Grapefruit* by Yoko Ono, 1964, Wunternaum Press, Tokyo (edition of 500). Given to John by Yoko on 3 September 1967 with her notes on his astrological birth chart and John's humorous response. Many of the pieces invite the reader to 'imagine'. 'Cloud Piece', is printed on the back cover of the *Imagine* album.

DRINKING PIECE FOR ORCHESTRA

Imagine letting a goldfish swim across
the sky.
Let it swim from the West to the East.
Drink a liter of water.
Imagine letting a goldfish swim across
the sky.
Let it swim from the East to the West.

1963 spring

TUNAFISH SANDWICH PIECE

Imagine one thousand suns in the
sky at the same time.
Let them shine for one hour.
Then, let them gradually melt
into the sky.
Make one tunafish sandwich and eat.

1964 spring

To John.

yoko
london
sept. 3 '67

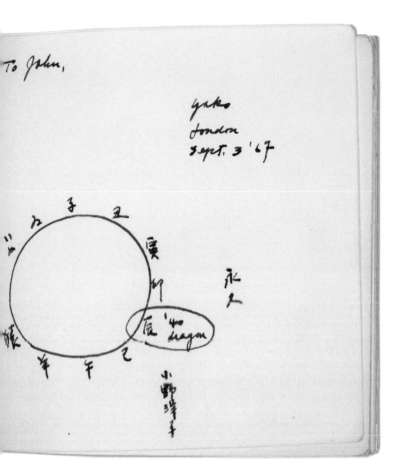

CLOUD PIECE

Imagine the clouds dripping.
Dig a hole in your garden to
put them in.

1963 spring

thank you

John
Edinburg
46 2 8 28

tea time

John & Yoko recording 'Imagine' in the White Room, Tittenhurst, 27 May 1971.

John: The Maharishi was good for me, like anybody who has something to tell you that you don't know enough about. He was no substitute for anything, though. There's a lot of good in Christianity but you've got to learn the basics of it, and the basics from the Eastern beliefs, and work them together for yourself.

The World Church called me once and wanted to say, 'Can we use the lyrics and just change it to "Imagine one religion"?' So that showed that they didn't understand it at all. It would defeat the whole purpose of the song; the whole idea.

It's one world, one people. And it's a statement as well as a wish. We're one world, one people whether we like it or not. We can pretend we're divided into races and countries, and we can carry on pretending that until we stop doing it.

Yoko: Imagine all the people living life in peace. I think that that's a very strong thing to do. It might be a very controversial thing to do. Because it's a very powerful thing to do. I think it's all right to say that. I don't think that goes against the policy of this country or anything like that. I think, in the end, all people in this country really want peace. But how to get there? Some people are thinking in a different way, of course. But imagining, that's something that we can all do, even when we have different opinions about how to get there. Imagining peace, imagining peace. That's okay. That we can all do, without feeling the conflict.

John: First of all, conceive of the idea of no nation, no passport. If you're not defending a nation, there's nothing to fight about. We've said it a million times. First of all we conceived of flying, then we flew. It took a long time to get up in the air, and it was a lot of sticking feathers together and melting under the sun and all that, but conceiving the idea is the first move.

We're not the first to say 'Imagine No Countries' or 'Give Peace a Chance', but we're carrying that torch, like the Olympic torch, passing it hand to hand, to each other, to each country, to each generation…and that's our job. Not to live according to somebody else's idea of how we should live – rich, poor, happy, not happy, smiling, not smiling, wearing the right jeans, not wearing the right jeans.

John: There was a time when you didn't have to have a passport to go from country to country. What kind of world are we creating, really? What is this game that somehow this is America and then just across the field is Canada and you have to have all kinds of papers and pictures and stamps and passports? When you think about it, it's insane carving up the world into little patches like that.

The concept of imagining no countries, imagining no religion – not imagining no God, although you're entitled to do that, too, you know? Imagine no denominations. Imagining that we revere Jesus Christ, Muhammad, Krishna, Milarepa, equally – we don't have to worship either one that we don't have to, but imagine there's no Catholic/Protestant. No Jew/Christian. That we allow it all. Freedom of religion for real. Just imagine it. Would it be terrible?

Yoko: George Orwell and all these guys have projected very negative views of the future. And imagining a projection is a very strong magic power. I mean that. That's the way society was created. And so, because they're setting up all these negative images, that's gonna create the society. So we were trying to create a more positive image, which is, of course, gonna set up another kind of society. Even in all this we always had this human race dream, you know?

John: Well, the other great dream of mankind, one was to fly – which might've taken us a long time, but it took somebody to imagine it first. The second was reach the Moon, right? Which we reached. Now, sure, it was an American in an American rocket because that was the way history was at that time, but mankind reached the Moon because they said, 'One giant leap for mankind', it was for all of us.

What we were doing then was projecting the future in a positive way. And people said, 'You're naïve, you're dumb, you're stupid.' It might have hurt us on a personal level to be called names, but what we were doing – you can call it magic, meditation, projection of goal – which business people do, they have courses on it. The footballers do it. They pray, they meditate before the game. They visualize themselves winning. We were early pioneers of that movement to project a future where we can have goals that we can reach. Right? People project their own future. So, what we wanted to do was say, 'Let's imagine a nice future.'

Yoko: Our mind has a strong plasticity. If you believe that it is important for you to make the world peaceful, it will happen. Don't start saying, 'No. It can't happen because….' And list a long line of No's and Nevers. It can happen and

We're not the first to say 'Imagine No Countries' or 'Give Peace a Chance', but we're carrying that torch, like the Olympic torch, passing it hand to hand, to each other, to each country, to each generation…and that's our job.

John, 1980

Filming *Imagine*: John sitting at Yoko's piano; the White Room, Tittenhurst, 21 July 1971.

Yoko's white Steinway 'O' grand piano with silver plaque:
'This Morning, A White Piano For Yoko, From John With Love, 18.2.1971'.
Opposite: order confirmation from Steinway & Sons, London, 29 January 1971.

BY APPOINTMENT TO
HER MAJESTY QUEEN ELIZABETH II
PIANOFORTE MANUFACTURERS

STEINWAY & SONS
INCORPORATED IN U.S.A. WITH LIMITED LIABILITY

PIANO MAKERS

STEINWAY HALL
1 & 2 ST. GEORGE STREET · HANOVER SQUARE
LONDON
W1R 9DG

TELEPHONE
01- 629 6641
(4 LINES)

TELEGRAMS & CABLES
STEINWAYS
LONDON W. I.

RA/IC   *Established in New York City 1853*   29th January 1971.

John Lennon's Secretary,
Apple Records,
3, Savile Row, W.1.

Dear Sir,
                re: Titenhurst Park, Sunninghill,
                    Ascot, Berks.
_____

We beg to confirm the pleasure of your telephone
call of 27th inst. and thank you for the valued order for
the Steinway "O" Grand, 419051, to be sprayed to a dull
white finish, the price of which will be £1,891.

In accordance with your request we are arranging
for a nickel silver plaque to be inscribed in script
reading as follows:-

                This morning   (indented)
                A White Piano   not indented
                For Yoko   (indented)
        From John with Love 18.2.1971.

This plaque will be fitted on the fall under the
name of Steinway & Sons.

With regard to delivery - in accordance with your
instructions this will be executed not later than the 12th
February. As soon as we receive advice from the Works
that the piano is ready, we will notify you, so that
delivery arrangements can be made.

Again thanking you for the order, and with
Compliments,
        We remain,
            Faithfully yours,

            STEINWAY & SONS. R. Allen

Over a Century of Service to Music

it will. We are just at the point that it will. So don't throw negative vibes to the world. There is enough of that.

John: The reason I got rich is because I'm so insecure. I couldn't give it all away, even in my most holy, Christian, God-fearing, Hare Krishna period, I got into that struggle – 'I should give it all away, I don't need it.' But I need it because I'm so insecure. Yoko doesn't need it. She always had it. I have to have it. I'm not secure enough to give it all up, because I need it to protect me from whatever I'm frightened of. I wasn't content with no dollars. I wasn't content with a million and I'm not content with $100 million. Contentment doesn't lie in money.

Money is energy. It's like electricity. You can kill people with it or you can light their house. The secret of money is circulation. That's one thing I learned. But you have to be responsible for it. My insecurity is to have too many clothes. That's a physical manifestation of my insecurity of childhood. But I understand it. I still have the clothes and I still dump them on the Sally Army once a year, whatever. But I understand that it's a neurosis.

You can transcend possessions without walking around in a robe. Possessions can be in the mind. And a monk who's off in a cave dreaming about fucking, sucking and eating is in a far worse position than me who has that money in his back pocket. When Christ says, 'It's easier for a rich man to go through the eye of a needle than to get to heaven,' I always took that literally to mean just his gold. That he'd have to dump the possessions to get through to Nirvana. But an intellectual has less chance of getting through than me. An intellectual with no money who doesn't even watch TV because they're too aesthetic and don't want that culture coming in their house. Well they're possessed of ideas. And I'm no longer possessed of ideas. So those were the possessions I had to get rid of, not the physical possessions.

Most people are choked to death by concepts and ideas that they carry around with them. Usually not their own, usually their parents' and society's. And those are the possessions you've got to get rid of to get through the eye of the needle and it has absolutely nothing to do with physical possessions.

Both Yoko and I have this dream of living in a small cottage in the country, eventually. But we ended up with this big Georgian house. I bought 70 acres and a beautiful house that looks like a miniature White House, and I took me wife there, but all the time she was complaining about why we had so much space when all we needed was two rooms. She wanted to live in New York in a loft. I said, 'Look kid, you were born rich; I was born poor, and I fought and made it.' But I sat in that house for a year, and I was not happy. I had all the possessions I wanted, but none of it was giving me any fun.

Yoko: When we were making 'Imagine' I felt that he was an extremely sensitive musician. And he was showing that side. Not the side of 'We're Beatles, aren't we?' He was a real musician. And I respected that. He was really very caring about the notes he was playing, the arrangement, the way that was recorded and the way it came through and all that. And I saw the kind of honest worker side of him. I loved it.

When I first heard the finished version of this song I was in a room in Ascot in England with John and my first thoughts were that it would be a hit. The lyrics were just so beautiful. We both liked the song a lot but we honestly didn't realize it would turn into the powerful song it has, all over the world. We didn't realize it would be that big. We just did it because we believed in the words and it just reflected how we were feeling.

I think 'Imagine' was prophetic, in a very positive way. I think it's all right that it's not fashionable or faddish and might seem simple.

We believed in peace. I think we were very ambitious in a sense that we wanted to see, finally, there would be world peace. I'd like to see that happen and I'd like to work my best effort for that. My feeling is that he's part of the big force, big power out there, and he's really helping us too.

John: I think my greatest pleasure is writing a song – words and lyrics – that will last longer than a couple of years. Songs that anybody could sing. Songs that will outlive me, probably. And that gives me my greatest pleasure. That's where I get my kicks.

Yoko: 'Imagine' is a very, very powerful song. And I think it is very interesting that it is still around and still giving power to people. And I'm very happy about that.

'That look', from the ending of the 'Imagine' music video; Tittenhurst, 21 July 1971.

'Imagine' should be credited as a Lennon/Ono song because a lot of it – the lyric and the concept – came from Yoko. But those days I was a bit more selfish, a bit more macho, and I sort of omitted to mention her contribution. But it was right out of *Grapefruit*, her book. There's a whole pile of pieces about 'Imagine this' and 'Imagine that'. And give her credit now, long overdue.

John, 1980

On 14 June 2017, the National Music Publishers Association presented John Lennon
& Yoko Ono, as co-writers of 'Imagine', with the Centennial Song Award. Photographed
on the balcony at the Dakota, overlooking Strawberry Fields, 14 June 2017.
Previous pages: John & Yoko in conversation with Mike Ledgerwood and
Roy Shipston from *Disc and Music Echo*, the White Room, Tittenhurst, 22 July 1971.

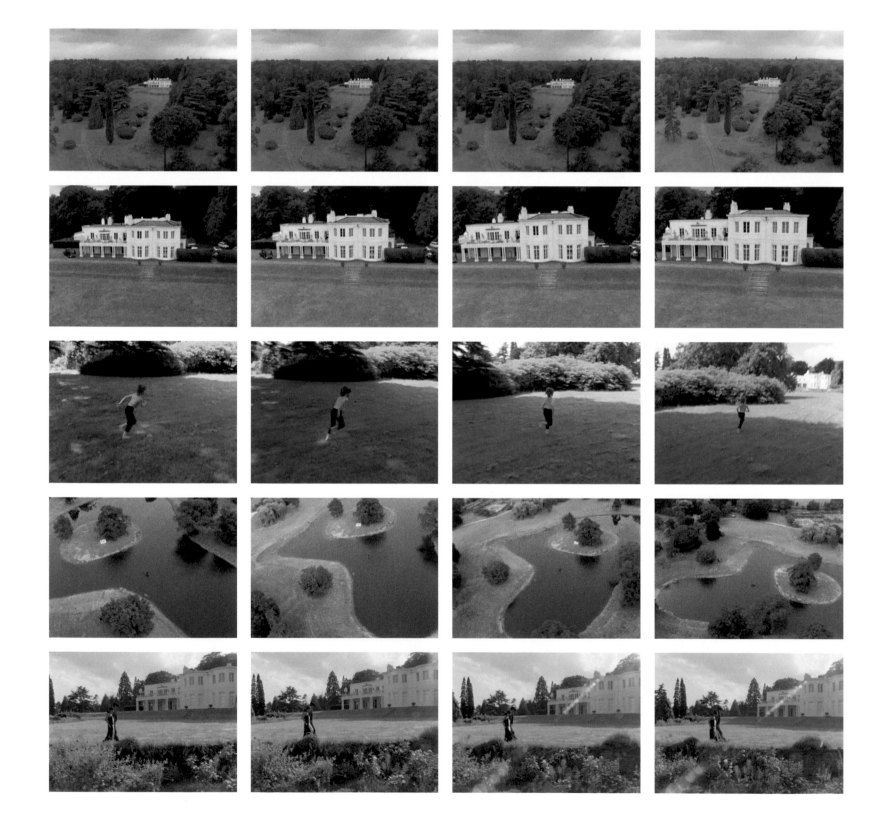

tittenhurst

John and I thought we would make Ascot our home and live there for many, many years to come. Otherwise, why did we plonk a huge lake in the garden and plant feeble-looking plum and cherry saplings around the lake, which promised to become trees in twenty years' time?

yoko, 1998

'Above us only sky' – the main house at Tittenhurst, 27 May 1971.
Previous pages: out-takes from the *Imagine* film, featuring the main house and grounds,
and including John & Yoko and Julian Lennon; Tittenhurst, 17, 20 and 21 July 1971.

tittenhurst park

◯ Trees

01	Cedar of Lebanon	50	Weeping beech
02	Lawson cypress	51	Pendent silver lime
03	Horse chestnut	52	Scarlet oak
04	Deodar	53	Western yellow pine
05	Cedar of Lebanon	54	Schwedler's maple
06	Maritime pine	54a	Pyrenean oak
07	Laurel-leaved holly	55	Whitebeam
08	Sweet chestnut	56	Ginkgo
09	Tulip-tree	57	Twisted pagoda tree
10	Douglas fir	58	Scarlet oak
11	Willow-leaved pear	59	Sweet gum
12	Purple beech	60	Wire-twigged cypress
13	Cut-leaf birch	61	Blue Algerian cedar
14	Cut-leaf birch	62	Golden Lebanon cedar
15	Spanish fir	63	Golden Lebanon cedar
16	Incense cedar	64	Young's cypress
17	Wissell's cypress	64a	Travers cypress
18	Wellingtonia	65	Golden-barred thuja
19	Wellingtonia	66	Arolla pine
20	Weeping blue cedar	67	Japanese white pine
21	Weeping blue cedar	68	Honey locust
22	Incense cedar	69	Black jack oak
23	Wellingtonia	70	Sweet gum
24	Cripps' Hinoki cypress	71	Pagoda tree
25	China fir	72	White fir
26	Monkey puzzle (male)	73	Japanese white pine
27	Monkey puzzle (female)	74	Weeping Wellingtonia
28	Weeping rosebud cherry	75	Weeping Wellingtonia
29	Scarlet oak	76	Weeping Atlas cedar
30	Swamp cypress	77	Weeping pagoda tree
31	Swamp cypress	78	Blue pencil 'cedar'
32	Variegated beech	79	Weeping hemlock
33	Sorrel tree	80	Golden Monterey cypress
34	Water oak	81	Mountain hemlock
35	Variegated elm	82	Golden-feathered cypress
36	Golden elm	83	Squarrose cypress
37	Blue Colorado spruce	83a	Lawson cypress
38	Monterey pine	84	Golden juniper
39	Black oak (covered by lake)	85	Deodar
40	Umbrella pine	86	Incense cedar
41	Umbrella pine	87	Deodar
42	Weymouth pine	88	Yellow cypress
43	Crested Japanese redwood	89	Wellingtonia
44	Manitoba maple	90	Incense cedar
45	Box elder	91	Yellow cypress
46	Scots pine	92	Coast redwood
47	Austrian pine	93	Filifera false cypress
48	Blue Algerian cedar	94	Versicolor false cypress
49	Norway maple		

← TO READING

FRONT GATES
ENTRY LODGE
GARAGES
STABLES
COTTAGES
STORAGE
TEMPLE
CONSERVATORY

PARKING
MEZZ
HOUSE
SWIMMING POOL

MAGNOLIA GARDEN

SILWOOD LANE

LONDON ROAD

TO LONDON →

TUDOR LODGE

GYPSY CARAVAN

ALLOTMENTS

STABLES

GREENHOUSES

STATUE OF DIANA

ISLAND AND SUMMER HOUSE

WEEPING BLUE CEDARS

CHERRY TREE SAPLINGS

LAKE

TENNIS COURT

HAY BARN

WHITMORE LANE

BARN

KILN LANE

TO GUILDFORD →

N

Deciduous (spreading)

Deciduous (conical)

Evergreen (spreading)

Evergreen (conical)

⅛ M   ¼ M

0.2 km   0.4 km

julian lennon

When Dad moved to Tittenhurst, it was the first time that he actually called me in quite a long time. It was an exciting thing for me to go and see him again after not seeing him for such a while. And at the time, I was living in, I won't say a small house, but it was a completely different situation.

It was on a street with lots of houses, lots of friends. And Tittenhurst was this enormous palace-like place with 99 acres, golf-cart buggies, a lake, a little island in the middle of the lake. It was like a house of fun. It was a completely different experience. It was wonderful. I loved the place. I recall so many people coming and going, other children too…. Dr Pepper was the drink of the

moment, which Dad and I both loved. There was a house lower down on the property that everyone thought was haunted so all the kids there, myself included, always teased each other about going into it.

I remember that Dad had a Mellotron in the main house, and I'd try to play it on occasion. It was such an inspiring instrument, and to this day, still one of my favourites. I believe it was passed on to Ringo, who in turn gave it to Ted Fields.

There were moments, though, where I felt very lonely there, at night, at bedtime. I recall being in a room halfway down the main staircase, which was on the opposite side to where Dad & Yoko slept. I was always

scared to go to bed, because in such a huge house/building, who knew if there were ghosts there or not? There were strange noises floating through the air of that place, all the time. As you can imagine, my thoughts got the better of me, on more than one occasion.

My time there is still vivid….

above: Julian with John & Yoko, rowing on the lake at Tittenhurst, 17 July 1971.

dan richter
personal assistant

In 1971, John & Yoko were at the height of their powers. They were looking for creative freedom from Apple. I was between projects and I was determined to help them find it at Tittenhurst.

I helped organize events, equipment, people and budgets – in much the same way that a line producer does in the world of film. Diana was their secretary, Stephen and Peter were general assistants who ran errands, Val was the cook, Les the chauffeur, and Frank the gardener.

Me, my wife Jill, and our first child Sacha lived at Tittenhurst from the very beginning – right up until John & Yoko left for New York. Initially, we had a room, John & Yoko had a room and all the other rooms were filled up with boxes, or falling apart with dry rot; we had to start from scratch. Later, we moved into the cottages.

John & Yoko had a very clear vision of what they wanted. We had the house remodelled – knocking down walls, adding black and white carpets, a recording studio, a sophisticated colour darkroom, film-editing and projection facilities – and I started creating a more organized archive of their music, films, artworks and possessions.

They wanted wide, natural-looking white carpet. So we had it loomed in China from natural, unbleached wool, with lanolin still in it, to get the right white. It was rich, thick and beautiful. They got white Empire marble fireplaces, a big round tub for the bathroom – and I found John a beautiful Queen Anne Chinoiserie desk.

The garden was a dendrologist's dream. It had been designed in the 18th century, and contained some of the most beautiful trees in the world. Beside each one was a little metal plaque stuck in the ground that described what it was.

While excavating the lake, we discovered unexploded bombs from the Second World War, which we had to have bomb disposal squads come in and get rid of. There were donkeys on the grounds, which my children – and Julian Lennon, when he visited – enjoyed riding.

Every time John went to America, he discovered something new that he couldn't get in England. He liked Dr Pepper, so we had cases of Dr Pepper sent over – and a freezer full of Häagen-Dazs ice cream.

We had a film-editing table specially designed so it could take 16mm or 35mm film. Stanley Kubrick (with whom I had worked on *2001: A Space Odyssey*) heard about the table and while John & Yoko were in America, they lent it to Stanley to use for editing *A Clockwork Orange*. Stanley was another great artist who was beating the studio system by setting up a creative centre at home – and he was similar to John. He could talk for hours about details over a wide range of subjects. If something wasn't right, even after months of research, he couldn't do it. It had to be true to his vision.

John & Yoko spent a lot of time in their bedroom, incubating ideas. Whenever they presented a new plan, they both had it all worked out in great detail; understanding every part. They were a real team that way. Whether it was a John project or a Yoko project, the other would be there in support. They were collaborators, and being together was liberating for them, not only emotionally, but as artists.

John was very keen to not just be a rock 'n' roll star, but also to do artistic music. The Plastic Ono Band albums (for which I photographed the covers) are now considered masterpieces, but they didn't sell so well at the time. Everybody said, 'What are you doing? You're destroying your career!'

The 'Imagine' film was beautiful – John playing the white piano he gave Yoko for her birthday, and Yoko opening the shutters and letting the light into the room. What a metaphor! And then, finally, as it wraps up, she's sitting beside him; the little smile, that little recognition. It's not a big smile. It's a little, gentle smile of understanding. What a gift to the world. And it was the two of them. That's the important thing. This woman who was being accused of destroying him and ruining him as a rock 'n' roll artist. She took so much heat for John during that period. It was almost as if they agreed upon it and it was okay by her to do that.

'Imagine' couldn't have existed without Yoko. The ideas – the aesthetic – all came from her; and John, as the artist, was able to incorporate those things and grow with them.

John was not like anyone before him. He was his own person completely. He had an honesty in his life that, in many ways, made him almost too vulnerable. He spoke his own language, he spoke his own thoughts and he had his own visions. For most of us, our thoughts are thoughts that many people think; the feelings we have are feelings that many people have. Everything about John was unique, and you just knew it when you were around him. You understood it immediately – and Yoko was just the same. They were so similar, yet completely unique.

To be with two such wonderful artists at the height of their creativity, when they were so excited about what they were doing…. It was a very special thing to witness, in a very beautiful place. They believed we have the power to change things if we all get together and love one other. It's a simple truth.

jill richter

I first met Yoko through Dan. She was very beautiful – she had this gorgeous, long black hair and a really nice smile. We became friends right away and soon found adjacent flats, so we could be neighbours.

After a while, Dan and I sold everything in London – gave everything away – and tried to make a life in America. But it didn't work out. When we came back to England, we needed somewhere to stay, and John & Yoko asked us to look after John's old house in Weybridge; because John and Cynthia had both moved out. There were about fifty wild cats there that John had been feeding.

When they bought Tittenhurst, we moved there with all the cats. Most of them ran off into the woods.

Dan oversaw the building work for the house and recording studio, and helped change that old house into a really efficient place for them to make music and art. They built a huge lake and put a little building on it – and all the Canadian geese moved in. There was a field with donkeys, and a little donkey shed, and other outbuildings. Squirrels got in and started eating the wiring.

The house had a wonderful kitchen. Yoko taught me how to cook macrobiotic food in that kitchen. I will never forget that – showing me how to slice carrots on the angle – that was wonderful.

Our son Sacha is in the *Imagine* film. He was thoroughly spoilt because he was the only child, until Mischa was born. And everybody had time for him – Diana, John & Yoko, the gardener, the people who were painting the house, all the musicians…. Everybody loved Sacha.

It was wonderful at Tittenhurst in the spring. The camellias and magnolia bushes were huge, and had grown wild, all in different colours. Magical. It felt like everything was blooming – including the people and the music. We were in this extraordinarily beautiful place, with beautiful people, creating something wonderful. I have camellias growing outside my flat in Brighton. Every year, when they start to bloom, I think of Tittenhurst Park. I love them so much.

When I think of 'Imagine', I think of John at that piano, with the music and the light in that room. Just beautiful.

Peter Bendrey in John & Yoko's limousine, on the way
to filming at Battery Park; New York, 4 September 1971.

peter bendrey
general assistant

I was nineteen years old and I wanted to go and see the world. I heard that the road was open to India. The idea of going to the Himalayas and hanging out with Buddhist monks was too much for me, so that's what I did. I had a lot of balls for a shy kid with a stutter. And somewhere that trip led to something transformational.

Dan Richter was the first real hipster I'd ever met. He was with a group of people living on a houseboat in Kashmir. It was so beautiful there with these wonderful people. It was nice therapy. I would just laugh until I almost pulled a stomach muscle. They were funny as fuck!

Around Christmas 1966, as I was leaving a pub in Notting Hill, I literally bumped into Dan again, with a Japanese lady in tow. Yoko had just arrived in England, and Dan was her contact. We ended up having Christmas lunch together.

I reconnected with them in 1968, when Yoko & John were falling in love. Jill was pregnant and Dan was sick, so I moved into their flat and looked after them until the baby was born. As a teenager, my thing was bicycle racing. I used to train every day, like a professional athlete. The discipline of that really helped me. I got to be very good at looking after people in extreme situations and being very understanding. Yoko was our neighbour at Hanover Gate Mansions and we used to talk a lot. I was basically an old hippy. A classy one. A good listener. Discreet.

In 1971, I came in off the road, driving from India through Afghanistan. Dan and Jill were at Tittenhurst with John & Yoko and they invited me to come and live and work there. The house was on fire but the view was fantastic. I was exactly what they needed and it was a quantum leap for me. I met some of the best minds of my generation – people away from the music business, very

much part of the spiritual world – and then New York City was literally insane. Wow! It was full of wonderful painters and artists and session musicians. I got over my stutter around then partly because of the incessant ringing of the telephone and the fact that I was around psychically very, very strong people. They were kind. They would take me aside and say, 'Don't be embarrassed about it; to us it means you show exceptional sensitivity.'

We always used to contemplate somebody doing a movie about the bright side of the drug culture. I was part of it and it changed the world. We're talking about red Lebanese hashish and the real American LSD. It was actually astonishing but we didn't treat it like a toy. It was like a medicine really, and I was fortunate enough, probably through the influence of Dan Richter, that I never abused the drug thing, especially around John & Yoko, because I had to work for them.

In those days, John & Yoko never threw parties. They hardly ever went out to other people's parties. They liked to stay in bed and watch TV and eat sushi. If you are something of a creative, after a while you get bored with that and you want to go and make something, you know? John never really lived out his post-adolescent growth fantasy – where you go and explore the world and try a bit of this, try a bit of that. John missed that and the agony of John Lennon was that he never got over his childhood.

Bob Dylan is my hero, bar none. My favourite record of all time is *Blonde on Blonde* (1966). It's that sort of visionary colloquial/hipster vision of the Kerouacian-Ginsbergian Beat Generation America. They were the new priesthood. We finally got away from the idea of 'god' and we were moving into an area where our spiritual development was using art as a medium for liberating our imaginations:

'Don't follow leaders, watch the parking meters.'

While John & Yoko were staying at the St Regis, we were constantly inundated with visitors and phone calls from people we didn't know. One day, this guy came by and said, 'Could you tell John that Bob's here?' and I said, 'Bob who? I don't know who you are!' I wouldn't let him in. John absolutely loved that. He was wearing a hat and a scarf, you really couldn't recognize him. Dylan has a song – 'Idiot Wind' – where he says, 'People see me all the time and they just can't remember how to act.' John really had that problem. He'd say, 'Peter, look, I see these hungry eyes, these people, it's like they want to eat a part of me.' People would always try and invade their privacy and I did everything I could to protect them from that. But mostly people were too curious. Of course they were.

Yoko is totally unique. She has a ferocious intensity. She can be shy and she can be fearless and she loves to overwhelm. The last time I spoke to her, she said, 'Peter, I can never get enough!' which sums her up beautifully. She wrote a song called 'Peter the Dealer' where she sings about me, 'The world can't give us answers 'cos it's stuttering in its mind.' That's quite something, isn't it? It's beautiful.

In June 1972, I hit the road again, driving their green Chrysler station wagon on a road trip from New York to San Francisco. John & Yoko were listening to an eight-track in the back seat – they particularly loved *Carney* by Leon Russell and *After The Gold Rush* by Neil Young. In the car, John was like a little boy, so excited to see America from the road. One day we went in to a motel, deep in the Colorado mountains and the old couple who ran the motel just didn't recognize him when he paid the bill by credit card. It was the first time he hadn't been recognized in years. He just loved that.

diana robertson
secretary

I was doing some temping in London. I walked into an agency and they said 'Oh, John Lennon's assistant wants an assistant, are you interested?' So I said, 'Yes!' and they sent me over to the Apple office to see Anthony Fawcett, who was their assistant at the time. He was in a rush and said, 'Oh I've got to go down to Ascot to see John & Yoko, just jump in the car with me.' And that was my interview.

The next day (25 November 1969), John sent back his MBE. That was the first thing I typed, sitting across the room from a tightly entwined John & Yoko in the Savile Row Apple office, with John dictating the letter for me to type. There was about to be a press conference. I'd never been to one in my life. It was all pretty bizarre. I was twenty-one.

I got to be very good at calling people and finding anything at any time of day or night. I mean, strange things like a Perspex tissue box – I had to find someone to make it and fast. They always wanted things immediately. We didn't have the internet in those days, so it was all a matter of getting on the phone, asking people, and getting referred from one person to another. I actually loved the challenge.

When the Beatles were splitting up, John & Yoko decided to move Bag Productions [their production company] to Tittenhurst, and I spent a lot of time going back and forth down the M4 in my little red Mini. There were no emails in those days, so everything had to be taken by hand.

By 1971, I was living down there. There were four workmen's cottages on the estate and I lived in one with my husband. It was a bit like living in a dream. It was so beautiful in the summer when the azaleas and camellias were in bloom in the 80 acres of that wonderful garden. The smell was so absolutely heady

– we felt high just on the scents. It was just so gorgeous. There was a swimming pool too – it was a brilliant time.

Val lived next to us in one of the workmen's cottages. She was very, very straight. She was the most down-to-earth woman you could ever imagine. She did not want to be in the limelight. She just got on with her job. She was lovely.

She was the cook and housekeeper, so she cooked meals, ordered the food, made endless cups of tea and changed all the beds for the endless amounts of people coming in and out of the house. She worked incredibly hard and was very committed. It was a big, big kitchen. A wonderful family farmhouse kitchen with a big, big table, and we had some lovely evenings when everyone sat around the table eating and drinking lots of cups of tea.

While the *Imagine* sessions were going on, I remember everyone working very hard, staying up all up all night, making food – we were all so busy. I remember being called into the studio at about five in the morning to listen to 'Jealous Guy' when it had just been completed, which was quite incredible. It just sounded so amazing, you know, the first time we'd all heard it, really beautiful. Everybody suddenly stopped and they said, 'Listen to this' and we were all completely silent and just listened to it. People were practically in tears, it was just so lovely, so pure. I feel very privileged to have been there on that day.

That whole album and era are really special for me. We were living in this extraordinary world with a bizarre mixture of a lot of interesting people in the most beautiful countryside. It was a very privileged job. I had a wonderful time and they always treated me very well.

John was very funny and witty. Both of them could be quite sharp and direct, very acid-tongued at times, but there was a gentle and funny side to them as well.

Yoko was very protective towards John and would make sure that people wouldn't try to take advantage of him. They were almost like one person. If he said something, she'd say something, they sort of said it together, really. One day he said to me, 'Bring your boyfriend over here, he doesn't have to stay over in the cottage, it's fine, he can come over here,' which was a nice thing to say. He was quite inclusive. He was also quite a joker in lots of ways and asked me and Val to lock the cupboards at night so he couldn't get at the chocolate.

I knew at the time that 'Imagine' was important; probably not as huge as it became, but it did feel amazing to me because it was such a very beautiful song and it said so much. I think I knew that the album would be so important just because it covered so much ground.

I'm not a religious person, but if somebody was to say, 'What kind of hymn would you listen to?', I think 'Imagine' would be it, because it says it all. It's completely inclusive of everything, isn't it? It's incredibly powerful and moving. If it comes on the radio now and I've not heard it for ages, it always stops me in my tracks and brings tears to my eyes and gives me goosebumps. It's gone very deep. I think it's going to get more and more important because John & Yoko were so ahead of their time with all this thing about peace, weren't they? We need it more than ever now. It is the hymn for non-religious people that says it all.

Diana Robertson at work with Peter Bendrey and Dan Richter (top),
Dan Richter and Steve Brendell (centre) and Peter Bendrey
(bottom); Tittenhurst office and kitchen, 16 July 1971.

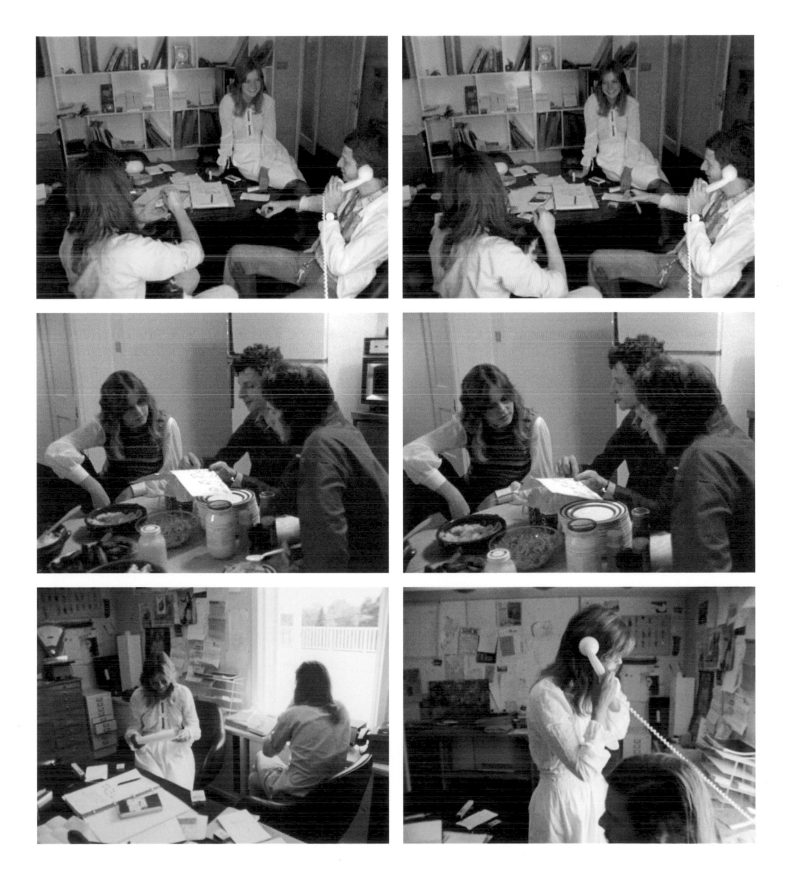

John & Yoko with Steve Brendell on the Northern Ireland
peace march / *Oz* protest march, Marble Arch, Mayfair
and Picadilly, London, 11 August 1971.

steve brendell
general assistant, upright bass

In 1967, I was the drummer in a band called Rupert's People. By 1969, I was Film and Tape Librarian at Apple and one day Dan Richter arrived in the office, introduced himself and told me John & Yoko needed someone to sort out their films at Tittenhurst.

Dan showed me around the house and I soon learnt that everywhere was carpeted in either black or white thick pile carpet – an indication as to where I could go in the house. Anywhere carpeted in black was fine – they were the office and general areas of the house. But anywhere carpeted in white should be avoided. These areas – a kitchenette, John & Yoko's master bedroom, en-suite bathroom and dressing room on the first floor – were their own private rooms, which only Dan, Diana and Val the housekeeper, were permitted to go in. In addition to those, there was the very large reception room where Yoko's white grand piano and artworks stood and everything else in the room was white.

Across a landing, outside of the master bedroom was a large empty, black carpeted room where Dan and I set up a bench for me to work at sorting out the films. That's where I met John for the first time. He didn't have a clue who I was or what I was doing there, but Dan soon explained and he gave me a friendly, welcoming smile. I found both John & Yoko had lots of charisma and would often be speeding around at what seemed like 100 miles per hour, working on their various projects, meetings and press liaisons.

Every day for eighteen months, I'd drive my MGB from home in Muswell Hill to the Apple office in Savile Row, collect the post, memos and any other documents for John & Yoko, including John's weekly petty cash and continue along the M4, through Windsor Great Park to Tittenhurst Park in Sunningdale, Ascot. At the end of the day I'd drive home again.

I also became involved with finishing off John's home recording studio and running errands to collect ashtrays and stools for it. I found John a jukebox and then sourced his choice of 45's to go in it. The best place I discovered for many of John's old favourites was a store in New York called The House of Oldies – still there today. Every time I was needed in New York I would take my list of records to the store and search through the racks for the more obscure ones and usually find a copy.

I always had free access to the studio and would often pop in at lunchtime to practise on the drums. This didn't go unnoticed; one day I'd just come in from a walk in the garden through the studio control room and John, Yoko and Dan were all fiddling around with the new console. John had decided to try out the studio with Dan engineering and Yoko producing, for a song John & Yoko had written a song for the three editors of *Oz* magazine who were awaiting trial for publishing an obscene cartoon drawing of Rupert Bear in their *Oz* 'School Kids' issue. John asked me to join him in the studio on congas, which is exactly what I did and we recorded a demo of 'God Save Oz'.

Once the studio was completely tested and ready, John was anxious to start using it for his second solo album. Mal Evans asked me if I knew any rhythm guitarists for these sessions and I recommended my old friend Rod Lynton (from Rupert's People) and he then brought in John Tout on keys (also from Rupert's), Ted Turner (from Wishbone Ash) and Andy Davis (from Stackridge). Rod and I had already played on sessions at Abbey Road with Phil Spector producing for George Harrison (*All Things Must Pass*) and his wife Ronnie Spector ('Try Some, Buy Some').

On one session I was spontaneously invited to play on 'Crippled Inside',

a fantastic moment for me. Phil wanted to create a kind of honky tonk, bar-room sound and suggested someone slap the strings of the double bass with drumsticks. John said, 'Steve's a drummer, get him in there.' So, swiftly armed with a pair of sticks, I joined Klaus who was standing there with an upright bass and I started to slap the strings as Klaus manoeuvred his way around the neck of the bass. We had a couple of run-throughs and then Phil decided to do a take.

At the end of a session when all the musicians had left and John & Yoko had gone up to their room, I would sometimes sit in the control room with Phil listening back to the night's recording.

I remember one very early morning finish when I was sitting on the sofa with Diana in the control room and Phil was playing back 'Gimme Some Truth' at an extremely high volume, over and over on the large studio speakers. We all listened in awe, it must have been about four or five in the morning.

'Imagine' is a song that lives on with me and so many others to this day. Whenever I hear it, it fills me with emotion and inner peace, and love for a most remarkable man. Someone who for a short time took me into his No. 9 Dream and gave me some of what he found there. Thank you, Dr Winston O' Boogie. The world misses you a lot.

Clockwise from top left: dining room view, 28 May 1971; the White Room,
3 August 1971; the kitchen – John's replacement 1971 Seeburg USC1
'Musical Bandshell' jukebox in the background – 3 August 1971; the library
and billiards room, 3 August 1971; the dining room, 3 August 1971;
the kitchen – posters of Che Guevara and Angela Davis, *War Is Over!*
and *U.S.A. Surpasses All the Genocide Records* on the wall – 3 August 1971.

ground floor

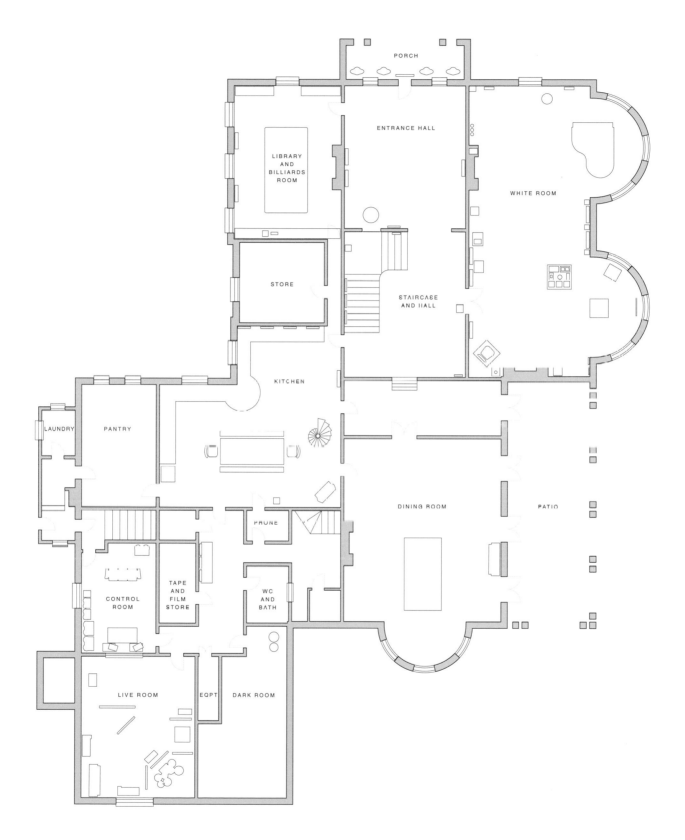

PORCH

ENTRANCE HALL

LIBRARY
AND
BILLIARDS
ROOM

WHITE ROOM

STORE

STAIRCASE
AND HALL

KITCHEN

LAUNDRY

PANTRY

PHONE

DINING ROOM

PATIO

CONTROL
ROOM

TAPE
AND
FILM
STORE

WC
AND
BATH

LIVE ROOM

EQPT

DARK ROOM

ground floor (detail)

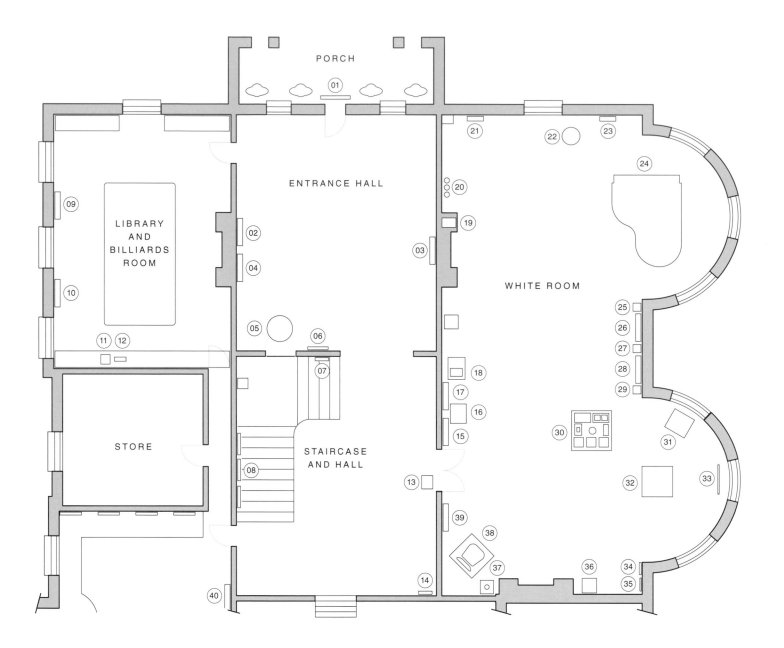

○ works of art | all artworks by yoko ono unless otherwise indicated

01 *This Is Not Here*, 1966/1968
02 *Bag One Drawing*, 1969, John Lennon
03 *Bag One Drawing*, 1969, John Lennon
04 *Bag One Drawing*, 1969, John Lennon
05 *Ceiling Painting (YES painting)*, 1966
06 *You Are Here*, 1968, John Lennon
07 *Bag One Drawing*, 1969, John Lennon
08 *Painting To Hammer A Nail In*, (x3), 1961/1967
09 *Mona Lisa*, n.d., John Lennon
10 *Mona Lisa*, n.d., John Lennon
11 *A Box Of Smile*, 1967
12 Indica Gallery catalogue, 1966
13 *Painting To Be Stepped On*, 1960/1966
14 *You And Me*, 1966/1971
15 *Add Color Painting*, 1960/1966
16 *Water Piece (Painting to be watered)*, 1962/1966

17 *Add Color Painting*, 1960/1966
18 *Danger Box*, 1965/1971
19 *Grapefruit*, 1964/1970 (London edition)
20 *Bag Piece*, 1960/c.1967–1968
21 *Glass Keys To Open The Skies*, 1967
22 *Mending Piece I*, 1962/1966
23 *Glass Keys To Open The Skies*, 1967
24 White Steinway 'O' grand piano
25 *Growing Piece I*, 1966
26 *Add Color Painting*, 1960/1966
27 *Growing Piece II*, 1966
28 *Add Color Painting*, 1960/1966
29 *Growing Piece III*, 1966
30 a. *A Box Of Smile*, 1967
　 b. *Disappearing Piece*, 1971
　 c. *Mind Object I Mix Them Well In Your Mind and Make An Object*, 1960/1966
　 d. *Cleaning Piece For A.P.*, 1966

　 e. *Shovel To Dig a Hole For the Clouds to Drop In*, 1963/1971
31 *Eternal Time*, 1965
32 *White Chess Set*, 1966
33 *Painting To Let The Evening Light Go Through*, 1961/1966
34 *Painting To Hammer A Nail*, 1961/1966
35 *Painting To Hammer A Nail In*, 1961/1967
36 *Three Spoons*, 1967
37 *Mind Object II Not To Be Appreciated Until It's Broken*, 1960/1967
38 a. *Wrapping Piece for London*, 1966
　 b. *Hide Me*, 1971
39 *Add Color Painting*, 1960/1966
40 *The Lodging House*, 1921, L.S. Lowry

Yoko in the White Room with her artworks: *Eternal Time*,1965; *Cleaning Piece For A.P.,* 1966; *Shovel To Dig a Hole For the Clouds to Drop In*, 1963/1971; *Mind Object I Mix Them Well In Your Mind and Make An Object*, 1960/1966; *A Box Of Smile*, 1967, *Disappearing Piece*, 1971; and *White Chess Set*, 1966.

first floor

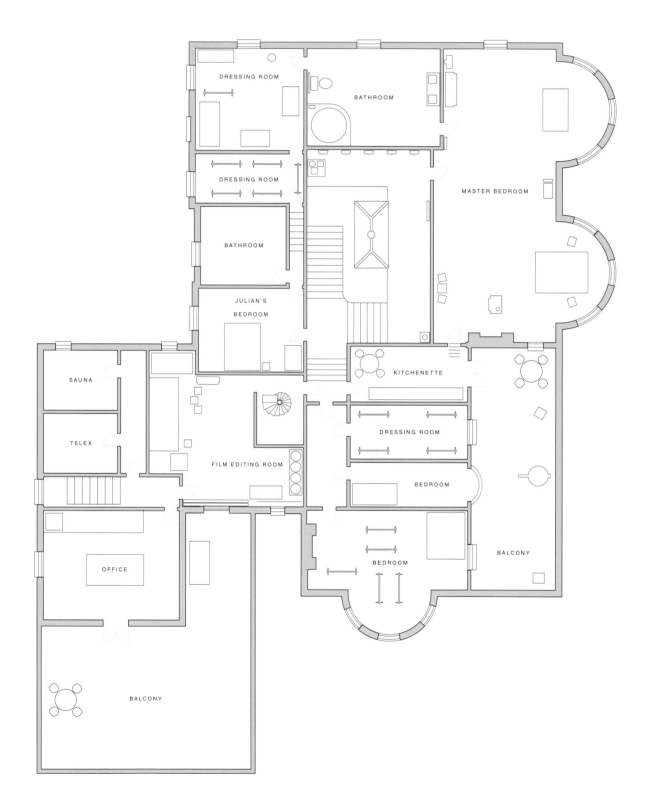

DRESSING ROOM

BATHROOM

DRESSING ROOM

MASTER BEDROOM

BATHROOM

JULIAN'S
BEDROOM

SAUNA

KITCHENETTE

TELEX

DRESSING ROOM

FILM EDITING ROOM

BEDROOM

OFFICE

BEDROOM

BALCONY

BALCONY

Clockwise from top left: spiral staircase to first floor from kitchen, 3 August 1971; master bedroom, 17 July 1971; bathroom, 3 August 1971; John & Yoko's balcony, 20 July 1971; north-west dressing room, 3 August 1971; and master bedroom, 3 August 1971.
Previous pages: Yoko in the White Room with her artworks.
Following pages: panoramic views stitched from original film footage, 16 July 1971.
The centre panorama includes the upright piano on which 'Imagine' was written.

master bedroom north view

master bedroom west view (with John's composing piano on which 'Imagine' was written)

bedroom/dressing room east view

kieron 'spud' murphy
photographer

I first met John & Yoko on 26 May 1971. It was one of my first jobs as *Sounds* magazine's in-house photographer. I hadn't that long arrived from Ireland and suddenly I was to be photographing my hero. I was very excited. I drove down in my little yellow mini and arrived about 5 o'clock in the afternoon.

John & Yoko were having breakfast in the kitchen. They'd been recording all night the night before, and hadn't had much sleep. They seemed to always be glued to one other. In common with a lot of people, I had fallen for the line that she was this dreadful woman who broke up the Beatles. I found her to be an absolute sweetheart. I really liked her and it was also obvious that the two of them were very much in love.

While we were all sitting round the kitchen table, George Harrison showed

up, and some people I didn't recognize, and suddenly Phil Spector seemed to appear in a puff of blue smoke. It was as if he'd come up out of the floor. He had such a heavy presence. And he stood there for a moment, and said something very quietly, like, 'I think we should maybe get started, John.' And John rushed around literally taking teacups out of people's hands, like, 'Phil wants us to start now' [laughs] and literally hustling us all to the studio, like herding cattle. He seemed to be as much in awe of Phil Spector as I was of John.

They were rehearsing 'How Do You Sleep?' in the studio all day. I can't remember at what point I left. I stayed there till midnight or maybe later. I don't think they recorded anything, because when I heard the album version, the arrangement was quite different.

On 17 July, he invited me back to hear the finished album. It was a beautiful summer's day and about half-past two when I got there. I really wanted to hear the album, but John kept putting it off, making excuses, like, 'Let's go for a walk around the park with a long stroll around the lake' and 'Let's have a cup of iced tea.' By this time it was 7 o'clock and I was wondering, 'What's the matter with him?' It was only many years later I realized he was so nervous about playing his new album to a member of the public.

Eventually, he took me into a little music room, just off the White Room, which had a state-of-the-art stereo, and he put on an acetate of the album. He said, 'I can't bear to hear it any more; I've heard it hundreds of times. We've mixed it, and I can't even tell if it's any good or not. You're the first

member of the public to hear it, so have a listen and come out and tell us what you think.' And I'm thinking, 'Fucking hell, I now have to give some feedback to John Lennon!', you know?

I listened to it through, three times I think. At this stage it was nearly dark outside. When I went back out to the kitchen, he literally buttonholed me. 'Well, what do you think? Is it any good?' He literally asked me about lots of different things. 'Did you like King Curtis's solo in 'I Don't Wanna Be A Soldier?' Any musician in the world would've cut off their right arm to play on this album, but he seemed to be as much enthralled by them.

He didn't seem to be convinced by everything I said, and at one point I said, 'Look, John, let me put it this way, I really like the previous album,

the one with "Working Class Hero" and all that old stuff on it. I play it every day in the dark room,' which was true. And I said, 'I hope you won't mind me saying this, it does have a kind of bleak feel to it. This new album is much more accessible.' And he put his head in his hands and said 'Oh no!' and I said, 'What?' 'I can see the headlines now: Lennon sells out!' [laughs]

I said, 'I really like that first song, "Imagine". People are gonna be listening to it in five or ten years' time' [laughs] and he said, 'Don't be fucking stupid, it's only a pop song!' I did recognize it was a special song and a hit single, but I'd be fibbing if I said I knew it was going to be such a massive anthem.

Some of the close-up portraits are on a 105mm lens and some of the wider

shots in the studio were probably on a 24mm wide angle. Probably Ilford HP4 film. There's one photograph I really like of the two of them sitting on the bed. It has that very late Sixties style with back lighting and flare, which was very 'in' at the time. He's yacking away, clearly in full motormouth mode, and he's got his right hand up making some sort of gesture. She's smoking a cigarette, just kind of looking down. I can still hear her saying, 'Yes John, yes dear.' It's one of my favourite photographs.

This and following pages: John & Yoko in the master bedroom, 17 July 1971; Kieron 'Spud' Murphy's favourite photo, overleaf.

pages 74–75: on the balcony, 21 July 1971.

john & yoko's balcony east view

balcony 2 north and east view

balcony 2 east view

John & Yoko in the woods at Tittenhurst, 22 July 1971.
Previous pages: stitched panoramic views from the
first floor balconies outside the bedrooms and office,
and dawn in the grounds; Tittenhurst, 16 July 1971.

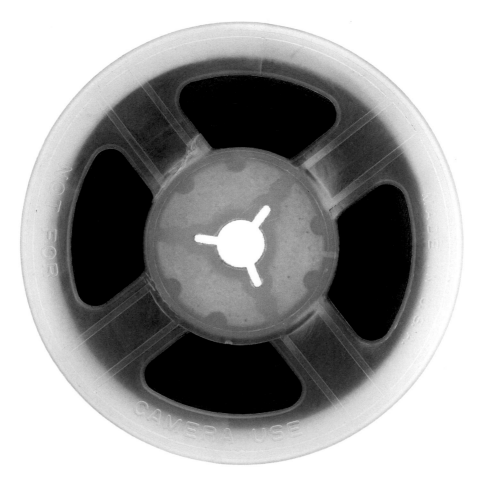

Somebody tell John I'll be at
Gatwick the 18th wearing a three
quarter brown sheepskin coat +++
Reply immediately before. Should
I come and wait or not? +++
I can't make the trip over unless
I know you'll be there +++ You say
you want to help and you know
I need help but I won't come there
until you wire back +++

Curt Claudio, telegram to John Lennon, 1971

Quarter-inch audio tape recording of a spoken letter sent from
Curt Claudio in Milpitas, California, to John & Yoko at Tittenhurst, 1971.

claudio

John: I had this guy called Claudio who had been sending telegrams for nine months to England saying 'I'm coming, I'm coming and then I'll only have to look in your eyes and I'll know.'

Dan Richter: We began to take Claudio seriously and we were able to trace the telegram back to a Veterans Administration hospital in the San Francisco area. Apparently Claudio was a shell-shocked Vietnam veteran who was due to be released from the hospital.

John: So last week he turned up at my house and he looked in my eyes and he didn't get any answer. He thought the whole thing was about him and I said, 'No, it's about me.' It might strike a corresponding chord in your experience because we all have similar experiences but it's basically about me and if it's not about me, it's about Yoko. I said. 'You better get on

and live your own life, you're wasting your time trying to live mine.'

Yoko: At Tittenhurst, there was no particular security and one of our assistants told us that there was this strange guy that was staying in our garden almost every night. John always felt responsible for these people because they were the result of his songs. That's how he felt.

Peter Bendrey: Dan and I would go around the grounds every morning to see if anybody was camping out and very often there were people there. And as we were escorting this guy out of the park through the main gate, John comes out of the front door and says, 'Hey, bring him in, I want to know what's going on in his head.'

Diana Robertson: Claudio would just appear out of a hedge sometimes. He looked rough but also incredibly beautiful, there was something about

him that was amazing. I think he was harmless really, but to begin with, people didn't want to have anything to do with him and didn't want him around. It was so lovely when John let him in and gave him a cup of tea. It was just so nice, this guy never really expected this was going to happen.

Yoko: He was no dummy. He was a spiritual person. Claudio was communicating to John on a high level. It's no bad thing; it was a good thing, actually. We knew he was a spirit and that's why John invited him in to have lunch with us. The food did it, though. It calmed him down. I don't think we heard from him again after that.

Dan Richter: John had a really special way with people. He also had a very honest, vulnerable quality, which always made me worry for him. It was part of the key to and price of his success.

John It's just a record. It might mean more to me or you than somebody else. It's still just songs. It's poetry.

Claudio: You didn't put it all together? You just....

John: I just write it like anybody writes anything. Either from my own experience or out of my own head.

Yoko: Many people get the same impression. They think, 'Oh, that's me.'

John: Think about when you were fourteen. Just imagine it. And imagine if one of your friends had come and said the Beatles, or Elvis, or anybody was writing songs only about them. What would you have thought of it?

Claudio: To be honest. I wasn't thinking that it was me, egotistically....

John: Well that's alright, but don't confuse the songs with your own life. They might have relevance to your own life, but a lot of things do. So we met, you know, I am just a guy, man, who writes songs. You can only say 'Hello', and what else is there?

Claudio: Yeah. I figured that if we met I would know just by reading you....

John: But know what?

Claudio: If what I was thinking was true.

John: Well, what…is it true?

Claudio: Well, I guess not.

John: Right! I am just a guy, man.

Claudio: But it all fits, you know?

John: Anything fits. If you're tripping off on some trip, anything fits. You can get tripped off by the stars [astrology] in the newspaper. when they say you're going to have a good day or a bad day. It could be your auntie's boyfriend writing the stuff. But if you get into it, anything fits.

Claudio: Yeah, I just had to meet you.

John: Well, here we are. We met. And I'm just a fellow and I am working.

And you met me and we say, 'Hello' and that's it. There's no secrets, really. You just have to try and remember what it was like when you were younger. Before you got tripped off.

Claudio: You know, like when you were saying, 'Boy you're gonna carry that weight for a long time', was that just…

John: Paul sang that, yeah.

Claudio: Paul sang that?

John: Well that belongs to all of us. He is singing about all of us. We've all got to carry it until we die, haven't we?

Claudio: I guess that's true. Yeah, I guess I was building it all.

John: Right. Yeah, but you have got to believe that or you're going to spend your whole life looking for dreams. The only way to do it is to try and remember when you were younger. What would you have thought of it then – all this mystic jazz? You would have told him where to stick it.

Claudio: Remember that one, um… 'You can radiate everything you are, you can penetrate anywhere that you go, syndicate everything….'

John: Yeah. That was just having fun with words.

Yoko: I thought of the 'radiate', 'syndicate' – all that.

John: Radiate. Yeah, she wrote that. Radiate. Syndicate. I was just having fun with words. It was literally a nonsense song.

Yoko: I wouldn't tell you, unless….

John: I mean, Dylan does that. Anybody does it. You just take words and you stick them together and it's like throwing the I Ching or something. You just see what happens. You take a bunch of words, you throw them out and see if they have any meaning. Some of them do, some of them don't. But it's not universally significant or anything.

Claudio: Yeah. And your 'Hare Krishna has nothing on you'?

John: Yeah, well he don't. I mean. You're it. You see, that last album of mine was me coming out of my dream.

Claudio: You really weren't thinking of anyone in particular when you were singing all that?

John: How could I be? How could I be thinking of you, man?

Claudio: Well I don't know. Maybe I don't care, me, but it's all, it's all somebody.

John: I have been thinking about me; or at best Yoko, if it's a love song. And I maybe think about an audience in general if I am singing 'Old Hare Krishna got nothing on you', I am talking to any old friends who have been listening to what we were saying, and saying, 'Look, well I think it's a lot of bullshit now, let's forget it.' I am basically singing about me and I am saying, well, I had a good shit today and this is what I thought this morning and, 'I love you, Yoko', or whatever. I am singing about me and my life and if it's relevant for other people's lives, that's alright.

Claudio: Yeah.

John: Are you hungry?

Claudio: Yeah.

John: Let's give him something to eat, come on.

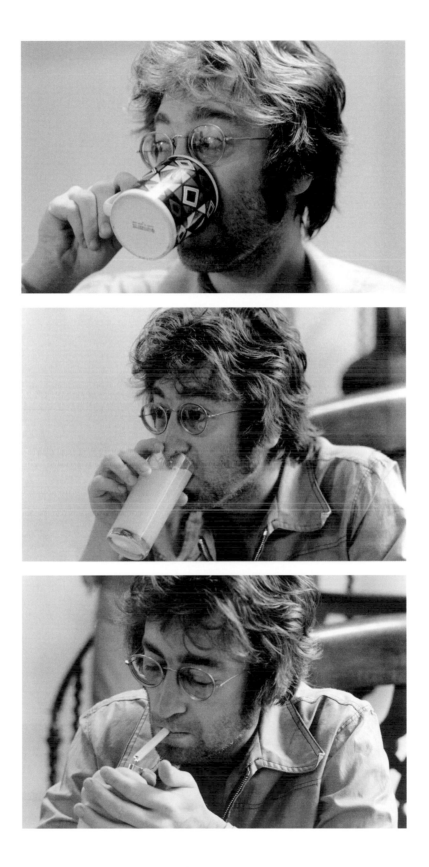

You can shine your shoes and wear a suit
You can comb your hair and look quite cute
You can hide your face behind a smile
One thing you can't hide
is when your crippled inside!

You can wear a mask and paint your face
You can call yourself the human race
You can wear a collar and a tie
one thing you can't hide
is that your crippled inside

You can go to church and sing a hymn
judge me by the color of my skin
you can live a lie until you die
one thing you can't hide
is when your crippled inside.

crippled inside

You can shine your shoes and wear a suit
You can comb your hair and look quite cute
You can hide your face behind a smile
One thing you can't hide
Is when you're crippled inside

You can wear a mask and paint your face
You can call yourself the human race
You can wear a collar and a tie
One thing you can't hide
Is when you're crippled inside

Well now you know that your
Cat has nine lives, babe
Nine lives to itself
But you only got one
And a dog's life ain't fun
Mama take a look outside

You can go to church and sing a hymn
You can judge me by the colour of my skin
You can live a lie until you die
One thing you can't hide
Is when you're crippled inside

Well now you know that your
Cat has nine lives, babe
Nine lives to itself
But you only got one
And a dog's life ain't fun
Mama take a look outside

You can go to church and sing a hymn
Judge me by the colour of my skin
You can live a lie until you die
One thing you can't hide
Is when you're crippled inside

crippled inside

John: Songwriting is like getting the demon out of me. It's like being possessed. You try to go to sleep, but the song won't let you. So you have to get up and make it into something, and then you're allowed to sleep. It's always in the middle of the bloody night or when you're half awake or tired, when your critical faculties are switched off.

'Crippled Inside' is a social comment. It talks about people having false fronts in society and really underneath there's something else. Satire. There was one review of that song that said, 'Oh, that kind of song has been done before…' but I wasn't even thinking about it. I was sitting down and this little riff came into me head, like an old Twenties song: 'One thing you can't hide is when you're crippled inside.' It just came to me, you know, like that, and I just finished it off. It's like whatever suit you're wearing, tie you're wearing, whatever face you're putting on, it always shows really in your face, in your eyes, what's really going on in your soul. And there's nothing you can hide.

People hide from each other all the time. Everybody's frightened of saying something nice about somebody in case they don't say something nice back or in case they get hurt. Everybody's uptight and they're always building these walls around themselves. All you can do is try and break down the walls and show that there's nothing there but people. It's just like looking in the mirror.

Yoko: Next time you meet a 'foreigner', remember it's only like a window with a different shape to it and the person who's sitting inside is you.

John: Paul's parents were terrified of me and my influence, simply because I was free from the parents' stranglehold. That was the gift I got of not having parents. I have cried a lot about not having them and the torture it was. Some people cannot see that their parents are still torturing them, even when they are in their forties and fifties; they still have that stranglehold over them and their thoughts and their minds and everything.

This image of me being the orphan is garbage because I was well protected by my auntie and my uncle and they looked after me very well, thanks. There were five women that were my family. Five strong, intelligent beautiful women, there were five sisters. One happened to be my mother. My mother just couldn't deal with life. She was the youngest. And she had a husband who ran away to sea and the war was on and she couldn't cope with me and I ended up living with her elder sister.

My mother was alive and lived a fifteen-minute walk away from me all my life and I saw her sporadically all the time.

I just didn't live with her. She got killed by an off-duty cop who was drunk after visiting my auntie's house where I lived, but I wasn't there at the time. So that was another big trauma for me. I lost her twice. Once as a five-year-old, where I was moved in with my auntie, and once again at fifteen where she actually physically died. I was at art school. So I must have been seventeen. And that was a really hard time for me and it just absolutely made me very, very bitter.

And the underlying chip on my shoulder that I had as a youth was really big then. Being a teenager and rock and roller… and mother being killed just when I was re-establishing a relationship with her. It was very traumatic for me.

Yoko: I remember the severe bombing in Tokyo, hiding in an air-raid shelter listening to the sound of the bombs coming closer and then going away, and feeling that my mother and I lived another day.

I remember being evacuated to the country; the food shortage, and starving; going to the next village to find rice for my brother and sister; being stoned by the village kids who hated people from the city; getting anaemic and being diagnosed as having pleurisy; being abused by a doctor, and having my appendix taken out without proper anaesthetics because of the shortage of medicine. I remember how I cried at the end of the war, how bombed out Tokyo looked when I returned from the country on the back of a truck, and what we went through daily, reading about the people in Hiroshima. The ones who died of burns went quickly. The ones who died of leukaemia went through a slow and agonizing death. We lived through their death.

When I had this apartment in New York, I was imagining myself all the time as a kite, holding on to a kite, and when I was sleeping, I'd lose my string and go off floating. That's the time I thought: I'll go crazy. I was just holding the string, making sure that I wouldn't let go.

Around the time that I met John, I went to a palmist – John would probably laugh at this – and he said, 'You're like a very fast wind that goes speeding around the world.' And I had a line that signified astral projection. The only thing I didn't have was a root. But, the palmist said, 'You've met a person who's fixed like a mountain, and if you get connected with that mountain you might get materialized.' And John is like a frail wind, too, so he understands all these aspects.

I'm not searching for the big daddy. I look for something else in men – something that is tender and weak and I feel like I want to help.

John: And I was the lucky cripple she chose!

recording imagine

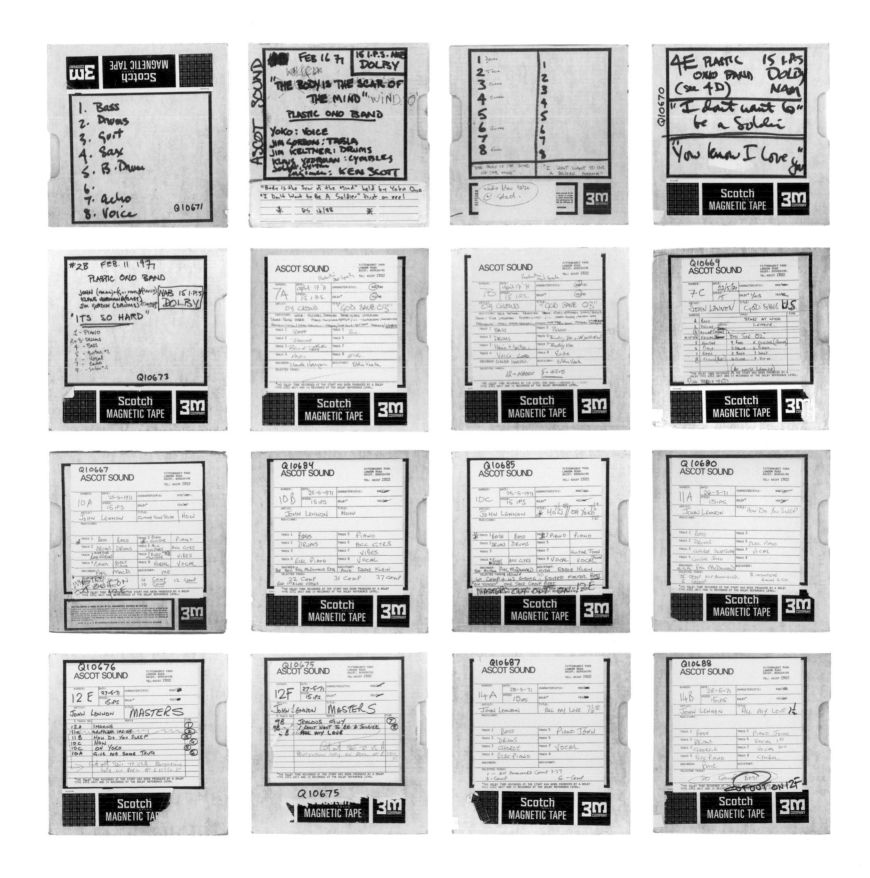

What's the point of going into town to record when you've got it in the house? The one in the office hasn't been finished, you see. And that's going to be sixteen-track, and this is eight-track. And it just means you can record when you want. And, you can go to bed. It's better than EMI's because it's got newer equipment.

John, 1970

John at the bespoke console built by Eddie Veale
and David Dearden; Ascot Sound Studios, 3 August 1971.
Previous pages: thirty-two 1-inch, 8-track audio master tape boxes
from Ascot Sound Studios, Tittenhurst, 11 February – 29 May 1971.

eddie veale
engineer, ascot sound studios

The brief was exactly that: very brief. The request from Neil Aspinall was, 'Please build a studio for John as good as Apple.' It was the first professional home studio in the UK.

I had studied acoustics at university, and then worked at de Havilland on aircraft noise control. After that, I went to Advision Studios for five years, to refurbish and then relocate their studios. They had the first eight-track in London. As new machines and effects were invented, I designed lots of black boxes to make them all work together.

When I remodelled the control rooms at Lansdowne Studios, Clive Green did the console. He had created the CADAC modules, replacing the valve parts of the desk with transistors, and readying them for eight-track. He also created the Gyrator EQ. When Clive put the desk in at Apple, he asked me to design and install the monitoring speakers above the window. I fixed a few other things in George Peckham's vinyl cutting room, and then Neil Aspinall asked me in for that chat.

We started at Tittenhurst in August 1970. John and I looked around various rooms that would fit the larger equipment like the Studer eight-tracks and the mixing desk. We converted a photographic studio near the kitchen into the music studio, and we took a wall out to make the control room large enough. Although John was anxious to have the studio done in three to four months, there was a lot of building work involved, and the single-storey roof section had some serious damp rot. We built in sound isolation – to keep the sound in – with an isolated sub-ceiling under the roof we had to refurbish. There wasn't much needed to keep external sound out, apart from the lawnmower and the occasional aircraft flying overhead.

John was spending more and more time at Ascot. He was extracting himself from the Beatles' emporium and he was anxious to get into the studio rather than have to go into London. I don't think a day went by without him visiting and saying, 'Well how's it going? Can I get in yet?'

Eventually, we came to an arrangement where we engineers could work mornings and John could have it for the rest of the day. This quickly developed into long days for me, because John wanted me around for the session in case anything went wrong, which it often did.

I found that, instead of getting on with things that I had intended to do, I was often spending time before everyone showed up, helping John to plug in mics, make things happen, or play tape back to him, so he could listen back to what he had done. I hadn't done that before. It was fun and I always like a new challenge. Later in the day, John would try to do something – or Phil would want a particular effect – or something wouldn't work – and we engineers would have to technically solve it. The engineers were very easy to work with. Good guys, with clear ideas. They had a very good understanding of what John wanted to do, because they had worked with him on so many Beatles recordings. It was a really good time.

Early on, John had started experimenting and laying down tracks. But when Phil Spector arrived, things started happening in earnest. Phil sat down at the desk on the first day and instinctively understood how it worked. I held him in some awe for his ability to do that.

Phil was very forthright. He quickly assembled, in his mind, a picture of what he wanted to achieve, and was very much on top of everything that went on. He was used to working in big, professional studios – not one that was in the middle of being built. So he expected everything to be there, ready. It was already a case of, 'Why haven't you plugged it up yet?' I very much liked his production ideas, and his approach. I thought from his influence and control on the musical work, he was right at the top of his profession.

To create his sound, Phil liked everything clear – distinct – and perfectly placed. He would have everything in mono, so the guitar appeared there, the drums appeared there and the strings were sort of a little bit across the top, with a bit of drums behind them. Everything was placed and then maximised, so you got this really big wall of sound. Often, for John, it was too much in your face – 'Can we just back that off a bit more, Phil?'

John was a very competent musician. Very astute with his ideas. He would start talking, verbalising something he wanted. And by the time he had finished talking, he had rationalised it and knew exactly what he wanted. So you could just go and do it.

At the time, I had no concept of what *Imagine* might turn into. It was a departure for John. When I heard the final product, I was very impressed. *Imagine* reminds me of some very happy times – I get quite emotional about some of it, where we all worked together so well.

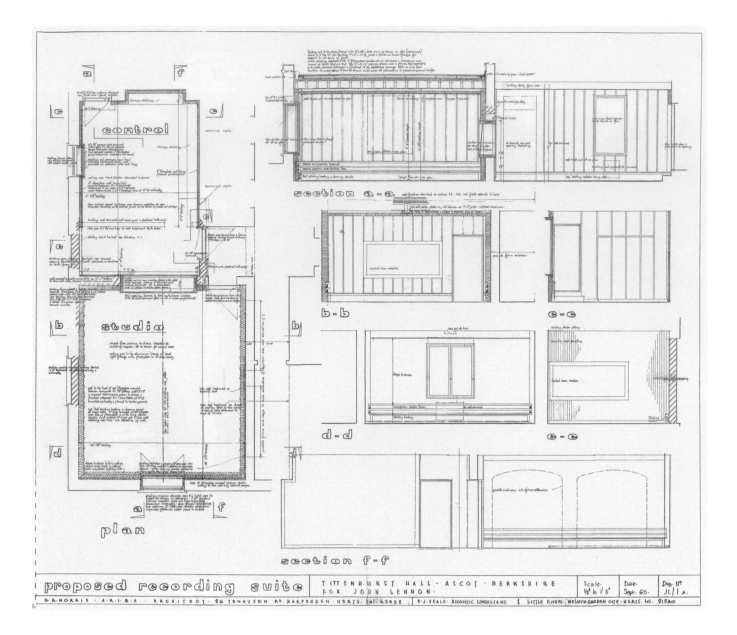

studio equipment

Eddie Veale: The music studio was designed so one side had more of a live feel than the other. I built the first desk from scratch, with David Dearden. It had sixteen channels, four echo returns, eight master outs, two foldback, two reverb sends. We couldn't get anything bigger in the room. The desk was all based on CADAC modules. It was a three-band EQ – a top and bottom, and a bit of a mid lift and cut – nothing too fancy.

The outboard at Tittenhurst was DBX and UREIs – a pair of each being the limiters and compressors. Generally, everything was recorded clean, and then any effects were either added in mixdowns or the final mix. Voice and piano were about the only things

pre-processed at the recording stage – a bit of EQ on the tracks just to get them sounding sweet. Very few additional effects were brought in.

Mics were Neumann KM84s, U87s, U47s, KM84is and a few AKGs. Amcron power amps, Crown DC300 and Quad 303s for the headphones and other amps. The speakers were Altec 604E Drivers in wedge-shaped, corner-mounted cabinets to get them out of the way, above the window – like at Apple.

To broaden the monitoring sweet spot, we set the speakers up so they were slightly wider than normal, and angled in – bringing the convergence point farther forward. So if you moved from centre to left, you would come

more into the field of the right-hand speaker and the change is not so obvious. The combination of that, with the earlier reflections in the room, deceived the ear into thinking the sweet spot was wider. Which was great for multiple people listening at the desk at the same time. Quad was the emerging thing at that time, so we hooked a couple of JBL speakers up at the back for them to play with.

There was a stereo echo chamber and stereo EMT 140 plate reverbs. The chamber was a Crown DC300 amp and loudspeaker, and a couple of mics, without a delay. We had a 3M-56 1-inch eight-track from Apple, and two Studer B62s for mixdown, and ADT with a 706 varispeed unit.

The newly built studio control room with speakers, console, 8-track and quarter-inch tape machines and turntable; Ascot Sound Studios, January 1971.
Opposite: original plan of recording studio by Eddie Veale Associates, September 1969.

ground floor (detail)

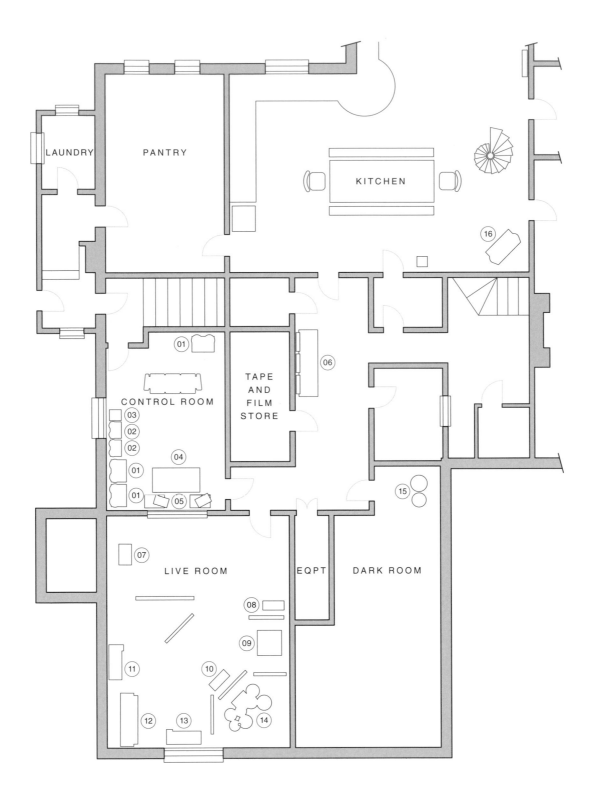

LAUNDRY

PANTRY

KITCHEN

CONTROL ROOM

TAPE AND FILM STORE

LIVE ROOM

EQPT

DARK ROOM

◯ musical instruments and recording equipment

01 3M56 1" tape machine
02 Studer B62 ¼" tape machine
03 Turntable
04 Control desk
05 Speakers (floor and wall-mounted)
06 Mellotron
07 Fender Showman amplifier
08 Fender Vibro Champ amplifier

09 Ampeg Portaflex BN-15N amplifier
10 Fender Twin amplifier
11 Wurlitzer 200 electric piano
12 Steinway Model Z upright piano
13 RMI 300B Electra piano
14 Ludwig Silver Sparkle drumkit
15 Conga drums
16 Wurlitzer 2500 jukebox

In the control room with John & Yoko, Phil Spector, Joe Marcini, Phil McDonald, Eddie Klein, Rod Lynton, Mal Evans, John Barham, Alan White and Klaus Voormann; Ascot Sound Studios, Tittenhurst, 24–29 May 1971.

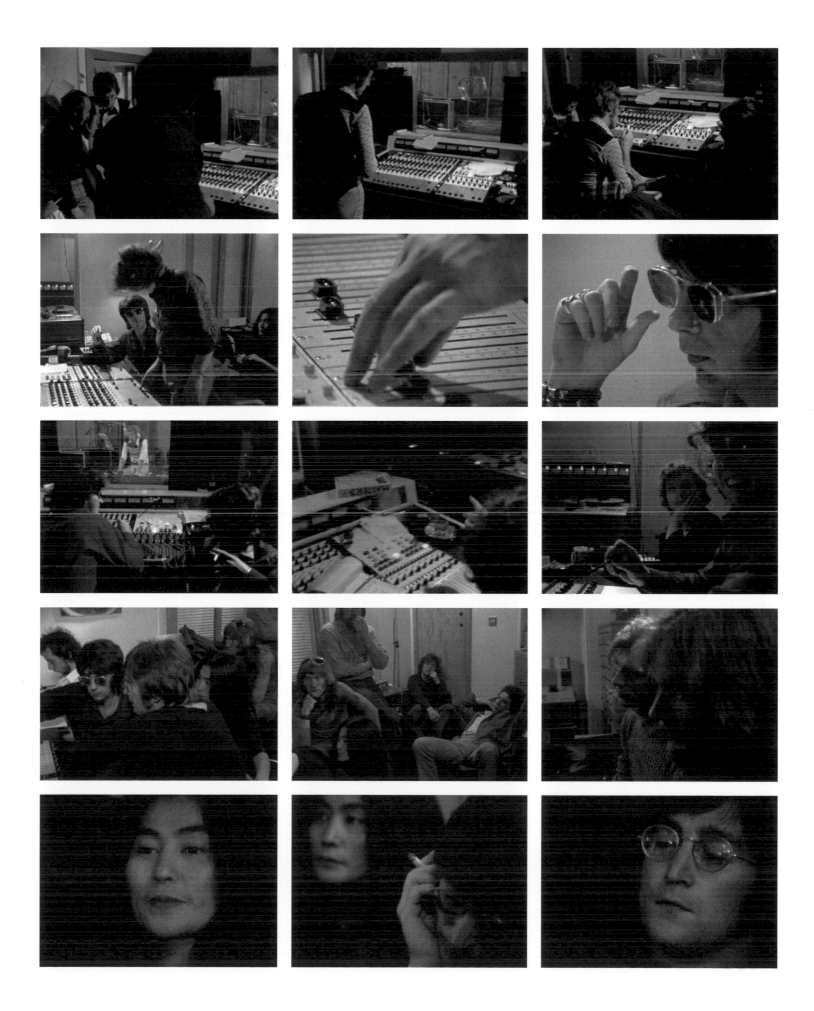

Recording 'How Do You Sleep?' – George Harrison (electric guitar), Ted Turner and Rod Lynton (twelve-string acoustic guitars), Klaus Voormann (bass), Alan White (drums), John Lennon (electric guitar and vocals), Nicky Hopkins (Wurlitzer electric piano), John Tout (upright piano); Ascot Sound Studios, 26 May 1971.

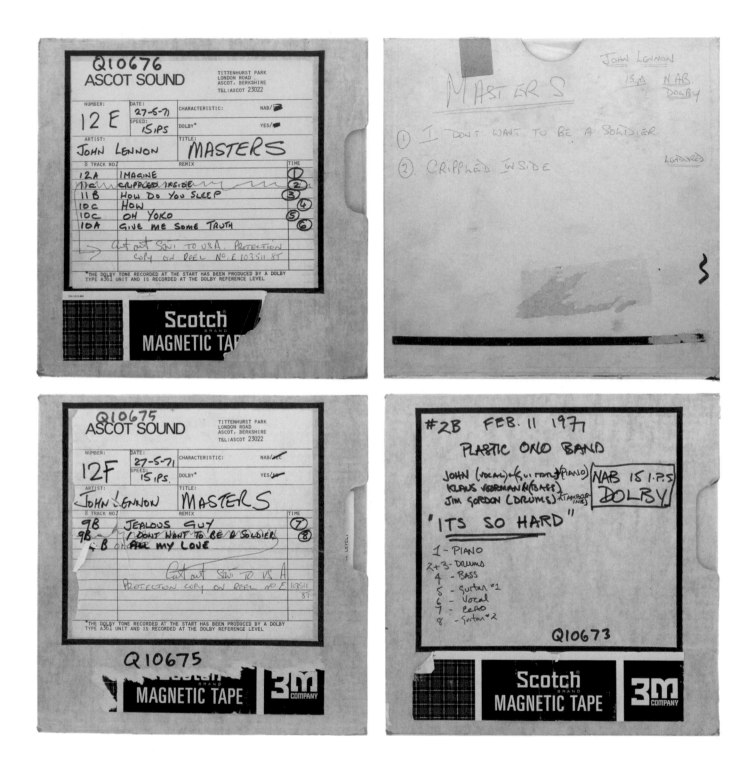

The four 1-inch, 8-track audio master tape boxes for the *Imagine* album
from Ascot Sound Studios, 11 February 1971 and 24 – 29 May 1971.

recording imagine

John: I have a group called Plastic Ono Band, which means anybody that comes to the session. I don't want to be trapped again with the same musicians making the same sound. Just whoever I like at the moment or whoever visits me. I always have the tune and the words. I like to just play it and just teach the group the basic song and then we play it.

We recorded it at home in our studio, Phil Spector produces with Yoko and I, so as we don't go overboard and he doesn't go overboard – we get a balance between the three of us. It was better than the first time, because now we know each other and we've done quite a lot of work together and we understand each other, so we know how to work better. That's why it's been quicker – we did the last one in ten days and we did this one in nine.

You can see the vast difference from when he works with George or he works with me or he works alone – I just take what I need from him and it doesn't get completely Spectorised. Spector produced 'River Deep Mountain High', which is one of the all-time class records ever, and that's completely Spectorised, and that's great. There's one or two where we just let him go.

Yoko: Not really.

John: Aren't there?

Yoko: Well even on 'Soldier' it's completely you, really.

John: Yoko's there completely. She never lets up, you know? You'll see in the film where there's dialogue between them, if we all three agree, then it's all right. We usually do, too. I don't know how we do, you'll probably see on the film – it's just sort of done. I'll get the arrangement – Phil doesn't arrange or anything like that – and she and Phil will just sit in the other room and shout comments like, 'Why don't you try this sound' or you're not playing the piano too well, try that,' something like that. I'll get the initial idea and say, 'Nicky, you get on piano, and someone else get on that' and then Phil will suggest three acoustic guitars strumming somewhere, and we'll just find a sound from it. It's quite easy working with him, isn't it?

Yoko: I think the funniest thing is that we're all three very strong personalities, but somehow it doesn't clash at all. It works in a very quick way and somehow we bring out each other's sensitivity rather that the aggressiveness. It's very nice, we all take different parts in a way.

John: This is still pretty simple – there's just some little pieces. The violins – I've kept them pretty simple because I don't want them to swamp the thing, but all I've done really is make the basic tracks and just lay violins on them.

Yoko: There are a lot of delicate things happening inside them musically that didn't happen so much in the last one.

John: We've bothered with it more this time. It was intense, that last one, it was just like getting it down like a shorthand message, and although this was fast, this was a more musical trip, really. You know, I'd bother to overdub Tibetan cymbals just to have it on with the real cymbals, or whatever, whereas on the last one I wouldn't bother.

I like to use different people on each track so that it doesn't get stilted. There's Jim Gordon on drums, Alan White on drums, Jim Keltner on drums, and they're fantastic. I would have used Ringo on drums, but he was away filming in Spain. George is on a good five or six tracks. Yoko's on whip, and that's very good; whip and mirror, actually.

Nicky Hopkins is a fantastic guy. It's just amazing how he lifts a whole track. Then we had John Barham on a few things and King Curtis is on sax. I think Mike Pinder even plays tambourine on one track. There's some rhythm guitarists from Badfinger and some from somewhere else. I used some of the New York Philharmonic Orchestra for the violins and we called them The Flux Fiddlers. I forgot to mention Klaus because he's on everything.

It's not a personal thing like the last album, but I've learned a lot and this is better in every way, technique and so on. It's lighter, too. I was feeling happy. It's a lighter and happier album than the last, and I've tentatively.0 titled it *Imagine*, which is the title of one of the songs.

Yoko co-wrote one of the tracks ('Oh My Love'). It's one of the best on the album, and she designed the album.

I did eighty per cent in the studio here. It took seven days, then I spent two days putting the violins on in New York. We'd already mixed everything and we just did it again over there down to another stereo or whatever you call it, like they used to do it in the old days. It took me nine days to make this album and ten to make the last one. So I'm getting faster.

There are ten tracks on it. I had more, but Phil suddenly said that I had no more room, so we stopped. We recorded some in Quad too, it's fantastic, I did the Quad in New York, it's beautiful. Quad Music!! Compared to the last one it's less introspective, in a way, and it's a bit light; there's some heavy stuff, but I call it commercial with no compromise.

Eighty per cent was recorded in Britain in seven days. I took them, re-mixed them, and took it to America like they used to do in the old days. It took me nine days to make this album, and ten to make the last one. So I'm getting faster.

John, 1972

John in the master bedroom at Tittenhurst, 17 July 1971.

Phil Spector about to record 'Oh My Love'; Ascot Sound Studios, 28 May 1971.

phil spector
co-producer

I graduated in 1958. It was a very quick change for me from student to artist to producer to whizz-kid. When I made my first record 'To Know Him Is to Love Him', I had the chance to be upfront. Nobody knew it was about my father and nobody knew it was about death and it was a love song to somebody up beyond.

I learnt a lot by being in The Teddy Bears. I learnt I didn't want to be a singer. I learnt about payola and distributors and manufacturing. I learnt about the Mafia. I wanted to be in the background but I wanted to be important in the background. I wanted to be the focal point. I knew about Toscanini. I knew that Mozart was more important than his operas, that Beethoven was more important than whoever was playing or conducting his music. That's what I wanted to be.

Most producers don't create, they interpret. When I went into the studio I created a sound that I wanted to hear. And I always compare it to what Da Vinci did when he went to a blank canvas. I always considered it not rock 'n' roll. I always considered it art.

I just knew that my calling was to be in the music industry and write songs – the best songs in the world – and make records and be a record producer. And if the songs didn't work and the artists didn't work, the records would be the art that would carry the weight of everything. The production always carried the power of the art, which was in the recording. That's why the recordings live on today.

The Spector 'sound' took a lot of work and creativity and it was a bitch to get. And it was in my mind. It would take me days and I'd have to throw away thousands of dollars of studio time. I had the 'Wall of Sound' but it took me forever. Brian Wilson aged sixty-five is still going through craziness,

he writes, listening to 'Be My Baby' every morning, going crazy, trying to work out how I got that sound, forty years later.

Even when the music became big, I never felt like I fitted in. I never did all the drugs and the parties. I didn't feel comfortable. I always preferred the studio. Going out was always the big ordeal. Too hard. It was like being in front of an audience. I just felt I didn't fit in. I was different. So I had to make my own world. And it made life complicated for me, but it made it justifiable. I look strange, I act strange, I make these strange records. So there's a reason to hate my guts – because I felt hated.

Pain is just there. It's a constant. Hurting is a natural phenomenon with art. It's like criticism. It's something to be expected before adoration. It comes with the music. It comes with the art. You expect to be criticized by the 'in crowd'. You don't expect the good reviewers to say anything nice about your music. You don't expect your heroes, even your musician heroes, to want to play your music. You expect them to make fun of you.

I am trying to get my life reasonable. I'm not going to ever be happy. Happiness isn't on. Because happiness is temporary. Unhappiness is temporary. Ecstasy is temporary. Orgasm is temporary. Everything is temporary. But being reasonable is an approach and being reasonable with yourself, it's very difficult to be reasonable.

I'm not addicted to applause because I live a life of reclusiveness. Those records, when I was making them, they were the greatest love of my life. I lived for those records. That's why I never had relationships with anybody that could last. That's why I can't figure out why they have so little significance for me today. John Lennon said that I kept rock

'n' roll alive for the two-and-a-half years while Elvis was in the Army, which was very flattering.

Lennon was the brother I never had. I just loved him. And we just loved each other. He loved the way I worked. He loved the way I thought. Perfect marriage. Just perfect.

I'm all for an international holiday every 9 October. Anything to remember John is just like remembering Martin. You know, they didn't want a Martin Luther King holiday. Reagan opposed it and it was Congress that got it through, and Stevie Wonder. So, you know, with just a little help from a couple of our friends, we could get it through. We just can't seem to get them together. We can't get them together to stop this war and we can't get them together to get a holiday for John!

When Kurt Cobain died, somebody phoned me from *Time* magazine and said, 'I haven't been this upset since John Lennon died.' I said, 'You don't know the difference between Kurt Cobain and John Lennon?' He said. 'No, what's the difference?' I said, 'That's too bad, because Kurt Cobain did.' It's all been done! It's all been done!

Following pages: John and Phil Spector rehearsing 'How Do You Sleep?'; Ascot Sound Studios, 26 May 1971.

Recording the backing vocals for 'Oh Yoko!'; Ascot Sound Studios, 29 May 1971.

Yoko: Phil Spector is a genius. He's a real genius. Everybody in the music world knows that.

John: He's a mysterious man, his woodwork to perform, my dear.

I think it was Klein's suggestion when we first used Phil Spector. I was pleased with the result of Spector's work and anyone who can make a record like 'River Deep, Mountain High' must be good. I was amazed at the amount of great records he had been involved with that had influenced me back in Liverpool. It seems that talented people must always be in pain – their sensitivity is what makes them great artists – but what a price to pay. He is and always will be one of the great originals of rock music. And it's true – to know him is to love him.

George Harrison: Phil was brought into London by Allen Klein when we did *Let It Be*. *Let It Be* was supposed to be just a live recording. We ended up doing it in the studio and nobody was happy with it. It was troubled times. Everybody listened to it back and didn't really like it and we didn't really want to put it out. So later down the line, Allen Klein brought Phil Spector and said, 'What do you think about Phil looking at the record?' At least John and I said, 'Yeah – we liked Phil Spector, we loved all his records so let him do it.' And he did what he did and everybody knows the rest. And so he was around and one day I was with Phil and I was on my way to Abbey Road to do 'Instant Karma!' and so I made Phil go with me and that's how he got to do that record as well. That was how we first started working with him.

John: It was good to work with Phil, because I always admired him, and he contributed a lot. He contributed the Spector touch. But of course if you play *John Lennon/Plastic Ono Band*, *Yoko Ono/Plastic Ono Band*, because he's involved in both, and you play Phil Spector's work, you see there's a vast difference. We never gave him his 'head', you know, because we didn't let him go free on it. Otherwise he would be all things....

Yoko: Allen Klein brought in Phil Spector right at the end of the recording sessions for the *Plastic Ono Band* albums, when John and I had already done everything production-wise. Phil said, 'All I'm going to do is just put a little touch to it' and we said, 'No, no, Phil just do it!' He was very modest about it and he mixed the album beautifully.

John: When I say to Phil what I want, he gets it me. You can hear him on the album.

Yoko: When it came to recording *Imagine*, we had more musicians and they were all incredibly talented and we didn't want them to get upset by Phil's working methods where he would sometimes treat musicians like paid staff to be ordered around, as they used to do in the studios in the 1950s and pre-Beatles generation.

John: He's got a tremendous ego. He considers the artist like that film director considers actors, just pieces of garbage...canned goods that you bring on and you wheel off. He'd like to bury the artist and so the production is the main thing. But we didn't allow him to do that to us. So on that level it was very good, because we used what we considered is his amazing ear for pop music and sound, without letting it become [deep voice] 'Spector', you know – thousands of castanets, 'The Wall'. We didn't want 'The Wall of Sound' but we wanted the outside input.

Roy Cicala: Phil would put everything into a reverb chamber with delay and come up with a sound – The Ronettes' 'Be My Baby', The Righteous Brothers'

'You've Lost That Lovin' Feelin'' – that was called the 'Wall of Sound' at the time. And that's Phil. He did so many records in the Sixties. That's the old rock 'n' roll that John loved.

John: The Beatles had a standard to live up to, and for that reason when the Beatles went into the studio they had to stay in for at least six months. Today I just couldn't stand being locked up in a studio for that length of time. I don't want a standard to live up to. Everybody was saying, 'If Spector gets involved, it's going to take six years to finish.' We finished the whole album in seven days.

If you do it the same night, you're still in the mood of the take and you romix it in that style. It often has the best feel, although some things aren't technically perfect. When you come back to it later and remix it technically, you might get a better sound but you might also lose the feel: I'd sooner have feeling than perfection. So would Yoko, and Phil's the same. We get on really well, and that's why we call ourselves the three musketeers. It's a great partnership.

george harrison
electric guitars, dobro

John: Paul introduced me to George. We asked George to join us because he knew more chords, a lot more than we knew. We got a lot from him. Paul had a friend at school who would discover chords, and these would be passed round Liverpool. Every time we learnt a new chord, we'd write a song round it. The first thing we ever recorded was 'That'll Be The Day', a Buddy Holly song, and one of Paul's called 'In Spite Of All The Danger'.

George: We grew up together. I was about thirteen when I first met John. He was a tough guy. John's mother had taught him some chords. His guitar was cheap, with a little round sound-hole. It only had four strings. John didn't even know that guitars should have six strings. He was playing banjo chords: big extended finger chords. I said, 'What are you doing?' He thought that that was how it should be. So we showed him some proper chords – E and A and all those – and got him to put six strings on his guitar.

He wanted to do something different and likewise so did I and Paul. So we gained strength from each other really, like that. He was always the noisy one or the cheeky one, the pushy one. He'd be a bit more outspoken than the others and at the same time I think that was important – that we had all these elements – John being a bit upmarket with the intellectuals, Paul being cute, Ringo being cuddly and I was the quiet one. So it all worked out. It would be hard to say in a minute because we grew up together and spent many, many years together.

John: George is all over my new album. He plays guitar – some real 'Mothers' [of Invention] solos. George's best guitar solo to date on 'How Do You Sleep?' is as good as anything I've heard from anyone, anywhere. Would you believe that George wasn't happy with these solos? He wanted to do them again! I told him that he'd never

get them any better if he tried for years. It's the best he's played in his life, but he'd go on forever if you let him.

George: The Sixties was a good period. We'd been born during the Second World War, and as we grew up we became sick of hearing about it. To this day the newspapers and television love the war and wars in general – they can't get enough of them. They keep putting programmes on about them. There's about fifty-four wars happening right now, and even if there's a lull in one of the fifty-four wars they'll show us the re-runs of the Second World War or Pearl Harbor.

We were more bright-eyed and hopeful for the future, breaking out of the leftover Victorian mould of attitudes and poverty and hardship. We were the first generation to experience that. And then we had Little Richard and Elvis and Fats Domino and all that music – because up until then it had all been pretty silly music from the Fifties. And then we bumped right into Vietnam.

I think that one of the things that I developed just by being in the Beatles was being bold and I think John had a lot to do with that. Because John Lennon, if he felt something strongly, he just did it. And I picked up a lot of that by being a friend of John's. Just that attitude of, 'Well, just go for it, just do it.' Like when Ravi wanted me and Peter Sellers to come and introduce the concert [for Bangladesh] and he could make twenty-five thousand dollars [for the cause]. Straight away I thought of the John Lennon aspect of it, which was, 'Film it and make a record of it and let's make a million dollars!'

Yoko: George introduced Indian philosophy and Indian music to all of us, and that was a really important thing. America didn't have that kind of knowledge, and he made people understand it and realize there

was some very deep music and philosophy there.

All four of them had a great sense of humour. George's was mixed with a bit more sarcasm, which you didn't expect from a pop star. He was an incredibly talented musician, a very sensitive guy, and I think, in a way, he was even more interested in philosophy than in music. He was the most handsome guy in the group in a general sense. Being younger than people like Paul and John was quite hard for him as a Beatle, although by the time we made *Imagine*, George was already on the top of his own incredible mountain.

George was technically so proficient. Of the four of them, he could really make it in that sense. In rock 'n' roll music, you don't need that so much – you go more for the 'feel'. George knew that too, of course. He played on five tracks on the album – all subtly different styles – from delicate and classical on 'Oh My Love' to the country slide in 'Crippled Inside' to that amazing guitar solo in 'How Do You Sleep?' – on all of them he used his incredible talent really beautifully, precisely and with so much soul.

George, we miss you! I hope you are hearing all this – in an Indian sense or in an Asian sense you are still with us, and you must be laughing about us!

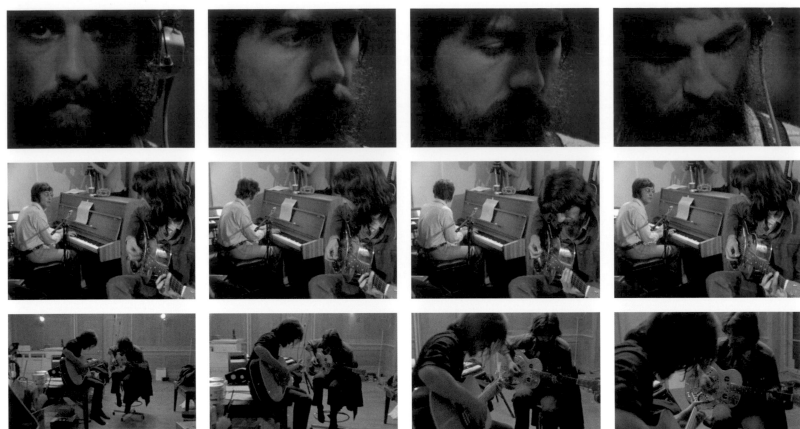

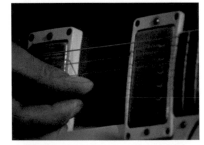

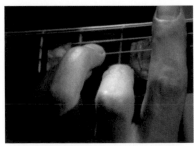

George Harrison tuning up before recording 'How Do You Sleep?' In the background, Alan White (drums) (left) and Rod Lynton (twelve-string acoustic guitar), John Tout, Phil Spector (co-producer) and Ted Turner (twelve-string acoustic guitar) (right). Ascot Sound Studios, 26 May 1971.

klaus voormann
bass, upright bass

I met John for the first time in Hamburg in 1960 and I was scared of him. I wasn't sure if he was going to hit me. I went into the Kaiserkeller Club and he was playing in a band called the Beatles. They were all rockers. I got all the people from my art college down to the club. I said, 'You have to see this band! You have to see this band!'

We went night after night and in the end they said, 'Klaus, you have to talk to them, you can speak English.' I walked up to John, showed him a record cover I had made and said, 'Look at this! I did this cover for you. What do you think of it?' And he said, 'Talk to Stuart – he's the arty one in the band.' We all became great friends and some years later in 1966, I designed the cover for the Beatles' *Revolver* album.

Later, in 1969, I had just finished touring in a band called Manfred Mann. John suddenly called me and said, 'Do you wanna join the Plastic Ono Band?' It was perfect timing. We took a plane to Toronto – Eric Clapton, Alan White, John & Yoko, Mal Evans and me. We were rehearsing in the last row of the plane, right next to the jets. I only had an electric bass and couldn't hear a thing! We rehearsed with John and then Yoko came up to us and said, 'Can I rehearse my song now?'

And John got up and said, 'No, no, no, let's have a cup of tea.' So when we got up on stage, we had no idea what was going to happen. She was in a sack and then she came out and started singing! We had no idea what was going to happen. No idea! That was the first time I met Yoko and we are still great friends today.

I was living at George's place at Friar Park in Henley-on-Thames. George and I often drove to Tittenhurst together. Tittenhurst was great. It was fun. Always something to eat and people hanging out.

On the *Imagine* album, I played an old Fender Precision electric bass and an Ampeg Portaflex B-15N valve amplifier with a 15-inch speaker. It was one of the suitcase ones; when you travel, you take the whole top off, turn it round 180 degrees and put it in the box.

On 'Crippled Inside', John said he wanted an upright bass. I had never played one before, but he said, 'No, you can play it!' So John sent me to London with Mal Evans and we rockers went into this classical music store, full of very neat people wearing bow ties! Mal bought a really good, huge, full-size upright bass. John realized he wanted it played like a slap bass, and I couldn't do it so I played the notes on the bass with my left hand and Alan White played the strings like drums, with his sticks.

When we were rehearsing, John would play the song on guitar or piano, and then we would start contributing what we thought was right. He was singing all the time. It was a great help and really made those songs work. If you pick the right people who can really play, they find their own way through. There's not that much said or manipulated. It's instinctive. Everyone is clever in his own way. You listen to everybody. You listen to the whole

thing. And for me in particular, I always listened to the song and the words. John had printed out the sheets with the lyrics on it really big, so you knew what the song was about.

When I think of those sessions, I always think of 'Jealous Guy'. I'm sitting there. I don't even know what key I'm in. I have no idea. I just play. It just goes like a dream, you know? It's such a beautiful song and it just flows. I close my eyes and listen to John, and just play. And then those notes come where there is space for them, or when I think they should be played at that particular moment.

Yoko was very important to John. The Plastic Ono Band was her idea and now there's the new Plastic Ono Band that she does too. Lots of people now know that Yoko was really something long before John Lennon was even in the picture; and that's really interesting. She had such an important part in everything John was doing.

Phil Spector was very thoughtful, patient and subdued. He was giving good comments. He was really, really right. He was not being a producer who was pushing anything on you. He let things go and happen, and was just perfect. Mostly I'd say, 'Is that okay, what I'm laying down?' And he'd say, 'Yeah, yeah, yeah. It's fine.' He never told me what to play. He and John communicated well together.

When we played 'Imagine' and heard the lyrics, the possibility that this was going to be such a big song was apparent. It definitely was. I even thought I didn't want to play on it because it was so amazing with just John playing piano. It was so true and honest. That would have been enough. I hope you've got a version of just John playing it.

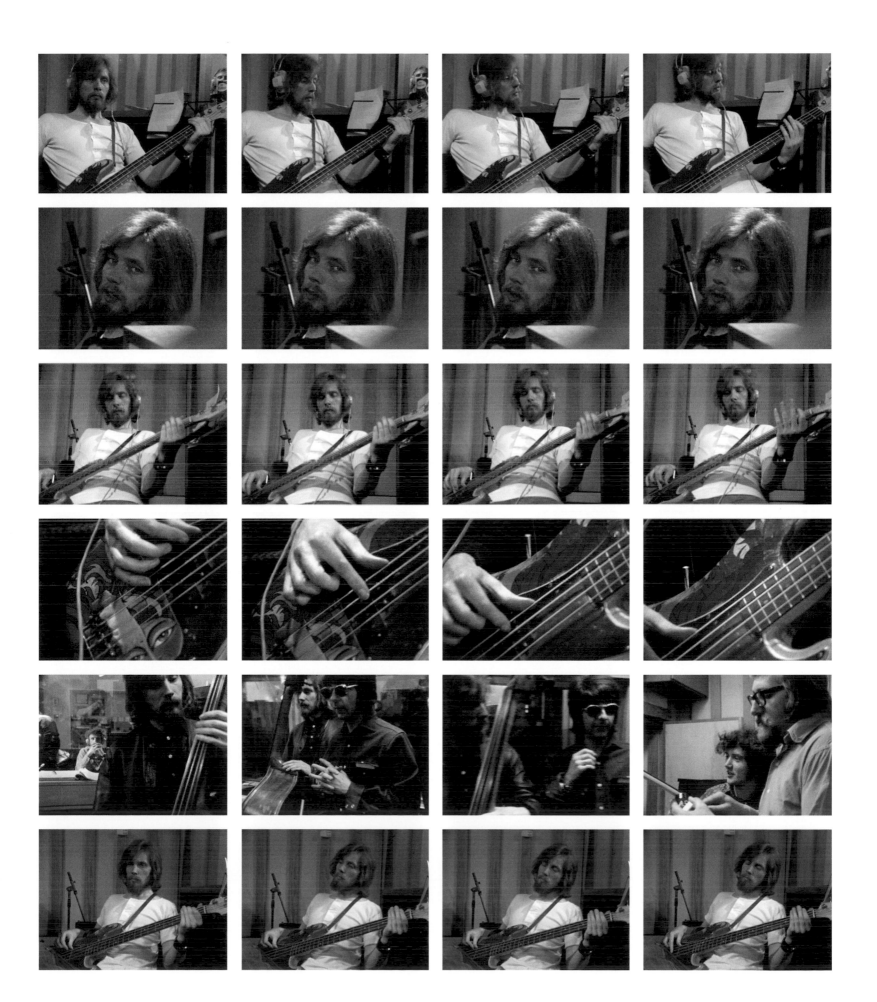

JOHN HANDS PLAYING
IMAGINE

John singing
Imagine
ASCOT TITTENHURST
PARK and
we was all
listening.

KlausVoormann 04

Drawings by Klaus Voormann (2004), depicting his memories of the *Imagine* album recording and mixing sessions at Ascot Sound Studios and Record Plant, New York, in May and July 1971. Following pages: Alan White, Klaus Voormann, George Harrison and John Lennon at the kitchen table, Tittenhurst, 26 May 1971.

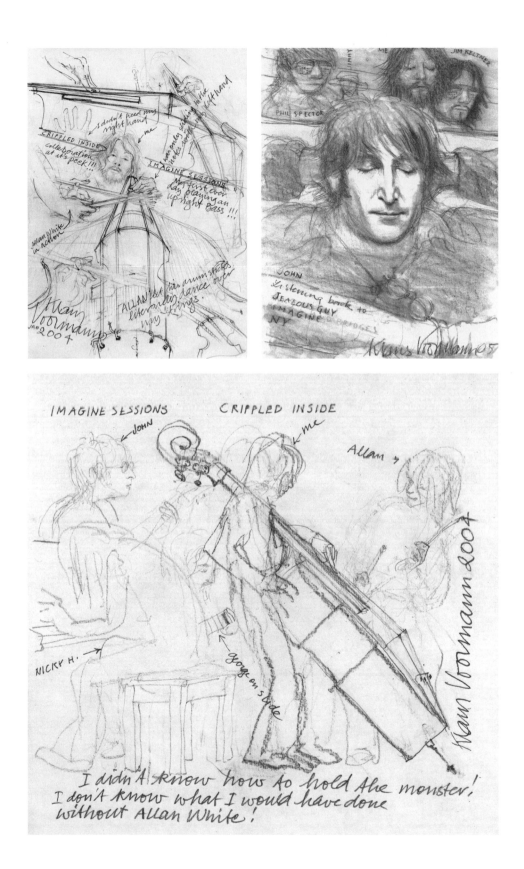

I was dreaming of the past
and my heart was beating fast
I began to lose control
~ I began to lose control

I didn't mean to hurt you
~~I didn't mean to make you cry~~
I didn't want to hurt you
I'm just a jealous guy.

I was feeling insecure
~~You might not love me any more~~
I was ~~shivering inside~~
I was ~~shivering inside~~
She is invisible
Chorus

I was trying to catch your eyes
Thought that you were trying to hide
I was swallowing my pain
I was swallowing my pain.

jealous guy

I was dreaming of the past
And my heart was beating fast
I began to lose control
I began to lose control

I didn't mean to hurt you
I'm sorry that I made you cry
I didn't want to hurt you
I'm just a jealous guy

I was feeling insecure
You might not love me any more
I was shivering inside
I was shivering inside

I didn't mean to hurt you
I'm sorry that I made you cry
I didn't want to hurt you
I'm just a jealous guy

I didn't mean to hurt you
I'm sorry that I made you cry
I didn't want to hurt you
I'm just a jealous guy

I was trying to catch your eyes
Thought that you was trying to hide
I was swallowing my pain
I was swallowing my pain

I didn't mean to hurt you
I'm sorry that I made you cry
I didn't want to hurt you
I'm just a jealous guy

jealous guy

John: 'Jealous Guy' was originally a song called 'Child of Nature'. The melody had been written in India. I never did anything with it but always liked the melody. The words were silly, anyway. I sang it to Yoko, Phil Spector and a few people and they always winced. I decided to change it – and with Yoko's help, I did.

Yoko: 'Jealous Guy' was a totally different song with the lyrics 'on the road to Marrakesh' and I said to John, 'That's a beautiful melody, but you have to think about something more sensitive. It's in you.' So whenever I hear 'Jealous Guy' I think 'Oh my god!' because he really did that.

John: I was a very jealous, possessive guy. And the lyrics explained that pretty clearly. Not just jealous towards Yoko, but towards everything male and female. Incredibly possessive. It's partly to do with childhood. A very insecure male who wants to put his woman in a little box and lock the key and just bring her out when he feels like playing with her and put her back in. And she's not to communicate with the world outside of me, you see? Because it makes me feel insecure. And that's not allowed, you know? So this is facing up to it.

I don't believe these tight-skinned people who are 'never jealous'. When you are in love with somebody, you tend to be jealous and want to own them and possess them one hundred per cent, which I do. I love Yoko. I want to possess her completely. I don't want to stifle her – that's the danger – that you want to possess them to death.

Yoko: I touched on the subject in my song 'Revelations' – 'Bless you for your jealousy, for it is a sign of empathy. Direct not to your family, direct not to your friends. Transform the energy to admiration and what you admire will become part of your life.'

John: All that 'I used to be cruel to my woman, I beat her and kept her apart from the things that she loved' was me. I used to be cruel to my woman, and physically. Any woman. I was a hitter. I couldn't express myself and I hit. I fought men and I hit women. That is why I am always on about peace, you see. It is the most violent people who go for love and peace. Everything's the opposite. But I sincerely believe in love and peace. I am a violent man who has learned not to be violent and regrets his violence. I will have to be a lot older before I can face in public how I treated women as a youngster.

Yoko: We would argue, of course. We were two very temperamental, very emotional, people. Friends and lovers, musicians and artists, man and woman, husband and wife. That was part of our communication. We were both shy, we didn't go out often, certainly not to parties or anything like that. So we were literally together for fourteen years with very few breaks. John and I stood for peace and love but standing for peace doesn't make either of us holier than thou. John and I together were human beings, and by no means were both of us totally peaceful. Anger, hurt, vulnerability, were all a part of John. When we met we were like two driven people and it was like a fantastic meeting of two crazy souls.

They say that Venus is jealous of lovers. Forget Venus. In our case it was the whole world. But as far as we were concerned, we felt so lucky that we had found each other. Aside from the fact that we were both rebellious and emotional, we were true opposites. John was tallish. I was smallish. John made music for the people. I made music for the avant-garde, though I did not think of my music in those terms at the time (I thought I was big time). John was humble, in a way only a very successful person could be. I was proud, like most people living in an Ivory Tower, who never had to test the big water. Coming from a semi-working-class background, John was street-wise. I was totally inexperienced when it came to the games of the real world.

And we felt so, so lucky that we fell in love with each other. It was a blessing neither of us expected at that time in our lives. We couldn't take our eyes off one another. We couldn't get enough of each other, But the outside pressure was very strong. It was so strong that sometimes we had to separate from each other in order to protect our love. We thought we were clever, that we did everything right, and nothing and nobody could tear us apart. But it happened: our separation. So sudden, too. He was taken away from me for good.

Even now, I think there are people who still cannot reconcile themselves to the idea that I had been in John's life. To those people, I'd like to say, I'm sorry that we had hurt you, But that's what happened. That's how it was.

John: It's a kind of jealousy. People can't stand people being in love. It's your self-absorption with each other; it's your contentment with each other that people can't stand.

Yoko: We're so ashamed of being jealous; so ashamed of being possessive. We're so afraid of having hate and all that. We shouldn't. It's all just different forms of energy.

John: Nicky Hopkins' piano is beautifully busked as is the bass and drums et al. Result – 'Jealous Guy'! (Nicky's name was somehow missed off the credits on the L.P. Sorry Mr and Mrs Nicky!)

All that 'I used to be cruel to my woman, I beat her and kept her apart from the things that she loved' was me. I used to be cruel to my woman, and physically. Any woman. I was a hitter. I couldn't express myself and I hit. I fought men and I hit women. That is why I am always on about peace, you see. It is the most violent people who go for love and peace.

John, 1980

John with his toy panda during a break in filming *Imagine* at Tittenhurst, 21 July 1971.

nicky hopkins
piano, keyboards

I started when I was three. When I was a little kid and when I was tall enough to reach up and play this… well, I didn't know what was up there, it was just this table thing, and all of a sudden these things on the top which were the keys started making a noise. And I got into it. Mum lifted me up and helped me for about three years and I picked it up.

The first pro gig I did was with this bizarre character called Screaming Lord Sutch in 1960. About 1967, The Rolling Stones had become incredibly successful and apart from their first album, all their albums had been done in the States. Olympic opened, it was the first eight-track studio in England, so they decided to start recording in England, and I got pulled in because I knew them and they liked what I did and that started a relationship that lasted from then till 1981, off and on – just about all the albums from *Satanic Majesties* to *Tattoo You*.

Yeah, I had a distinct style. Plus, there were only a few players in England who could play rock 'n' roll piano in those days, but none of those others ones could read music. So I was able to take on all sorts of work because I had the ability to write down the chord charts, since bands like the Stones never knew how to do that.

I get along very well with Lennon. John is egotistical to some extent but he tells you that. He's a very honest cat. His album was such a gas to do.

It was all put together in about a week at the studio in his house. For years John has been part of a band where each member contributed a great deal. Now when he forms a band it will be to perform his own material. It will be a cooperative album but very much John's. That is understandable because he is such a prolific songwriter. He just wants to sing his songs.

I have very fond memories of John. He was just able to get things done properly in a record amount of time.

They had the 'apparency' of being somewhat laid-back and yet, at the same time, there was a tight control on it. It's the funniest thing because John was able to get things done very quickly but with no sacrifice at all to quality and without bullying. Once, when one of the sax players opened his case, pulled out a bag of grass and was gonna roll up a number, John said, 'Could you just leave that till after the session? Then we can all sit back and relax. In the meantime, if we can just get on with it or else we'll all forget where we are.'

To me, John was a great guy. He was fallible, he was human so he had his problems, but he was a great dreamer. He had great visions of how he would ideally conceive the world to be. There's a great quote from L. Ron Hubbard, in which he said: 'A culture is only as great as its dreams. And its dreams are dreamed by artists.' I think that sums up Lennon better than anything else.

John is very definite about what he wants and there is no uncertainty working with him . He doesn't want to spend much time recording. I played electric piano on [an out-take of] the 'Imagine' track and the main piano track on 'Jealous Guy' is me too. My name was missed off the credits for that one through a mistake. I was on 'Crippled Inside,' 'Oh Yoko!' and 'Soldier' too.

Lennon is fast. I did two LPs with him, *Imagine* and *Walls and Bridges*. I played on both and it was almost the same. We recorded them in a week: *Imagine* was done in seven days and two days to put strings and mix it. Nine days in all. Not bad, huh?

Yoko: Nicky Hopkins's playing in 'Jealous Guy' is so melodic and beautiful that it still makes everyone cry, even now.

Jim Keltner: Nobody in the world ever played piano like Nicky Hopkins – the way he played chords. A piano is a piano, and the keys are the keys, and the chords are chords, but one individual can make that same piano sound so different from another person and Nicky embodied that whole thing, man. Nicky played like nobody else. Nicky always sounded like he was in a cloud somewhere. He always sounded dream-like. He was kind of a frail guy. He had a lot of health problems. His playing was astonishingly beautiful. Everybody sounded better when they were playing with Nicky Hopkins. Nicky just had that ability. Some musicians have that, and some don't. Nicky Hopkins was always like that. When you had him playing, everything went up a notch. That was what Nicky did. There are few players like that. He always elevated everybody.

Original film footage of Nicky Hopkins recording piano and keyboard parts for the *Imagine* album; Ascot Sound Studios, 24 – 29 May 1971.

alan white
drums, upright bass, tibetan cymbals, good vibes

The first time I spoke to John Lennon was in September 1969. He called me on the phone and asked me to play drums with him at a live show in Toronto. I thought it was a friend playing a joke, so I hung up. Thankfully, he called back a few minutes later and convinced me it really was John Lennon. Apparently, he had seen me play at a club in London the night before. I had no idea he had been in the audience!

The next day, he sent a limo, which took me to the VIP lounge at London Heathrow Airport. None of us (including Eric Clapton and Klaus Voormann) had done any rehearsal – nothing! On the plane, I played with a pair of sticks on the seat in front of me. We got there and all of a sudden, we were on stage. [laughs]

John was a very nice, accommodating guy. I always felt he kind of took me under his wing. I was only twenty years old, a little bit naïve, and jumped in the deep end. He made me feel very comfortable; and so did Yoko. She was extremely nice. She spoke in a very quiet voice and adored John. You could tell they were madly in love. It was a great experience.

Following Live Peace in Toronto, the first thing I was asked to record with John & Yoko was 'Instant Karma!'

Then along came *Imagine* and we went down to Tittenhurst to rehearse the music. Every song we did on *Imagine*, John would make us read the lyrics and insist that we understood the meaning of the song before we started playing it. That had quite an impact for me.

John worked fast. He knew when something was right and was definite about his ideas. He knew what he wanted – and he knew when he had it. I remember him saying to me, 'Whatever you're doing, just keep doing it.' He didn't try to control what I was playing; he seemed to trust my musical interpretation and allowed me the freedom to play what I felt. I got on with the job, listening to a song and then translating it into my style. Once we had a great take, it gave us all such a great feeling.

Yoko was always at John's side; giving him advice and ideas to make it better. She was very much part of the whole thing. Phil Spector was a bit of a strange guy. He seemed extremely paranoid, but he was totally into the project. John would talk to him and, gaining confidence, say, 'Am I doing the right thing?'

I had never met Klaus Voormann before we played Live Peace in Toronto, but we got to be really good friends. While playing 'Crippled Inside', there was an unusual situation where Klaus was playing upright bass and I sat on a chair beside him and played the drumsticks on his bass strings. It produced the unique 'slap' sound effect for the song.

When we did 'Jealous Guy', Jim Keltner played the drums and I ended up playing vibraphone in the toilet in the corner of the studio. It had a little door, with a four- or five-inch crack, and I could see everybody through there. It was, 'One, two, three, four...' and then we were playing. John gave me a great credit on the album. On the sleeve notes inside the record, he wrote, 'Alan White: Good Vibes', which meant a lot to me. It was all good vibes when we were making *Imagine*. Everybody was really happy. And when everybody is happy in a studio, the happiness comes through the music – and there is a lot of great music on that album.

One of my favourite moments was when we cut the track 'Imagine'. There seemed to be a feeling in the room that the first recorded track was a good one. We didn't need to do any more – that was as good as we were ever going to play that song. It was a mutual feeling; something I recall and stood out in my mind.

I am proud to have played on 'Imagine', because its message is for the world, has been played worldwide and is well understood. It is a song of hope – for then, for now, for the future. The message is still so relevant. For me, it's the most important piece of music I've ever recorded. Timeless. I've been asked several times to re-record 'Imagine' with different artists, but always decline. I can't think of any reason I would ever do that. The original recording with John and the other musicians is exactly what it should be. It could never be improved upon. I perform the song with other bands to keep it alive and share it with the world, but will never re-record it. It had an amazing impact on my life and continues to inspire me every time I play it.

John had great insight into things that were happening then and into the future. It was like all the politicians who are trying to make the world a safe place rolled into one. And he seemed to say it all in one statement. Occasionally, when it applies to the news you see on TV now, you say, 'Wow! John was right! And in the beginning, you know.'

jim keltner
drums, tabla

I first met Yoko at Tittenhurst on 16 February 1971. I was playing drums and tablas on a session for her *FLY* LP – with her, Klaus Voormann, Jim Gordon and Bobby Keys. She was an avant-garde New York beatnik, dressed in a black turtleneck, and I was a bit of a beatnik myself. I wasn't a rocker like the rest of John's friends. I came from the jazz world and I had known about Yoko's New York days as an artist. She hung out with a lot of the great jazz guys. There we were at the Ascot mansion and Yoko was describing to Bobby Keys the sound that she wanted him to play with his mouthpiece out of his saxophone; which was 'the sound of the wind rushing over the back of a frog sitting on top of the world'. I remember thinking, 'Wow. I know exactly what that sound is.' I got on with Yoko really well.

Later that evening, I met John. He was recording 'It's So Hard' and an early version of 'I Don't Wanna Be A Soldier', with Jim Gordon on drums. Jim was struggling a bit, trying to find his way into the suggestions that John and Phil were giving him. The following week, John invited me to come back to redo the track.

John was so strong a personality and so charismatic. I was floored to meet him. He was so smart, and always so beautifully in charge, in a really practised way. His songs were always so well written. You didn't need a chart. There was always a funny bar, like a little 5/4 bar. Great songs by great artists play themselves. First, he would play you a new song on the guitar, or piano. He would mostly work on telling the guitar players what to do – play this here, play that there – but with the bass and the drums, he left us pretty much alone. It really loved that he had that kind of faith in us.

Playing on 'Jealous Guy' was like being in a dream. Nobody in the world ever played piano like Nicky Hopkins, and Klaus has such a tremendous deep feel on the bass. Having John's voice in your headphones, glancing up and seeing him at the microphone – 1971 – fresh from the Beatles and such a tremendous musician and songwriter – singing this beautiful, haunting little song. You only have a few of those moments in your life as a musician and that was one of them.

I've always believed in the genius of Phil Spector. I got to see it first hand, in his prime, with John and George; and also with Leonard Cohen, The Ramones and Celine Dion. I've done nothing but make records since I was a kid, and the producer and the arranger are the most important people – other than the artists. I consider it one of the great good fortunes of my life to have worked with Phil Spector as a producer.

I loved 'Imagine' from the moment I heard it. But when I first heard John sing, 'Imagine there's no heaven' and 'no hell', it made me feel uncomfortable. Now I realize what he's saying is the way mankind has put together our consciousness of God has become a 'yours against mine' situation, like a big football match. I believe John meant the words to 'Imagine' to be healing words.

john barham
harmonium, vibraphone

I first met John Lennon in March 1967, when the Beatles were recording George Harrison's 'Within You, Without You', for *Sgt. Pepper*. He was really friendly, and interested in talking about my piano compositions – based on Indian classical ragas – even though I was wearing a Burton's suit!

In the spring of 1970, I got a phone call from Apple to do some sessions for John. So of course, I said, 'Yes!' John sent a huge white Rolls-Royce to pick me up. I was impressed with Tittenhurst – especially the cutting rooms upstairs, where Yoko had all her film equipment – and the huge table of food in the kitchen.

I was at Tittenhurst for two days. I played harmonium on 'Jealous Guy' and vibes on 'How?' I'm not sure of the make of the harmonium; it was a very old one.

In the studio, John was very, very focused and didn't waste time. He was firm, friendly and gentle – as was Yoko. Phil was pretty withdrawn. He didn't talk a lot, to any of us. He seemed to be quite introverted.

'Imagine' is a wonderful utopian dream, which sets the standard by which we can judge reality, when reality gets too bad.

rod lynton
acoustic guitars

I first met John at Abbey Road in 1967. I was in a band called Rupert's People. Our drummer, Steve Brendell, worked for Apple. So I met each of the Beatles through him. After Rupert's People disbanded, I worked with John Sherry and Miles Copeland – who did management and PR in an office off Oxford Street, in London – doing, amongst other things, the PR for Wishbone Ash.

The first time I worked with John was on the *Imagine* sessions. Mal Evans rang me and asked me to organize some musicians. So I brought Ted Turner from Wishbone Ash, Andy Davis from Stackridge, and John Tout from Renaissance. I spent three days at Tittenhurst.

I had previously played with George, and Ringo, and worked with Phil Spector. There was something – an extra quality – with John. It was very hard to describe. He was just more intense about the recordings and yet very relaxed about it. I knew the songs really meant a lot more to him. It was more about getting the 'feel' right, using the guitar as rhythmic percussion. We'd talk it over and John would say, 'What feels comfortable? What feels right? Do what's right.'

I played on 'Crippled Inside', 'Gimme Some Truth' and 'Oh Yoko!' We also tried parts on 'How Do You Sleep?', extra vocals on 'Oh Yoko!' and John even asked me to put a guitar on 'Imagine'. I tried strumming, finger picking, folk, and little phrases, but the contrast always made the piano sound dull – and the track was so beautiful without it. I am very grateful for the whole experience.

When you stand up to be counted, like John & Yoko did, you get put down a lot. God knows Yoko got put down so unfairly in the early days and so did John. As people who grew up in that generation, we could understand it. But the older generation didn't have a clue what was going on. To them it just looked odd.

'Imagine' is a complete philosophy lesson in one record – if only the world would listen! The lyrics have a very strong message, and it had a profound effect. I don't think there is a person on the planet who loves that song that wouldn't agree with that. There are a lot of people out there who have found solace in listening to that track. In moments of despair, it puts things into perspective. It is such a unifying call to common sense. It's so powerful. The bagpipes are one end of what music can do – a call to arms, stirring the blood to violence. Put 'Imagine' on, and you go the other way. There are very few songs you can say that about.

Years later, when I was in New York in 1974, I had ten minutes before my taxi was due to get me to the airport and fly me home. I called John and he wanted me to go around see him that evening. I couldn't do it because I only had about twenty dollars left and I had a press reception lined up the following day in the UK. I felt really bad about turning him down.

ted turner
acoustic guitar

John Lennon walked in the room, sat down on the stool in the centre, looked around and asked, in that inimitable Liverpudlian accent, 'Is everybody ready, like? One, two, three….' And that was it. One take! I was smiling like a Cheshire cat! It felt like no time at all, but in that moment, me playing with two of the Beatles…it was magic!

When we were listening to the tracks, I remember Phil turning up the reverb and John immediately turning it down. I interpreted this as an example of John's confidence that he was going to have this done in his way, even when working with a mastermind producer.

I would not be here without music. Playing guitar and writing songs has got me through some of the darkest experiences of my life – including the death of my beloved son, Kipp. Contributing to the 'Crippled Inside' track has taken on a new poignancy for me, over the years. I feel I was being given a message about how to survive and heal when faced with personal tragedy.

John Lennon was a genius. A poet. A troubadour. A messenger. And he was right. LOVE is all we need. That was why I chose this anthemic song to walk down the aisle after marrying the love of my life.

joey molland and tom evans
acoustic guitars

mike pinder
tambourine

In 1971, Tommy and I were playing in Badfinger and signed to Apple. 'No Dice', 'No Matter What' and 'Come And Get It' had been hits and we were about to tour the world.

We had played acoustic guitars on George Harrison's *All Things Must Pass* album. George was now working with John on *Imagine* and recommended us, so John's driver rang us to ask us to come – and of course we said, 'Yeah!'

The limo dropped us off at the front door. We were both really excited, but there was nobody there. We walked through and there was the step ladder with the magnifying glass in the vestibule. Up the black carpeted staircase were artworks – big gold picture frames with hammers. We got lost in the house, and ended up in a library with no doors and a huge Indian snooker table. Eventually, we found our way out, past a smaller room full of cases and cases of Dr Pepper, and into the kitchen with that great jukebox.

John came into the studio and played us 'Jealous Guy'. We had brought our acoustics; mine a Gibson J50 and Tommy's a Martin D41. We ran through the song once or twice, all very simple and natural. Tommy suggested a significant chord – a minor 9th or 6th.

Yoko suggested it needed an intro, which Nicky played so beautifully.

After we recorded about three takes of 'Jealous Guy', John jokingly said, 'You can fuck off now!' [laughs] But we didn't want to. And it didn't seem like he was throwing us out. So we stayed and played on 'I Don't Wanna Be A Soldier', too.

It was one of the thrills of my life, having headphones on and John Lennon sitting five feet away, playing with us. The whole thing was magic.

I was enthralled with John and the songs he wrote. 'Strawberry Fields' was like Salvador Dalí music. He was changing the form and it was easy to grab; still communicating ideas to you. It was a magic thing that he had. The room got warmer when he was in it.

'Imagine' is another great Lennon song. The beautiful simplicity of it. It's like a melody we all know. The idea of the 'dreamer' and not being 'the only one' was always strong to me. I look on myself as a dreamer and I'm sure a lot of us do.

Tommy co-wrote 'Without You' with Pete Ham. I think it was John who told Harry Nilsson to play it.

I met John around 1964. We were very young, musically driven and having fun at the clubs in London. Ray Thomas and I would often hang out at the studio with John and the guys. When we finished a Moody Blues album, we would go to John's flat to play it for him. We often shared our work and ideas; that was the beauty of that time.

When John called me to come to the studio, I thought I was going to be playing Mellotron. I had turned John onto the Tron and knew he had one in the studio. However, when I got there the Mellotron was in tatters. They had put the Tron on its back and all the tapes had gotten jumbled up inside. Given the time, I could have fixed it. But there was no time and they were ready to do the session. So I grabbed a tambourine and played into Jim Keltner's hi-hat microphone. The engineer got a balance and away we went. Besides Mellotron, I happen to be king of the tambourine!

Playing with John was always a pleasure, as I loved John for his humanity first and foremost. John and I shared the same philosophy that we humans are interconnected – that love is all there is – and that life on the planet and beyond is a cosmic occurrence – and we are all sharing the experience.

jim gordon
drums

john tout
piano

andy davis
acoustic guitars

I did a lot of records. Maybe two hundred albums. I liked Phil Spector a lot. I played percussion on a lot of his music. Some of The Righteous Brothers and The Ronettes. I thought Phil Spector was real good. He was crazy. He'd have six guitar players, three piano players, two drummers, five percussionists and we'd all get in there and play a tune for four or five hours and get this incredible sound.

Jim Keltner and I really started together. We were good buddies. I was about twenty or twenty-one when we met. Jim's probably a little older. But he plays so different than I do. He came from like a real jazz influence where I was more influenced by rock 'n' roll. So, when we played together we fit in real well. When Delaney & Bonnie broke up, I got a call from George Harrison to go over and do his *All Things Must Pass* album in London.

Tuning was, and still is, a big part of my sound. I try to get that sound that I like. For starting out, I guess rudiments are the most important thing. Get a metronome and play a little bit with that. I used to come home from school and play my rudiments all night long.

Rod Lynton: When Mal Evans asked me to bring a keyboard player to the Imagine sessions, John Tout was the obvious choice. We had played together from 1967 to '69 in Rupert's People, as had drummer Steve Brendell. John's exceptional abilities on Hammond organ were integral to our sound.

Quiet and unassuming, John was a musician's musician. On one occasion, in 1967, hit-record-maker Manfred Mann was impressed enough to struggle through a packed audience (while we were playing) to ask him how he got 'That fantastic sound!' The answer lay mostly with John's keyboard ability. So precise, fluent and evocative.

In 1971, John joined Renaissance, where his classical training gave this progressive band their final musical identity. When he left the band following a personal tragedy, they ceased touring as he was impossible to replace. They only reformed years later when John felt able to perform again.

John's quietly humorous and considerate manner was apparent on the day he was present at Tittenhurst. During a break in recording, John mixed easily with helpers and the famous alike.

There was a spiral staircase in the middle of the room and John, Yoko and Phil Spector slowly came down from the floor above. When Yoko walked down that spiral staircase, I thought she looked absolutely stunning. Fantastically beautiful. The sort of face you couldn't take your eyes away from.

'Oh Yoko!' was the first song we did. The three of us sat down with acoustic guitars and we learnt the chords and the shape of the song a few times. It was fantastic. The room was full of impressive musicians and I was young enough to know that the mark of a good musician, in those situations, is always what you don't play. Keep it simple. When John played it to me, I just kept it to totally what he did.

I was there for two days. I also played on 'Gimme Some Truth' and a version of 'How?' and Rod and I tried some extra backing vocals on 'Oh Yoko!'

I could've gone down a third night but I had to play with my band, Stackridge, at the Winter Garden in Cleethorpes. I'm not kidding! Ted Turner went instead. I found out George Harrison turned up on that session, so I could've played with two Beatles, but I couldn't let the boys in my band down. The show must go on!

H ASSINA'S

Phone:
667-3694

26 Christina Gardens,
Arima,
Trinidad, W.I.

IMAGINE

IMAGINE THERE'S NO HEAVEN
IT'S EASY IF YOU TRY
NO HELL BELOW US
ABOVE US ONLY SKY
IMAGINE ALL THE PEOPLE
LIVING FOR TODAY...

IMAGINE THERE'S NO COUNTRIES
IT ISN'T HARD TO DO
NOTHING TO KILL OR DIE FOR
AND NO RELIGION TOO
IMAGINE ALL THE PEOPLE
LIVING LIFE IN PEACE...

IMAGINE NO POSSESSIONS
I WONDER IF YOU CAN
NO NEED FOR GREED OR HUNGER
A BROTHERHOOD OF MAN
IMAGINE ALL THE PEOPLE
SHARING ALL THE WORLD...

YOU MAY SAY I'M A DREAMER
BUT I'M NOT THE ONLY ONE
I HOPE SOME DAY YOU'LL JOIN US
AND THE WORLD WILL BE AS ONE

MARCH '71
LONDON, MADRID, TRINIDAD

CRIPPLED INSIDE.

YOU CAN SHINE YOUR SHOES AND
YOU CAN COMB YOUR HAIR AND LO
YOU CAN HIDE YOUR FACE BEHIND
ONE THING YOU CAN'T HIDE
IS WHEN YOU'RE CRIPPLED INSID

YOU CAN WEAR A MASK AND PAINT
YOU CAN CALL YOURSELF THE HUM
YOU CAN WEAR A COLLAR AND A T
ONE THING YOU CAN'T HIDE
IS THAT YOU'RE CRIPPLED INSID

YOU CAN GO TO CHURCH AND SING
JUDGE ME BY THE COLOUR OF MY
YOU CAN LIVE A LIE UNTIL YOU
ONE THING YOU CAN'T HIDE
IS WHEN YOU'RE CRIPPLED INSID

WELL NOW WE KNOW THAT YOUR CA
NINE LIVES TO ITSELF
BUT IF YOUONLY GOT ONE
A DOG'S LIFE AIN'T FUN
SO MAMA TAKE A LOOK OUTSIDE

I DON'T WANT TO BE A SOLDIER,

WELL,I DON'T WANT TO BE A SOLD
WELL,I DON'T WANT TO BE A SAIL
WELL,I DON'T WANT TO BE A FAIL
WELL,I DON'T WANT TO BE A SOLD
oh no el
WELL,I DON'T WANT TO BE A RICH
WELL,I DON'T WANT TO BE A POOR
WELL,I DON'T WANT TO BE A LAWY
WELL,I DON'T WANT TO BE A SOLD
oh no
WELL,I DON'T WANT TO BE A BEGG
WELL,I DON'T WANT TO BE A THIE
WELL,I DON'T WANT TO BE A CHUR
WELL,I DON'T WANT TO BE A SOLD
oh na e

T
CUTE

E

LIVES BABE

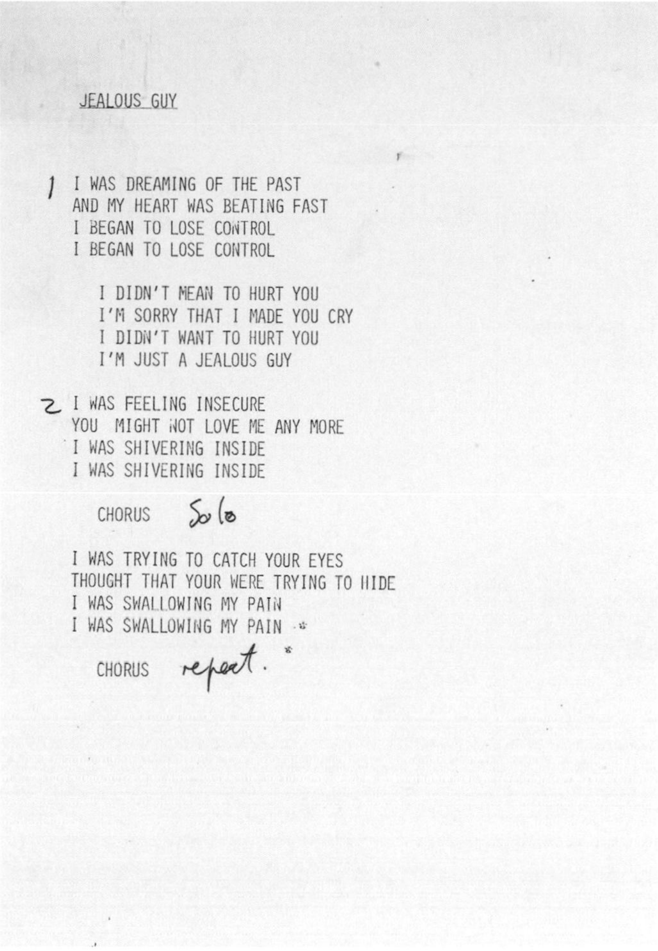

JEALOUS GUY

1   I WAS DREAMING OF THE PAST
    AND MY HEART WAS BEATING FAST
    I BEGAN TO LOSE CONTROL
    I BEGAN TO LOSE CONTROL

       I DIDN'T MEAN TO HURT YOU
       I'M SORRY THAT I MADE YOU CRY
       I DIDN'T WANT TO HURT YOU
       I'M JUST A JEALOUS GUY

2   I WAS FEELING INSECURE
    YOU MIGHT NOT LOVE ME ANY MORE
    I WAS SHIVERING INSIDE
    I WAS SHIVERING INSIDE

       CHORUS   Solo

    I WAS TRYING TO CATCH YOUR EYES
    THOUGHT THAT YOUR WERE TRYING TO HIDE
    I WAS SWALLOWING MY PAIN
    I WAS SWALLOWING MY PAIN

       CHORUS   repeat.

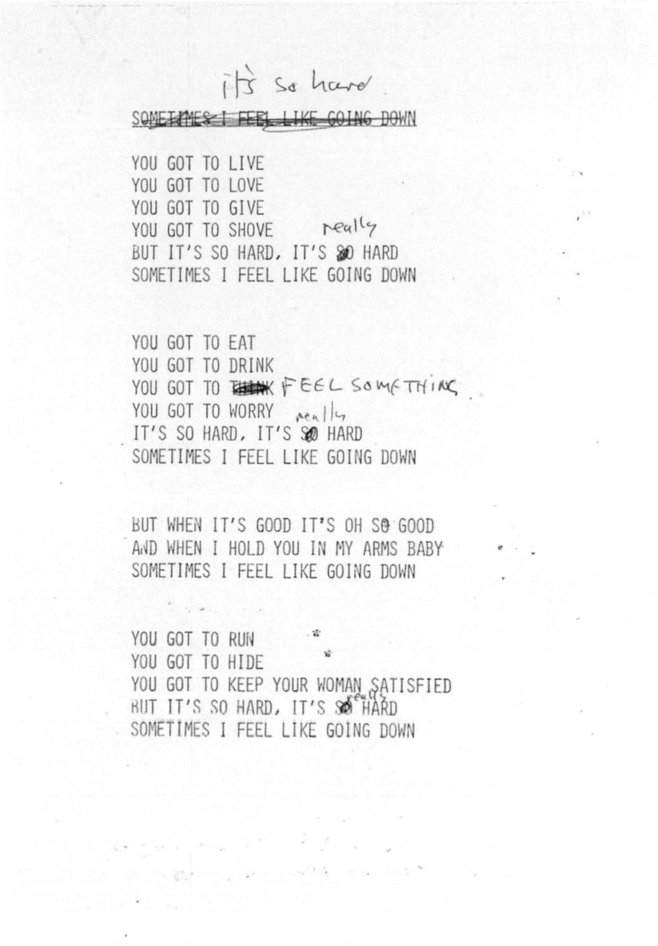

it's so hard

SOMETIMES I FEEL LIKE GOING DOWN

YOU GOT TO LIVE
YOU GOT TO LOVE
YOU GOT TO GIVE
YOU GOT TO SHOVE   really
BUT IT'S SO HARD, IT'S SO HARD
SOMETIMES I FEEL LIKE GOING DOWN

YOU GOT TO EAT
YOU GOT TO DRINK
YOU GOT TO THINK FEEL SOMETHING
YOU GOT TO WORRY   really
IT'S SO HARD, IT'S SO HARD
SOMETIMES I FEEL LIKE GOING DOWN

BUT WHEN IT'S GOOD IT'S OH SO GOOD
AND WHEN I HOLD YOU IN MY ARMS BABY
SOMETIMES I FEEL LIKE GOING DOWN

YOU GOT TO RUN
YOU GOT TO HIDE
YOU GOT TO KEEP YOUR WOMAN SATISFIED
BUT IT'S SO HARD, IT'S SO HARD
SOMETIMES I FEEL LIKE GOING DOWN

I DON'T WANNA DIE
  DON'T WANNA FLY
I DON'T WANNA CRY
I DON'T WANNA DIE.

  I DON'T WANNA CRY
  I DON'T WANNA FLY
  DON'T WANNA LIE
I DON'T WANNA DIE

  DON'T WANNA DIE
, I DON'T WANNA FLY
, I DON'T WANNA CRY
I DON'T WANNA DIE

HOW

1   HOW CAN I GO FORWARD WHEN I DON'T
    KNOW WHICH WAY I'M FACING?
    HOW CAN I GO FORWARD WHEN I DON'T
    KNOW WHICH WAY TO TURN?
    HOW CAN I GO FORWARD INTO SOMETHING
    I'M NOT SURE OF? OH NO, OH NO.

2   HOW CAN I HAVE FEELING WHEN I DON'T KNOW
    IF IT'S A FEELING?
    HOW CAN I FEEL SOMETHING IF I JUST DON'T KNOW
    HOW TO FEEL?
    HOW CAN I HAVE FEELINGS WHEN MY
    FEELINGS HAVE ALWAYS BEEN DENIED?

3   HOW CAN I GIVE LOVE WHEN I DON'T
    KNOW WHAT IT IS I'M GIVING?
    HOW CAN I GIVE LOVE WHEN I JUST DON'T KNOW
    HOW TO GIVE?
    HOW CAN I GIVE LOVE WHEN LOVE IS SOMETHING
    I AIN'T NEVER HAD?

    YOU KNOW LIFE CAN BE LONG
    AND YOU GOT TO BE SO STRONG
    AND THE WORLD IS SO TOUGH
    SOMETIMES I FEEL I'VE HAD ENOUGH

4

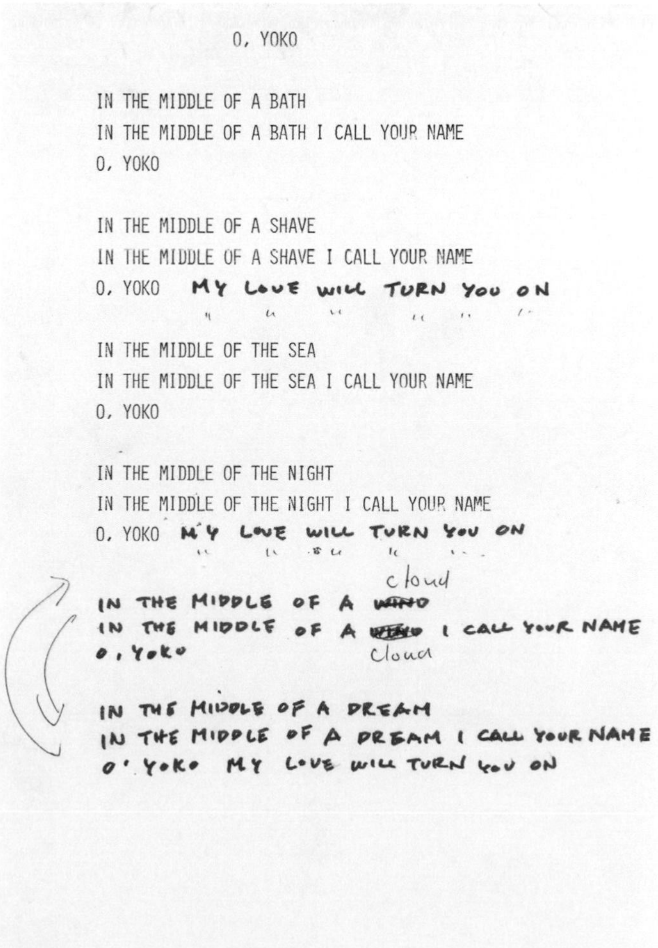

4   repeat with
    'we' instead of 'I'

O, YOKO

IN THE MIDDLE OF A BATH
IN THE MIDDLE OF A BATH I CALL YOUR NAME
O, YOKO

IN THE MIDDLE OF A SHAVE
IN THE MIDDLE OF A SHAVE I CALL YOUR NAME
O, YOKO   MY LOVE WILL TURN YOU ON

IN THE MIDDLE OF THE SEA
IN THE MIDDLE OF THE SEA I CALL YOUR NAME
O, YOKO

IN THE MIDDLE OF THE NIGHT
IN THE MIDDLE OF THE NIGHT I CALL YOUR NAME
O, YOKO   MY LOVE WILL TURN YOU ON

IN THE MIDDLE OF A   cloud   WIND
IN THE MIDDLE OF A WIND I CALL YOUR NAME
O, YOKO   cloud

IN THE MIDDLE OF A DREAM
IN THE MIDDLE OF A DREAM I CALL YOUR NAME
O' YOKO   MY LOVE WILL TURN YOU ON

mal evans
road manager

I was in Liverpool window shopping one day, down Mathew Street where The Cavern was, and I heard this wonderful music coming from under my feet. Paid a shilling, went in, became a firm fan, and that was it. That was about 1960.

I was a telecommunications engineer for the Post Office in England and I'd been there eleven years. All my life since I was a kid, I wanted to be an entertainer and being road manager for the Beatles was the next best thing. I was a fan for three years before I joined them, so it was really the dream of a lifetime.

I did anything for them they needed. I set up the equipment, tested everything, you know, checking the security. On tours in England I ended up at four o'clock in the morning washing stage shirts and polishing boots because I wanted the group to look their best. I was so proud of the boys, I'd do anything for them.

I do love people. I think that might be my gig all my life – people. I really get on with people, generally. That was the great thing about the Beatles. They always involved you in everything they did. That really endeared them to me. The first time I drove down to London with them, and they were just about to break then,

everywhere we went there was always five of us. Even though I was just standing in for their regular road manager, Neil. That's what really endeared me to them in the beginning. They included me in the family. So I never felt like I worked for the Beatles, I always felt like I worked with the Beatles, which was really great.

We grew up together. They had just had a number one record in America when I joined them. And everything escalated but we went through it together, so you're too busy doing it to feel anything at the time. It was better than food or drink. You do a six-week tour of America and you get three hours' sleep a night if you're lucky. They were virtually prisoners for a long time, locked in hotel rooms. All they ever saw were policemen, security guards, management of theatres, and they were the ones that got the autographs. And the poor fans didn't get too close to them. They made the Beatles prisoners because of their own devotion.

Songwriting is a means of communication to people. We're all combinations of other people's attitudes. That's what Yoko got into. She took that art thing a step further because she made the public or the audience join in – the audience participation with her, which is another step in art because you take a piece of art whether it's a painting, a statue, whatever it is, a piece of music, and the audience will add something to it.

I kept a lot of diaries over the years. I'd look through the diaries and I'd come to one day and it'll say – 'Went round to Paul's house to pick up Paul and John and take them to the studio, and Paul says to me, "Mal, we've been talking. John and I have been talking about you and we think you're the straightest guy in the whole world!"' [laughs]

Recording's not the easiest thing in the world. I was always making tea or sandwiches or scrambled eggs to look after them and keep them working well. The whole thing being – you go do the music and everything and I'll do anything in the world to make you feel comfortable doing that. We'd do sessions at EMI and I'd be cooking dinners – egg and beans – at three o'clock in the morning, making sandwiches and things for them; really just wanted them to have no worries about anything except making music and being the group.

We'd try and start at two o'clock in the afternoon and say, 'Let's finish at twelve. Let's keep it regular hours, eh?' So the first couple of nights they'd finish about twelve, and the following nights they'd be really hot and cooking in the studio so they'd go on till three. So we'd start later and eventually they'd end up where we'd start at seven or eight o'clock at night and finish at eight o'clock in the morning. [laughs] We always had good intentions.

Sergeant Pepper was originally 'Doctor Pepper' until we found out it was a trade name.

Yoko: He was our family. A very sweet guy. And we all miss him. That's all I can say.

Original film footage of Mal Evans during the *Imagine* recording sessions at Ascot Sound Studios. Bottom row: Mal Evans with Steve Brendell, Rod Lynton, Phil McDonald and John Barham in the kitchen; Tittenhurst, 24 – 29 May 1971.

phil mcdonald
engineer
ascot sound studios

eddie klein
engineer
ascot sound studios

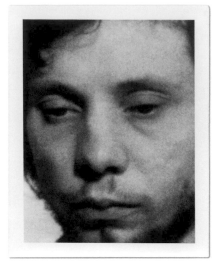

Imagine was not an easy album to record. Ascot Sound Studios was in its infancy and had a few teething problems. John was at his best running through a song two or three times. After that he would tend to wane, so if you didn't get the song on take two or three, then goodbye.

John sang a run-through of 'Oh My Love' just on piano as I was still setting up. It sounded so good, I wish I had recorded the song as it was! After that incident, I recorded everything that was played.

'Imagine' was one of the easiest tracks to record, almost all live in a few takes. We mixed the track at Tittenhurst and Phil Spector added strings on top of the stereo tape in the USA.

Phil Spector wasn't the easiest of producers. He wanted to hear the multi-track recording like a finished product and worked everybody hard to achieve this.

I was honoured to work with the best at the time and I can say brilliant albums don't come easy. You know what they say, 'All engineers want to be musicians, and all musicians want to engineer.' I will not get into the musicians saga. As you know, they are a breed of their own….

Prior to recording *Imagine*, Phil McDonald and I worked together at Abbey Road on a number of projects including John & Yoko's *Plastic Ono Band* albums and George Harrison's *All Things Must Pass* album. At Tittenhurst, we recorded 'Power To The People' (although the backing singers were overdubbed at Abbey Road) and 'God Save Oz', when the place was crowded with so many people – I seem to remember Mike Pinder playing a Mellotron in the hallway and Yoko singing in the bathroom! It was a fun session, and quite a zany experience with Phil Spector at the helm on both occasions.

I remember the five days of the *Imagine* sessions with great affection. I would pick Phil up each morning and drive through Windsor Great Park towards Ascot. It was a welcome relief to be in such beautiful countryside and leaving the noise and smoke of London behind. If I remember rightly we had taken EMI's JBL monitoring speakers and maybe some of Phil's favourite microphones. Most engineers get used to a particular sound and know what to expect with equipment they are familiar with.

During the sessions, John was anxious to get started and finished as quickly as possible. In the studio, he would lay a basic track, come into

the control room and listen back to it, see how it had transferred to tape and what he'd want to overdub or change, then go out and do a few more takes to capture it. Yoko mainly sat with Phil Spector in the control room. Phil McDonald was a stalwart at recording and quickly adapted to the CADAC desk, which was quite different from the EMI desks he usually worked with. Recording onto tape is very different to recording onto a computer. It's not like today where everything is instant. These were large clunky machines with unwieldy spools of tape. It seemed to take ages to wind through to the end of the reel just to change tapes. I think John would have loved the immediacy of ProTools.

As the tape op, everything went swimmingly for me until it came to some tricky overdubs. There's one particular time where John and Phil Spector were overdubbing backing vocals on 'Oh Yoko!' and John got angry and had a go at Phil McDonald for playing the wrong part of the song. You can see it in the *Gimme Some Truth* film. But to Phil's right, just out of shot, is me and I don't know where the hell in the tape I should be. The 3M eight-track tape machine didn't have a timing clock readout, so I wasn't able to accurately go to the part of the song they wanted. I had no option but to mark the moving tape with a white chinagraph marker. Spooling backwards and forwards created a number of ghost marks and it was easy to spool past the correct mark because the tape machine's wind and rewind speed was difficult to control. Eventually, I had so many white marks everywhere that I didn't know which bloody white mark was what! I became quite agitated because John was getting a bit short-tempered and impatient to get on. I was very fond of John, but I was wary of him losing his temper. Phil Mac, like all engineers at EMI, had served his own apprenticeship as a tape op and knew

what I was going through. He was
very laid back about it.

I remember for 'Crippled Inside',
they got Steve Brendell in to play on
Klaus's double bass with drumsticks
– such a novel idea – like Jerry Allison
slapping his knees in the Buddy Holly
record of 'Everyday'. My memory is
that it was Klaus fingering the bass
and Steve playing it with sticks and
it was played live.

When George arrived to play guitar,
he was very surprised to see Phil
Mac and me outside of Abbey Road.
I think a 'light bulb' came on in his
head because soon afterwards he
got Eddie Veale to build him a studio
at Friar Park. I also remember George
wanting to redo his guitar solo on one
track, particularly because his finger
slid off the fretboard. John loved the
sound it had made and so George
didn't get a second chance.

During the sessions we would
have a well-earned break. We'd all
sit around the kitchen refectory table
and be provided with lovely food and
drink. Everybody was in an amiable
mood, musicians and engineers alike.
These were moments to unwind and
were most welcomed. We recorded
every track at Tittenhurst except for
the basic track of 'I Don't Wanna Be
A Soldier', which was recorded by
Eddy Offord, and we overdubbed
onto that. After finishing recording
they went to New York to add some
string arrangements. I was impressed
by what they had done and was really
pleased with the album's final mixes.
Several years ago, Yoko and Sean
came to The Mill to see Paul McCartney.
I mentioned to her that I had never
received a copy of her *Plastic Ono
Band* album. So she sent me a copy
on which she wrote 'To Eddie – After
so many years – Yoko '95'. it was
a really kind gesture and was much
appreciated. It now sits alongside
Imagine in my record collection.

eddie offord
engineer
ascot sound studios

I was one of the first engineers to work
at Ascot Sound Studios. I would get
there around two in the afternoon and
work until eleven or twelve at night. It
was just me and John & Yoko producing.
I set up the mics myself, I ran the tape
machine myself, I didn't really have
any help. It was a few months before
their sessions with Phil Spector. John
was very confident. For him it was
more of a band 'thing' and he liked
to work fast. It was just a matter of
getting the sound right, getting
everyone to hear each other and
getting everyone comfortable. Once
we started rolling, it was all done in
one or two takes.

I did a few tracks with John and
a few with Yoko over three or four
full-day sessions, but unfortunately
I had to leave as I was booked on the
Tarkus sessions for Emerson, Lake
and Palmer at Advision. We had
bonded really well and I felt they
were sad to see me go.

John & Yoko really complemented
each other – John had this amazing
rough-around-the-edges street-smart
thing about him and Yoko was the
opposite – very sophisticated and
very well educated. They had a
communication and a tightness that
was very obvious; they were very
much in love and it was a nice
atmosphere there.

ken scott
engineer
ascot sound studios

John's thought process with regard
to recording was very different.
Often he wouldn't know how to
describe things and at times it
was difficult to try and understand
what it was he was after. But
with perseverance and often
experimentation we would eventually
manage to get to it and it nearly
always ended up being incredible.
In collaboration with the engineers,
the Beatles pioneered or popularised
so many cutting-edge studio
techniques: half-speed recording,
random tape loops, sound effects,
feedback, distortion, strange
equalisation, multitrack overdubbing,
compression, phasing, flanging
and Artificial Double Tracking
(ADT), as well as using completely
innovative microphone placement
and techniques.

After I moved to Trident, I mixed
'Give Peace A Chance' and recorded
'Cold Turkey' for John. John's vocal
on that was quite amazing. Completely
'in the moment'. I went to Tittenhurst
once, to do a session. John and the
musicians were rehearsing 'I Don't
Wanna Be A Soldier'. It started late
and I felt there was too much of a
'party' atmosphere going on to capture
a take good enough for an album.
So I said I had another job booked
the following morning and left early.
It was sadly the last time I saw John.

Sometimes I Feel like Going Down

You got to live
You got to love
You got to give
You got to share
but it's so hard. ~~so fucking~~ hard
Sometimes I feel like going down

You got to eat
You got to drink
You got to think
You got to worry it's so hard
its so hard, ~~so fuckin hard~~
Sometime I feel like going down

You got run
You got to hide
You got to keep your woman satisfied
but it's so hard , ~~it's so fuckin hard~~
Sometime I feel like I'm going down.

but when it's good it's oh so good
and when I hold you in my arms baby
sometimes I feel like going down.

it's so hard

You got to live
You got to love
You got to be somebody
You got to shove

But it's so hard
It's really hard
Sometimes I feel like going down

You got to eat
You got to drink
You got to feel something
You got to worry

It's so hard
It's really hard
Sometimes I feel like going down

But when it's good
It's really good
And when I hold you in my arms baby
Sometimes I feel like going down

You got to run
You got to hide
You got to keep your woman satisfied

But it's so hard
It's really hard
Sometimes I feel like going down

John at the kitchen table. On the table Yoko's mirrored *A Box Of Smile*, 1967/1971.
In the corner in the background, John's 1961 Wurlitzer 2500 jukebox with a colour
photograph of Elvis Presley in army uniform on top. Tittenhust, 22 July 1971.
Opposite: partial track listing from John's replacement 1971 Seeburg USC1
'Musical Bandshell' jukebox; in the kitchen at Tittenhurst, 3 August 1971.

it's so hard

John: I like to sing blues-rock or whatever it is. The words were written with the sound in mind rather than meaning, although both are useful. I also like playing guitar. This was the first finished record I made at Ascot Studios in our home, we didn't have any limiters at the time, etc. – but it sounded alright to me! King Curtis (who was killed a week later, R.I.P.) and The Flux Fidders were overdubbed at Record Plant New York. I like to sing the blues occasionally, so I just wrote a blues. And it is so hard sometimes.

I was an art student and I was an artist and a writer all my life. I did occasionally dig into music. Apart from meeting Yoko, the biggest experience of my life was hearing rock 'n' roll and black rock 'n' roll. Liverpool was a port where there were many black people and they still have the slave rings on the front of the docks there. But one thing about being a port is that it's usually a bit hipper. The next biggest town is Manchester – big industrial town – they ain't half as hip as us. The music – the sailors would bring it in. We were hearing old funky blues records in Liverpool that people across Britain or Europe had never even heard because they didn't know about them.

I grew up with blues music, country and western music which is also a big thing in Liverpool. One of the first visions I had was one of a fully dressed cowboy in the middle of Liverpool with his Hawaiian guitar, you know? That's the first time I ever saw a guitar in my life. He had the full gear on. The first music I got hooked on was blues. My earliest influences – the first black music I heard – was Leadbelly, Robert Johnston, Sleepy John Estes, people like that. From that I went into Bo Diddley, Chuck Berry and the early R&B artists, whether they were rhythm & blues or rock 'n' roll or whatever you'd call it then. It wasn't until the Sixties that we discovered B. B. King and Albert King.

The first thing that amazed us about America was – when we came over here in '64 – all the reporters said, 'Where's your influences from? What kind of music do you like?' Everything we said was black except for Elvis Presley and Jerry Lee Lewis. And they didn't know what it was and we didn't know about all this race record business. We had no idea there was a separate division. Music was music. It comes off the record. That's it. It's music, man.

We were talking about all these black people and all their faces were changing. 'Oh right, you don't go for The Beach Boys and Jan & Dean and all that?' We said, 'Come on man, that's rubbish!' So one thing we always did was to tell where we got our music from. In fact when we arrived in '64 we only ever talked about Chuck Berry, Bo Diddley, Little Richard. And by then they were not as big as they had been in the Fifties. They had already

been and gone but we virtually resurrected them. We did their songs again. The Stones did that again and made a really interesting amount of music. The only whites I ever listened to was Presley on his early records who was doing black music. The body movement. Presley was in Memphis. Obviously he was listening to the music . I don't blame him for wanting to be that music because that's what I wanted to be. I copied all those people and the other Beatles did, and all the groups did until we developed a style of our own.

People talk about the Beatles and *Sgt. Pepper* and all that jazz. It doesn't mean a thing. All I talk about is 1958 when I heard 'Long Tall Sally', when I heard 'Johnny B. Goode', when I heard Bo Diddley. That changed my life completely. I dropped my art, I dropped out of school, I got me guitar and that was the end of it. I dropped everything. And my auntie who brought me up all my life, all the time she was saying, 'The guitar is all right as a hobby, John, but you'll never make a living at it.' So I got that on a plaque for her and sent it to her in the house I bought her.

Black music was my life and still is. Of course, there's lots of good white music these days and they've learned a lot. One of the black guys said, one of the black leaders, 'We blacks loosened them young middle-class white kids, we gave them back their bodies.' And I was given back my body in the Fifties and I appreciate it, and I never stop acknowledging it. I met Chuck Berry for the first time in my life and it was a beautiful experience. It was like meeting a Soul Brother. It was like we'd known each other forever. And I was nearly crying meeting him because he'd been my idol all my life.

Black music started the revolution in the world. This so-called youth revolution, the whole change of style was started by rock 'n' roll. And rock 'n' roll was black. They created the best 20th-century art that has released more people than any other kind of art, ever, in the history of man.

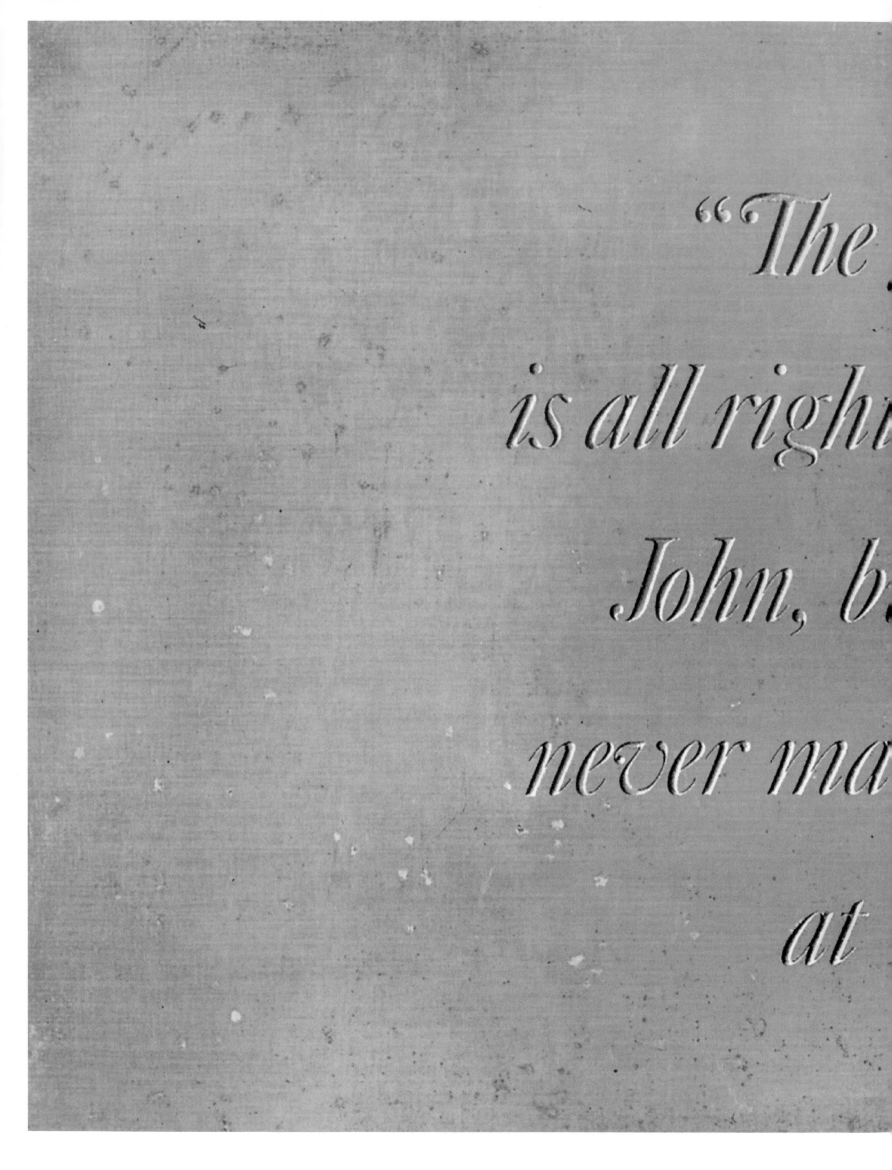

guitar

as a hobby,

t you'll

e a living

t!"

AmericanAirlines

In Flight... yes

Altitude; puzzled.

Location; yes.

14th Sep. (71.)

Dear Craig McGregor

'Money', 'Twist'n' Shout', 'You really got a hold on me' etc, were all numbers we (the Beatles) used to sing in dancehalls around Britain, mainly Liverpool. It was only natural that we tried to do it as near to the record as we could – i always wished we could have 'done them even closer to the original. We didn't sing our own songs in the early days – they weren't good enough, really – the one thing we always did was to make it known that there were black originals, we loved the music and wanted

John's letter to journalist Craig McGregor in response to his article accusing the Beatles of imitating and exploiting black music; written on a flight from New York to the Virgin Islands, 14 Sept 1971.
Previous pages: the plaque John gave his Aunt Mimi in 1965, inscribed with her own words.

AmericanAirlines

In Flight…

Altitude;

Location;

---

to spread it in any way we could.
in the '50s there were few people listening
to blues – R&B – rock and roll,
in America as well as Britain.
People like – Eric Burdon's
Animals – Micks Stones – and
us drank ate and slept the music,
and also recorded it, many
kids were turned on to black
music by us.
it wasn't a rip off.

it was a love in
John Lennon

P.S. what about the 'B' side off money?
P.P.S even the black kids didn't dig
blues etc it wasn't 'shop' or something.

roy cicala
owner and engineer
record plant

Yoko: John and I loved Roy Cicala. He was an incredibly good producer and we worked with him a lot in New York. He was not very talkative, and so not that many people may have heard of him. Roy was very rock 'n' roll. He would always go for the 'feel' of the sound, rather than being too technical and we really liked that.

Shelly Yakus: Roy Cicala first met John & Yoko on 4 July 1971, at The Record Plant; and it was the beginning of a friendship that lasted forever. Roy was a very experienced engineer, and a great producer and mixer. In the late Sixties, he and I were working at A&R Recording Studios on album after album, six or seven days a week, all hours of the day and night. The studios were so busy; and with our clients, the more success we had, the more people wanted to work with us. Roy really got to trust me – and I trusted him – so we worked together really well. We both came over to The Record Plant in 1970; it was a natural transition.

Roy had his hands on the faders and I would help him get to where he was going – because, when you're Roy in this, you've got your hands full. You've got Phil and John talking to you, saying, 'The mix isn't quite right.... Let's try to make it sound like this.... We need a little more of that....

A little more violin....A little more viola....' Whatever it might be. My job was to help Roy get his job done and to keep an overview of the sessions, to make sure everything ran smoothly.

We had learned from Roy, early on, that it should always be all about the music and the people creating it. He would whisper something to me – and between Jack, myself and Roy, we were able to solve problems, and get things done quickly, without the technology getting in the way of progress.

Roy and I did a lot of John's stuff together. Even after hours, we'd work on stuff, either with or without John, to try to make it better – to remove hiss, fatten up the sound, and improve the quality of the mix. We put in so many hours on this thing, that late one night I was so tired, I said to Roy, 'I've just got to lay down for a few minutes.' I fell asleep on this shag rug – and next thing I know, this flash is going off, and John and Roy were standing over me laughing. One of them had taken a picture of me – the one on the inner sleeve of the album – and John put 'Shelly Yakus (sleep)' in the credits.

Roy had a really unusual way of teaching. It wasn't like school. It wasn't like he would say, 'Hey, Shelly, do this and this will be the result.' He would make you think about it. If I went out to get pizza for everyone and came back without pepperoni on it, he would say, 'So I guess you don't like pepperoni.' It was never like a scolding. Everybody would laugh and it would make you think about what you did. I never saw him yell at anyone. Roy would always draw it out of you from the deepest part of you. Being yelled at makes it harder to learn, because then you feel bad about yourself and get embarrassed.

Roy would tell the techs, 'When you fix a microphone, or a limiter, or compressor – or whatever – you've

got to put music through it and make sure it sounds right.' You can't put tones through it and expect it to be correct.

Once, I was assisting him in a session, early on in our relationship, and the meters were just smashing the pin – I could hear the clicking over the music – and I said to him, 'Roy, your levels are really hot.' And he turned to me and said, 'How does it sound?' And I said, 'It sounds great!' And he said, 'OK, good.' At that moment, I realized that that's what it's all about. It's not what you read in books. It's not what people tell you. It's, 'How does it sound?' No matter what you're seeing and what you're told about how it should be. Instead, use your instincts – that's the gift he gave me. And that's who Roy was.

Jack Douglas: Roy was a gentle man with a very, very subtle – and sharp – sense of humour. He absolutely had the best bedside manner. He was very calm and he was doing things where you would wonder, 'How is he doing that? How does he get things to sound like that?' There were so many mysteries with his technique, and he just wanted you to watch and learn from him. But there was certain things that he did that you just couldn't learn, because you couldn't get inside his head. He was not a composer or a musician, but he had an ear and imagination that was incredible.

Shelly and I just marvelled at Roy's brilliance. It was like he immediately and instinctively knew exactly what John wanted out of it. He didn't even seem nervous at all. A lot of engineers would start barking at assistants if something was going wrong, but a guy like Roy...he would just turn around and smile, and you knew he had it under control. He was extremely humble and just so lovely. I learnt so much from him.

It's the Fourth of July 1971 at The Record Plant, New York. I'm twenty-five. We have John Lennon and Phil Spector – two giants of the music business – who represent every reason I got into this business – sitting at the console. Roy Cicala, Jack Douglas and I are all at attention; all our senses heightened beyond belief. I am sat there saying to myself, 'OK, what's it going to take so that this session doesn't go wrong? Is the tape machine going to stop? Is it gonna eat the tape? Is the board gonna crackle? Is someone going to knock a cup of coffee into the board, like I did with Roy's coffee when it was new?' [laughs] All of us wanted to be sure that when the session is over, John was going to say, 'Guys, this was really great. I got what I came for. This really works for the song. Thank you.'

I grew up in the business – my dad had a studio in Boston. By 1967–70, I was living in the West Village, in New York; working with Roy at Phil Ramone's studio, A&R Recording. I had had some success engineering albums like *Music From Big Pink*, by The Band, and *Moondance*, by Van Morrison. We moved to The Record Plant together in 1970.

John Lennon had a presence about him where, if he was standing in a crowd of five hundred people and you didn't know who he was, you would pick him out first. He wanted to make the best music that he could make, for all the right reasons; so that it was right for him and him only; and not based on the opinions of other people. And his music reached millions and millions. It was just about, 'Well listen, how does this take feel?' And, 'Are there any mistakes from the musicians that I'm not hearing right now – or anything we've got to correct or redo?' It was 24/7 about the music. Incredible. Just incredible.

Phil didn't say too much. He was very quiet. He did his part and then John did his part – together, yet separate. I think Phil was used to always being in control of his own sessions; where he was the lead guy who did everything. Now they were finishing the job, he had John sitting next to him saying, 'You know, I don't think that's going to work.' And I don't think Phil was used to working like that. Phil was respectful to everybody – very quiet and reserved – and yet his influence is all over that album; with the overdubs and the overall sound.

Yoko understood how the studio dynamic worked. If she had something to say to John about the music, she would say it to him quietly, in a way that was really respectful to everyone. And if he agreed, he would then say it to either us or the musicians. I thought she had good ideas and she handled herself really well in those sessions. It's not an easy thing, to be close to John and be quiet about stuff you might be hearing that's bothering you.

There was something about the freshness of John's music; how each instrument was important. For example, on 'Imagine' there's only a few instruments: bass, drums, a doubled piano and John's voice. Each instrument is so powerful – not in volume, but in its own part. It hit me like a truck. A lot of record makers just throw the kitchen sink at the production and hope something sticks. John didn't. That's what John had that made him special. The separate parts and the sum were very different than anything I had worked on before. This music coming out of the speakers felt extraordinary and it was getting to me in a way that was more immediate.

John had a very definite style. He was never distracted by anything, and his mission was to get the best out of the song by being totally immersed in it, but still keeping perspective – which is very difficult for creators to do. At the same time as listening to an individual part, he was listening to it as a whole, so he could quickly tweak the parts to improve the whole. I've seen successful people do it, but with John it was at a far higher level.

If you listen carefully to John singing 'Imagine', he uses a different vibrato on the end of every phrase. The only way a person can do that is if they're not thinking about the song; they're just singing from the deepest part of their being. It's not staged. It's not pre-planned. It's just real and in-the-moment – totally feeling the song. For John, it was incredibly natural to do this. That's what was so great about working with him. Nothing was ever forced. He never tried too hard. It just flowed out of him.

How do you reach the deepest part of a person with your music? I have this thing that I try to teach young people I work with. I say, 'Look – do not make perfect records. Perfect is boring.' Great records are exciting. Great records sometimes have mistakes. Sometimes they have tempo movements. Sometimes they have things that wouldn't be in there if you were making the perfect record. But a perfect record puts you to sleep. And John just had this ability to make great music.

jack douglas
engineer
record plant

I was extremely nervous about meeting John, being a big fan of the Beatles, and I was so surprised how comfortable he immediately made me feel. He seemed like a regular guy and just totally relaxed me. It was amazing. I was twenty-four and on staff at The Record Plant. I had started as a janitor, then a tape librarian, and now I was an assistant engineer – about to become a full engineer.

We hadn't had Phil Spector or John Lennon there before, so we wanted to make sure that everybody involved was experienced and reliable; so it would all go smoothly and not screw up. John and Roy really hit it off and quickly zeroed in on the sound of things. Shelly Yakus, who was already an accomplished engineer, would be backing up Roy; controlling compressors, and equalisers, and just following up on whatever Roy would say – 'Plug in the Pultec...', 'Give me a little 10K...', 'Give me 3dB of compression....' My job would be to set up the studio, placing microphones and operating the tape machine. It was a great team. We were just having a blast. But you know, both Shelly and I just marvelled at Roy's brilliance. It's like he just knew exactly what John wanted out of it.

John was ready to get right to work when he came in. He was very studio savvy; he knew how to get exactly what he wanted. Yoko was very involved in everything that John did. She was really listening to what was going on and had a handle on the whole process. It was such an honour – and a pleasure – to have them there.

Phil Spector seemed a little bit lost when he got there. But once things got rolling, he was able to join in with it. Phil had come from a much older school of producing, which involved putting all the right ingredients in to a pot – the right artist, the right arranger and the right engineer – and then stirring it up; much more like a movie producer than a modern music producer. He seemed a bit insecure, because suddenly there were some really strong-minded people in the room – that John seemed to be very comfortable with – who were getting what John wanted, without argument, in a very New York, organized way.

We recorded the strings in Studio 8, which was rather a small room. It didn't have a high ceiling and was over-padded. We did some tricks like placing plywood in the room to brighten it up, and Roy got a great sound out of it. The arrangements were so incredible that it was really breathtaking to be in the room with John – and, you know, I had to pinch myself a few times.

When Roy captured the sound of King Curtis's amazing performance on the saxophone, the amount of delay on it and the compression on top sat right in the track perfectly. It was very fast and very exciting. He just laid it down and got John exactly what he wanted.

The most fun was watching Roy mix it. The way he used his arrays was incredible. He did very unusual stuff like putting delay across all the drums – bass, drums, snare – the whole thing.

arlene reckson
night manager
record plant

I had just started with Record Plant as the night-time receptionist. Roy Cicala said to me, 'Can you work on Sunday? I have some Philharmonic people coming in.' And I said, 'Sure.' That Sunday morning – 4 July – all these musicians came in with strings, followed by John & Yoko. They were already so visible in our lives that we thought we knew them; and there was already a familiarity there.

John was quite anxious and impatient. He didn't like passing joints around; so I would roll lots of very thin joints, so everyone could have their own. That was my credit for 'this and that' on the album.

When they finished mixing 'Imagine', they invited me to come into the control room – to listen to *Imagine* as an album for the first time – with John & Yoko. There was only a handful of us. We were smoking the joints I had rolled and I remember saying, 'It doesn't get better than this.' It's my favourite moment of my life.

There is a weird connection I have with 'Imagine'. When something important happens and there is going to be some kind of shift in my life, that song will come on the radio; and I know it marks a time for me to move on to something else.

king curtis
saxophone

It was Louis Jordan playing alto saxophone. I heard it on the radio and told my mother I wanted to play that instrument more than anything. Six years later I was in high school, playing gigs in the evening and earning $240 per week – more than the principal of the school. I listened to Gene Ammons, Dexter Gordon, Lester Young and Sonny Stitt and tried to gather the good things from each of them. I also dug Ben Webster and Coleman Hawkins for ballads, Getz for his facility, Parker for technique and phrasing. I also loved Arnett Cobb, a very fine tenor player. Another guy who influenced both myself and Ornette Coleman was a Texas tenorman called Red Connor. He was a Coltrane ahead of his time. I used to argue that if I could play what these giants were playing, then I must be as good as they were. I know different now. They had to think of it first!

I saw music was dividing and I had the commercial business sense to realize that way-out jazz wasn't getting to the public. I realized that, good as those big-name jazz musicians were, they would always be coming out where I was working. That meant they didn't have jobs themselves. And when they'd ask me to lend them a couple of bucks, I couldn't believe it! All those great musicians not working! But I realized it was because most

people just couldn't grasp what they were doing. If you haven't had any experience in music, you can't really understand that way-out jazz. So I decided I wasn't going to be asking anybody for two bucks. I knew I wasn't as good as they were; they often showed me things on the horn which I could apply to the kind of music I was doing.

Around 1956, Sam 'The Man' Taylor and myself were doing all the tenor work. He really initiated the style, but I learned a lot from him when we both played in the Alan Freed band. I could always imitate him. I was doing sixteen record dates a week and getting 41 dollars and 25 cents for a three-hour session, but I could see that if I kept on that way I'd burn myself out. So I made my minimum session price $100 – and still the work kept coming in. So I cut down to eight sessions a week.

If [someone] wants to become a complete musician, I feel he must dedicate his complete self [to it]. I particularly like the authentic rhythm and blues, I think it has more soul than any of the other music.

Allan Steckler: John knew he wanted a sax player and it was his idea to use Curtis. He asked me to get him. I found his agent and booked him. John played him the tracks and told him the kind of feel he wanted. He went into the studio and played his ass off. John loved it, as did Phil and all of us. John asked for a few more takes and finally Phil said let's mix them all together – which is what he did.

John: I haven't seen you since, when was it, Shea Stadium? [laughs] This intro I want you on ['It's So Hard'] – it just comes in – it goes from A to D, and it's just that I've heard it before, it's either honky tonk or some old one, probably one of yours, I dunno. But there's just a bit where it definitely comes in and just trips out again.

As funky as possible – they called it dirty when I was a boy!

King Curtis: Hey John, if you want something in particular I'd like you to hum it because, see, there would be a different line that I would ordinarily hear, you know? Guitar players like y'all hear different lines and if it's something different that you want other than what I'm playing, just hum it.

John: No, no that was fine. That was beautiful. I want it like a sax player, not a guitar player. As soon as I say 'Hit it' [on 'I Don't Wanna Be A Soldier'], just come in on the top and play as wild as you can. I want you to try and come in on the highest note you've got. You know usually you start in the middle and go up to a beat. I want you to come in on that beat and stay up there as long as you can, even if it's one note all through. This time we'll be dropping in and we're keeping the first one. Come in on that very strong one. Yeah, that's it! And then after that, do what you like. Give me that and you're forgiven!

King Curtis: Alright, rolling! I think that made it.

John: I like the intro. Try and make the long notes longer, you know? There's just a little bit on the end where the tailout…something towards the end you could fill in. I'll wave to you when it comes. OK, keep that one. We'll give you a smoke. That was a beauty, especially that second one was out of this world. That was beautiful.

King Curtis: Thank you.

John: Now I know why they call you King! [laughs]

King Curtis: Alright, alright. [laughs]

torrie zito
conductor

the flux fiddlers

Allan Steckler: I took Morgana King's *With A Taste Of Honey* album down to play to John. Torrie Zito had arranged and conducted the orchestral parts. And John said, 'Yes! That's who I want! Get him!' So I contacted Torrie, we went over to the St Regis Hotel and I introduced him to John & Yoko. John played Torrie the mixes from the recording sessions at Tittenhurst and started describing and singing the arrangements that were in his head: 'This is where I want the strings to go, and this is basically how I want them to go, here and here.' Torrie made a load of notes, and returned with those beautiful orchestrations based on John's arrangements.

Torrie Zito: I was born in upstate New York in 1933. When I was twenty I moved to New York City. As a player, I stopped performing publicly about 1969, went into the writing side, and stayed with it, which led to my working with a lot of people. In 1961 I did an album with James Moody; then some work with Herbie Mann – these were strictly instrumental kind of things. Others I worked on backgrounds for in the record field: Morgana King, Frank Sinatra, André Kostelanetz, John Lennon – I scored his *Imagine* album; that was very enjoyable. I also spent some time in the commercial jingle field.

Allan Steckler: After the meeting with John, Torrie and I went for a coffee and discussed who we would use. I said I would try to get the best 'studio' fiddlers available. These are the guys who did almost all of the recording work in the NYC area. Torrie was extremely pleased with my choices.

Aaron Rosand: Torrie Zito was a very gifted man. I did a lot of recordings for him. Torrie Zito dates were extremely important, so you would have definitely had some of the top musicians available in New York playing there.

Torrie Zito: When I really got attuned to the orchestral thing, I was greatly influenced by the Impressionists – Debussy, Ravel, Fauré, etc. – and somehow I tried to marry that within the pop thing. I feel that some of the arrangements I've written really have an Impressionistic flavour to them. This was particularly so in the things I did with Morgana King, because she has this ethereal way of singing. I would say I've developed a special technique of string writing. At least, people tell me it's unique to me in some ways. It came from listening, but mainly from just doing it. I mean, you can experiment with so many things, but after doing so much of it, over and over, you kinda fall into your favourite sounds and so on. In my case, anyway, I became zeroed in to a certain approach to writing orchestral backgrounds for singers. It wasn't something I was even particularly looking for, I'd say; it just sort of evolved.

John Lennon: The first record [*John Lennon/Plastic Ono Band*] was too real for people, so nobody bought it. Now I understand what you have to do. Put your political message across with a little honey.

John: I put strings on in America. I used some Philharmonic people, I just tried to get the best players. On 'Imagine' and on 'Jealous Guy' it's very straight, and a bit sort of funky on 'It's So Hard' in the solo in the last verse. 'How Do You Sleep?' has also got the violins on. We called them The Flux Fiddlers – there's a group [of artists] that Yoko used to be with called Fluxus.

Aaron Rosand: In those days, some of the top New York musicians were doing recordings of this kind – musicians that wouldn't even dream of going to the New York Philharmonic because it didn't pay enough money. We made the highest rates of that particular time for jingles and things like that. I was doing it in between my touring as a concert violinist. We did so many of them! We played the sheets in front of us. That was all. It was all prepared. The players would have been in a C-shape. Violins usually on the left-hand side and cellos on the right-hand side with basses to the farther right or behind the cellos; the violas more towards the centre.

Conductor: Torrie Zito

Violins: David Nadien, Julius Brand, Frederick Buldrini, Peter Buonconsiglio, Paul Gershman, Harry Glickman, Emanuel Green, Leo Kahn, Stanley Karpienia, Harry Katzman, Joseph Malignaggi (Malin), John Pintavalle, Raoul Poliakin, Matthew Raimondi, Aaron Rosand, Julius Shachter

Violas: Alfred Brown, Harold Coletta, Theodore Isreal, Emanuel Vardi

Cellos: Charles McCracken, Kermit Moore, George Ricci, Anthony Sophos

Basses: John Beal, George Duvivier, Jack Lesberg

Copyists: Ben Ginsberg, Morris Gluckman

Original score for 'Imagine'. Arrangement by John Lennon, orchestration by Torrie Zito; St Regis hotel, June 1971.

① Well, I, don't want to be a soldier mama, I don't wanna die
Well, I, I don't want to be a sailor mama, I don't wanna fly.
Well, I, don't want to be a failure mama, I don't wanna cry.
Well, I, don't want to be a soldier mama, I don't wanna die.

② Well, I, don't want to be a rich man mama, I don't wanna cry.
Well, I, don't want to be a poor man, I don't wanna fly
Well, I, don't want to be a lawyer mama, I don't wanna lie.
Well, I, don't want to be a ~~soldier~~ mama, I don't wanna die.

③ Well, I, don't want to be a beggar mama, I don't wanna ~~shit~~ die.
Well, I, don't want to be a thief now mama, I don't wanna fly.
Well, I, don't want to be a churchman mama, I don't wanna lie.
Well, I, don't want to be a soldier mama, I don't wanna die.

(oho no?
oh no.) chone?

i don't wanna be a soldier mama
i don't wanna die

Well, I don't wanna be a soldier mama, I don't wanna die
Well, I don't wanna be a sailor mama, I don't wanna fly
Well, I don't wanna be a failure mama, I don't wanna cry
Well, I don't wanna be a soldier mama, I don't wanna die

Oh no oh no oh no oh no

Well, I don't wanna be a rich man mama, I don't wanna cry
Well, I don't wanna be a poor man mama, I don't wanna fly
Well, I don't wanna be a lawyer mama, I don't wanna lie
Well, I don't wanna be a soldier mama, I don't wanna die

Oh no oh no oh no oh no oh no

Well, I don't wanna be a soldier mama, I don't wanna die
Well, I don't wanna be a thief now mama, I don't wanna fly
Well, I don't wanna be a churchman mama, I don't wanna cry
Well, I don't wanna be a soldier mama, I don't wanna die

Oh no oh no oh no oh no oh no oh no

Well, I don't wanna be a soldier mama, I don't wanna die
Well, I don't wanna be a sailor mama, I don't wanna fly
Well, I don't wanna be a failure mama, I don't wanna cry
I don't wanna be a soldier mama, I don't wanna die

Oh no oh no oh no oh no oh no oh no oh no oh no

i don't wanna be a soldier mama i don't wanna die

John: Started off in the 'Working Class Hero' days, finished virtually in the studio. This was another first take (obviously). It's an amazing jam session track because there's a very funny rhythm in the song – it doesn't stay on the offbeat – it goes off somewhere – but Jim Keltner does some great drumming on it and sort of holds it together so you can still dance to it, although the beat's very strange. The words are lost or wrong sometimes. I also sing it in many keys at once! But it still has a nice feel – it depends on what mood I'm in, to like it or not. Yoko sticks up for it (each song takes on a personality when it is finished and we get possessive!). There's lots of echo on it, and on the solo bits there's three King Curtises on each solo – we recorded him three times on each solo – so that's really far out.

I remember 'The End Of The World Is Nigh' cartoons from when I was twelve. Our whole generation was brought up with the H Bomb and Bertrand Russell. All we ever heard as kids in England is how lucky we were because of the fucking war. Well, that war is over, man. The war is over, and the Sixties is over, and the Beatles is over, and it's all the same.

Male children in England were brought up to defend the country. A boy was really programmed to go in the army and you had to be tough. You're not supposed to cry and you're not supposed to show emotion. There's that Calvinist Protestant Anglo-Saxon ethic which is, 'Don't touch, don't react, don't feel'. And I think that's what screwed us all up. And I think it's time for a change.

I wouldn't fight. Not for Queen and country and all that. Up to eighteen there was still call-up, and I remember the news coming through that it was all those born before 1940, and I was thanking God for that, as I'd always had this plan about southern Ireland. I wasn't quite sure what I was going to do when I got to southern Ireland, but I had no intention of fighting. I just couldn't kill somebody, you know? I couldn't charge at them. I don't know whether I could kill somebody who was actually trying to kill me in the room. I couldn't just kill somebody for the nation and thank-you-very-much, here's your medal.

I can't understand how highly educated people, middle-class mainly, are so unaware as to think the game is really down to street fighting, because the game is a lot subtler than they imagine. That's what I mean when I suddenly get reminded that it's to do with oil in Biafra. What's the street fighter going to do about that? How can you fight big business? Only by attacking the shares or their image.

I think the thing we should really be talking about is the violence that goes on in this society; not in Vietnam but just right here in England or Northern Ireland. That's a far more important subject to talk about than 'Where's your hemline?' and 'Did you sleep with someone when you were fifteen or sixteen?' I think that humans always tend to talk about rubbish because they don't really want to talk about the reality that British citizens and British soldiers are getting shot down in Northern Ireland.

If we don't keep shouting PEACE, there could be war. Peace is big. War is big business. They like war because it keeps them fat and happy. I'm anti-war, so they're trying to keep me out of the USA. But I'll get in because they'll have to own up in public that they're against peace. We're all responsible for war. We all must do something, no matter what – by growing our hair long, standing on one leg, talking to the press, having Bed-Ins – to change the attitudes. The people must be made aware that it's up to them.

I want to see the plan. Count me out if it is for violence. Don't expect me to be on the barricades unless it is with flowers. The reason they don't dig it or understand it is because they're so conditioned to believe that it's inevitable, and man is a violent animal that always kills things, and we will always have it like that.

Yoko: John was a war child and so was I. He was born during the bombing of Liverpool while I was in a bomb shelter in Tokyo. In a war (which is another name for organized killing), civilians are the ones who suffer the most. Don't be misled by euphemistic expressions such as 'The attack was made with surgical precision.'

In the wars of the 20th century approximately 62 million civilians have perished, while nearly 43 million military personnel were killed. Soldiers came second on the death list. But then one must remember the soldiers' families. How they cope with the change in their lives as a result of the loss – emotionally, physically, and financially.

The war profiteers are strong because we allow them to confuse us and cause suspicion of each other. Divide and conquer. Their policy of deception, manipulation and intimidation is working. Find peace in your heart and it will spread over the world. The effect of it is strong and immediate. Keep your quiet centre, and stand for peace, instead of fighting for peace. We can do it.

We tried to find a common goal in life because she couldn't rock and roll with me and I couldn't avant-garde with her. I mean we can, but that's what we thought at the time. So we decided the thing we had in common was love and from love came peace. So we decided to work for World Peace.

John, 1969

This and previous pages: John & Yoko pose in front of a giant bronze eagle sculpture by Albino Manca at the East Coast Memorial in Battery Park during the filming of the *Imagine* movie; New York, 4 Sept 1971.

allen klein
owner
abkco

When I started in this business, I was an accountant. I'd go to an artist and say, 'let me go to your record company and do an audit for you' – to see if they were really paying him five cents on a record or whatever the contract said. I'd go over the books and I'd find that the companies were always short. Whenever I caught them at it, I'd take 50% of whatever I found for the artist. Which was fine with the artist, but I was making the record companies look like crooks even if it was an honest mistake on their part. They hated my guts.

I called John. Sometime in early 1969, I read that he had made a statement to one of the papers saying that if the Beatles didn't do something soon, Apple would be broke in six months. That was my opening.

John: We earned millions and millions. The Beatles got very little of it. We've all got houses, we've managed to pay for them finally after all these years, and that only really happened since Klein came in. They used to tell Paul and I that we were millionaires. We never have been. We didn't get the money. George and Ringo are practically penniless.

Allen Klein: *Yoko told me that when she and John came to me, they were looking for a real shark – someone to keep the other sharks away. He made more money for the parasites around him than he made for himself. Between bad advisors and a situation at Apple that just let the money flow, and taxes, it's easy to wind up with nothing. And John's very generous with his money. Too generous. There were houses that he bought – and never say – with his friends living in them. There were cars he bought that disappeared and times when he's given away, like, £25,000 out of his own pocket. Because of taxes, he's got to make £250,000 to give away £25,000, you know? And that's just too damn generous. But John does this kind of stuff from the heart. He gives things to people he cares for. You can't fault somebody for wanting to believe everybody and love everybody. That's just John Lennon.*

So, we worked out a new contract. We got the boys increased royalties, but more important than that, we got them total control and ownership of their product in America. And you know, finally, even Johnny Eastman said, 'Allen, I don't know how you did it, but this is the best record deal I've ever seen.'

Allan Steckler: He took their Capitol contract, threw it out the window and renegotiated a new one. I think they were then making 17.5% a record and he upped it to over 40% on average. It was a huge increase. The highest royalty any artist had ever received. He got Apple Films 50% instead of 20% of gross from United Artists. He also got them a huge chunk of money they were owed in back payments, and total control and ownership of their product in North America while managed by ABKCO.

Allen Klein: *There's only one thing that gives me an edge: I'm the best. I know more about this business than anybody else. I'm always better prepared than the guy across from me. Everything else is bullshit. I go into a negotiation knowing everything I can about the situation – my artist, who he is, what he wants, who the guy I'm dealing with is, who his company is and what they want. I'm the best, and that's why I can charge the Beatles 20%. I'll tell you. Under Epstein – by the way, he took 25% – when they were touring, selling millions of records, making movies they made £6,500,000 in six years. With me, they've earned £9,000,000 in 19 months. How's that?*

John: Mr Klein's contracts are amazing. He's a naughty boy, and he's too greedy, and he didn't do what he said he'd do, which was manage our affairs, which are in a worse state than when...well, according to the accountants, anyway.

Allen Klein: *There are good people in this business and there are scum. And when there's a lot of money involved, there are bound to be suits. Lawsuits are tools of the trade and you use the tools you have to survive.*

John: There seems to be an awful lot of lawsuits involved with rock 'n' roll… about twenty – he's suing me, and Yoko, and all the ex-Beatles, and everybody that ever knew them! And he's suing me individually, me collectively, any version of me you can get hold of is being sued – all just money. Somehow a deal will be made. Ask any rock star about lawsuits. And the more money there is, the more lawsuits there are. The bigger the artist, the more suits.

Allan Steckler: Despite all the crap that was said about Allen, and some of it was true, he had a very strong, positive feeling about John & Yoko. He really loved them and he completely turned their fortunes around.

All italicized text taken from an interview with Allen Klein published in *Playboy*, 1971.

1971

Polaroid of Yoko with Andy Warhol, signed by John, Yoko and Andy (above left),
Polaroid of John & Yoko to George Maciunas, signed by John & Yoko (above right).
Opposite: photos by Stanley E. Michels (pictured in the white shirt with Yoko, bottom left).
All taken at Betty Klein's birthday party; Riverdale, Bronx, New York, 12 June 1971.
As well as John & Yoko, Allen and Betty Klein's guests included Abbie Hoffman,
Allan Steckler, Al Aronowitz, Andy Warhol, Donna Jordan, Fred Hughes, Harold Seider,
Howard Smith, Jack Nicholson, Jane Forth, Jerry Rubin, Jill Johnston, Jonas Mekas,
Marty Ostrow, Miles Davis, Pete Bennett, Robin Klein, Shirley Clarke,
Stanley E. Michels and Molly Michels, The Boys In The Band and Viva.

pete bennett
manager
abkco

'Imagine' was a song I first heard at Phil Spector's house in California. My instant reaction to both Phil and John was that if it was properly recorded, 'Imagine' and the rest of the album would skyrocket to the top of the charts. My prediction turned out to be quite accurate as a result of my commitment to John, Yoko and Phil to make this a top record.

We told John he had to go more commercial if he wanted to get a big smash. An artist has to put out what he feels, but I'm sure an artist wises up, and that's why John put out this new type of album.

I'm a Bronx boy who, from nothing, broke the British Invasion in America.

The Animals, The Dave Clark Five, Herman's Hermits, The Zombies, Jeff Beck. I broke the Stones wide open. I took them to see the Beatles at Shea Stadium in the dugout in 1965. There were bottles and cans being thrown. We were scared!

We shaped the whole music industry. You gotta understand something. In 1963, our beloved president John F. Kennedy got assassinated and the whole country's morale was very down. And all of a sudden in '64, Boom! the Beatles come out. That was the biggest thing we needed in this country. That was timing. That was timing when Ed Sullivan put them on the TV.

Before that, I'll be honest with you, all the radio stations didn't wanna play the Beatles. They put them on a contest, they came in fifth: 'I Wanna Hold Your Hand'. I even told Murray The K, who was a big DJ at that time, 'I know something's gonna happen,' and it did. Ed Sullivan put them on the TV.

Today you have *American Idol*, which is a good outlet – a couple of sustained artists have come out of it, and a couple of one-shot wonders. But I don't think those days of the Ed Sullivan shows will ever come back again.

The Beatles trusted me. I broke their records and worked hard at promoting them. I was honest with them and they liked me. They felt secure with me and they could talk to me. We had a lot of laughter together. The Beatles were no different from other rock groups. Everybody thought a Beatles record would always sell. Without the right marketing and promotion, it's not gonna happen.

There was the Yoko Ono factor. She's a great gal, wonderful really, but the others resented that John had married her. She had a big influence over John, she wanted to sing but they could not see it. After the Beatles split, I worked with all of them individually.

One thing I learned since I got into promotion was that I didn't give anybody lip service. That's the way the Beatles liked me. I didn't go out and say their record was a smash if I didn't think so.

The industry hasn't changed, OK? What I love about the industry today is that there are more areas to promote a record. 'Cos now you got a lot of television, you got videos, you got more stations, everybody's playing different things. I love the business.

allan steckler
a+r
apple new york

Allan Steckler: In 1968, I was the creative director at Allen Klein's organization, ABKCO. They were mainly royalty specialists, lawyers and accountants – numbers people. I was more of a 'music' person and could relate with the bands, so if The Rolling Stones, The Kinks or Bobby Vinton or one of our other acts needed something, I was the one who handled it.

One day in September 1969, Klein said to me, 'I'm going up to Canada, will you come with me?' That's when I first met John & Yoko – in Toronto before they did the live show. I was amazed at John's humour. He had this really cutting, funny wit about him, which I loved.

Klein could be the most charming and interesting person you'd ever meet. One of the big reasons that he got on so well with John was that he had such a huge knowledge about music. He loved music, loved songs and loved lyrics. He would have been the most brilliant psychologist of all time, because in ten or fifteen minutes he would know you inside out. He would know what you wanted and he could get you to do anything he wanted. He was a street guy. He had no pretences. He was who he was and I think John could relate to that. But he could also be crude, rude and very uncaring. That's a strange mixture of qualities, but it was what made him a brilliant businessman.

Klein took the control of all North American music product away from Capitol, over to ABKCO, and over to me. I was responsible for getting all that product finished – the albums, the artwork, the advertising, the promotion – all of it. We supervised all the mastering, the graphics and the printing. We supplied Capitol with complete product. We were so busy with Apple product in 1971 that I had a period of about eight months where I never saw my wife except for one weekend when I brought her down to the city from where we lived in the suburbs.

When John & Yoko were staying in New York, we would send my secretary's assistant, May Pang, over to their hotel to help them with their day-to-day needs. I would go down once or twice a week, usually in the afternoons and stay for as long as they wanted me to. John had this really gentle, playful humour as well as this totally fearless side. One day in my New York office, he grabbed a pen and spontaneously drew a cheeky little doodle of him, Yoko and me on a white ceramic plant pot on my desk.

When they wanted to do recording sessions in New York, I found them The Record Plant and engineer Roy Cicala, with whom they became dear and trusted friends. And it was there that I first heard 'Imagine'.

There are times when you see something so beautiful – a sunset, a face, a child – that makes you stop and inhale the beauty and understand, at least for that moment, that God, or what you believe in, is responsible for this. Such moments remain with you for the rest of your life, and are as clear as the moment they happened, no matter how old and forgetful you become. The night I was in the studio and heard 'Imagine' for the first time was one of those moments. John had brought tapes from England and wanted to redo vocals before adding orchestration to the tracks. We listened to the song 'Imagine' with John's original vocal and knew that this was a perfect performance. Nothing could improve on it. Those amazing, simple, eloquent lyrics. I knew that this was a song 'for the ages'.

Phil Spector was a fucking genius. You can't really describe what Phil did. You have to listen to it. He always created such an amazing sound.

For example, he could layer fifteen tracks of strings to get the sound that he wanted. When we were doing the *Imagine* album, King Curtis came in to do the sax solos. He must've done eight or nine different takes for 'I Don't Wanna Be A Soldier' and Phil said, 'We should mix them all together.' And that's what they did.

John's innate sense was always the musicality. If there was some technical thing that didn't quite work, he'd say to Roy Cicala, 'It's fine, it doesn't have to be perfect. If it feels right, it's right.' And it was. I don't think many people understood what Yoko was trying to do, but John did. John and I were in the studio on a break and it was a very rare occasion where Yoko was out somewhere else – with Jackie Kennedy, I think – and I said to him, 'Explain something to me. I've been married for a number of years. When I have to go away on business, there are times I look forward to it. Sometimes it's good for me and my wife to be apart for a week or so. But you and Yoko are inseparable. You're with each other all the time, 24/7. How do you do it?' And he looked at me and said, 'She makes me think. I'm always thinking when she's with me.' I'll never forget that.

ALLAN STECKLER

APPLE
1700 Broadway
New York N.Y. 10019
(212) 582 - 5533

may pang
general assistant

Yoko: The first time I met May was in Allen Klein's office. She was working at ABKCO as an office assistant and she came in to give some papers to Allen.

In December 1970, John and I were in New York, and, to help us out, Allan Steckler sent May and Paul Mozian over from ABKCO to assist us while we were making films such as *Up Your Legs Forever*. May's job was to ring up many of my friends in the New York art world to ask them if they would be kind enough to come down and have their legs filmed for our new film. Then I suddenly noticed May had beautiful legs, like no other. She had a really pleasant, easy-going manner with people as well. It was very nice for us to have someone working for us who was like that.

We next saw her in July of 1971, when ABKCO sent her over with some film reels to Ascot from New York. In those days all our films and tapes had to be hand-delivered by a person to ensure they didn't disappear in transit. That's just how it was.

When we returned to New York in mid-August, May assisted us again while we stayed at the St Regis hotel. I was editing the *Imagine* film at the hotel and I was still adding a few new scenes – filming around New York and in the rooms at the hotel. We found out that Fred Astaire was staying at the hotel, so we sent May up to his suite to ask him if he would be in our film.

We had a lot of visitors. We met Dick Cavett then, whom John and I both liked very much. As a result, John and I were guests on Dick Cavett's TV show and when we talked about Bagism and my Bag Events, May and Paul Mozian showed the audience what we meant by both coming on stage, each of them wearing one of my bags.

May was always full of energy and good humour. She had a great love of music and told us she knew about a lot of the young hip bands in New York. When George Harrison and Bob Dylan came over to the hotel to visit, she told us she got a really big thrill out of that. She was also a very good secretary and I liked her very much.

May Pang at Tittenhurst on 22 July 1971 and at the St Regis hotel, New York, on 10 September 1971;
John & Yoko photoshoot at David Bailey's home studio, Primrose Hill, London, 18 July 1971.
Opposite: excerpt from John & Yoko's film *Clock* made for the Everson Museum show.
Filmed in their hotel suite, John is playing his guitar and talking to Yoko on the sofa.
May is on the phone. Posters from the *Imagine* and *FLY* albums are on the walls.

John & Yoko with George Harrison at the St Regis hotel, New York, 2 September 1971.
Opposite: the first 1,000 copies of the *Imagine* album sold in Japan included
a postcard to order this limited edition, promo, 7-inch interview disc
conducted by Kenji Mizuhara (Apple's label manager in Japan).

gimme ~~the truth~~ some truth

(1) i'm sick and tired of hearing things
from ~~sea~~ uptight - short ~~of~~ sighted - narrow minded.
hypercritics
    all I want is the truth
    just gimme some truth

(2) i've had enough of reading things
  by nevrotic - phsycotic - pig headed politicians
    all i want is the truth
    just gimme some truth

(8) no short haired - yellow bellied, son of tricky dicky
is gonna mother hubbard soft soap me
with ~~just~~ a pocketful of hope - money for rope
money for rope

(3) i'm sick to death of seeing things
from tight lipped - condescending - mommies little
chauvanists
    all i want is the truth
    just gimme some truth

psy
psychotic psycotic
    psch

gimme some truth

I'm sick and tired of hearing things
From uptight, short-sighted, narrow-minded hypocritics
All I want is the truth, just gimme some truth

I've had enough of reading things
By neurotic psychotic pig-headed politicians
All I want is the truth, just gimme some truth

No short-haired, yellow-bellied, son of Tricky Dicky's
Gonna Mother Hubbard soft soap me
With just a pocketful of hope
Money for dope, money for rope

I'm sick to death of seeing things
From tight-lipped, condescending, Mommy's little chauvinists
All I want is the truth, just gimme some truth

I've had enough of watching scenes
with schizophrenic, egocentric, paranoiac primadonnas
All I want is the truth, just gimme some truth

No short-haired, yellow-bellied son of Tricky Dicky's
Gonna Mother Hubbard soft soap me
With just a pocketful of soap
Money for dope, money for rope

I'm sick to death of hearing things
From uptight, short-sighted, narrow-minded hypocrites
All I want is the truth now
Just gimme some truth now

I've had enough of reading things
by neurotic, psychotic, pig-headed politicians
All I want is the truth now, just gimme some truth now
All I want is the truth now, just gimme some truth now

All I want is the truth, just gimme some truth
All I want is the truth, just gimme some truth

gimme some truth

John: Side Two starts with 'Give Me Some Truth', which is one I started a year or two back – probably in India. We wrote a lot there. It was an old lick that I had around a long time but I again changed the lyrics. I like the track because it sounds good but it didn't get much attention, so it's a personal track that I like the sound of. The guitars are good and the voice sounds nice and it says whatever it says. George does a sharp solo with his steel finger (he's not too proud of it – but I like it).

It's about politicians, newspaper men and all the hypocrites of the world. And male chauvinists, it's about them too. I think that music reflects the state that the society is in. There is nothing to hide. Not really. I mean, we all like to shit in private and we certainly have things we prefer to do in private, privately. But in general what is there to hide? I mean, what is the big secret?

I think it's like this whole game of the press. When the whole drug thing came out about the Beatles, what actually happened was the press cornered Paul one day with the TV cameras and all the press and asked him, 'Have you taken LSD?' And he said 'Yes.' And they said, 'Don't you think that you have a responsibility to society?' And he said, 'Yes I do, and so do you, so please don't publish this or print it.' And they had it on every newscast that night with him saying, 'Please don't publish it.' Now what the hypocrisy of the press is like, what I was saying about the *News Of The World* is they're always going on about other people's responsibilities and pop stars selling sex to people when they're the ones keeping the whole mill rolling. They have as much responsibility as us so-called 'stars' and that was a prime example.

There was a famous picture of me in one of the Beatle books and it said, 'No phoney politician is ever going to get through to me.' That still stands, although I dabbled in so called 'politics' in the late Sixties and Seventies. More out of guilt for being rich and guilty, thinking that maybe perhaps love and peace isn't enough, that you have to go and get shot or something, or get punched in the face, to prove I'm one of the people.

I think our society is run by insane people for insane objectives. And I think that's what I sussed when I was sixteen and twelve, way down the line. But I expressed it differently all through my life. I think we're being run by maniacs for maniacal ends. If anybody can put on paper what our government and the American government et cetera and the Russian, Chinese – what they are

actually trying to do, and what they think they're doing, I'd be very pleased to know what they think they're doing. I think they're all insane but I'm liable to be put away as insane for expressing that. That's what's insane about it.

Somebody comes along with a good piece of truth and instead of the truth being looked at, they look at the person that brought it. It's like when the bad news comes, they shoot the messenger. When the good news comes, they worship the messenger and they don't listen to the message – whether it be Christianity, Mohammadism, Buddhism, Confucianism, Marxism, Maoism, everything. It's always about the person and never about what they said.

Yoko: What's more important – the poet or the poetry? The poetry. Be honest to yourself. Very few people are. Others will take notice of you. And maybe become a bit more honest themselves, as well. We try to be honest. And the point is – if we are really honest, just to make it between us is really a lifetime thing. And if we can't make it together and endure each other, the world is nowhere. If ordinary couples can make it together and make it with their children and so forth, love-wise, then you can look after the world.

John: My function in society is to be an artist. The artist's function is to be as true to himself (and therefore the people he communicates with through his art) as he can, and survive. Art is a functional part of society. If you don't have artists, you don't have society. We're not some kind of decadent strip show that appears on the side. We're as important as prime ministers or policemen.

Yoko: I cannot stand the fact that everything is the accumulation of 'distortion' owing to one's slanted view. I want the truth. I want to feel the truth by any possible means. I want someone or something to let me feel it. I can neither trust the plant-likeness of my body or the manipulation of my consciousness.

John: Register to vote. If you register to vote, it doesn't mean you have to vote. At least you have it. And then if there's somebody around that you can believe in, you've got that vote. But if you don't register and it comes, and you wanna do something, you've missed it. Because there's one inch in which we breathe differently between the two parties. And everybody's saying they're all the same. They are all the same, but there's one inch in which they let you breathe.

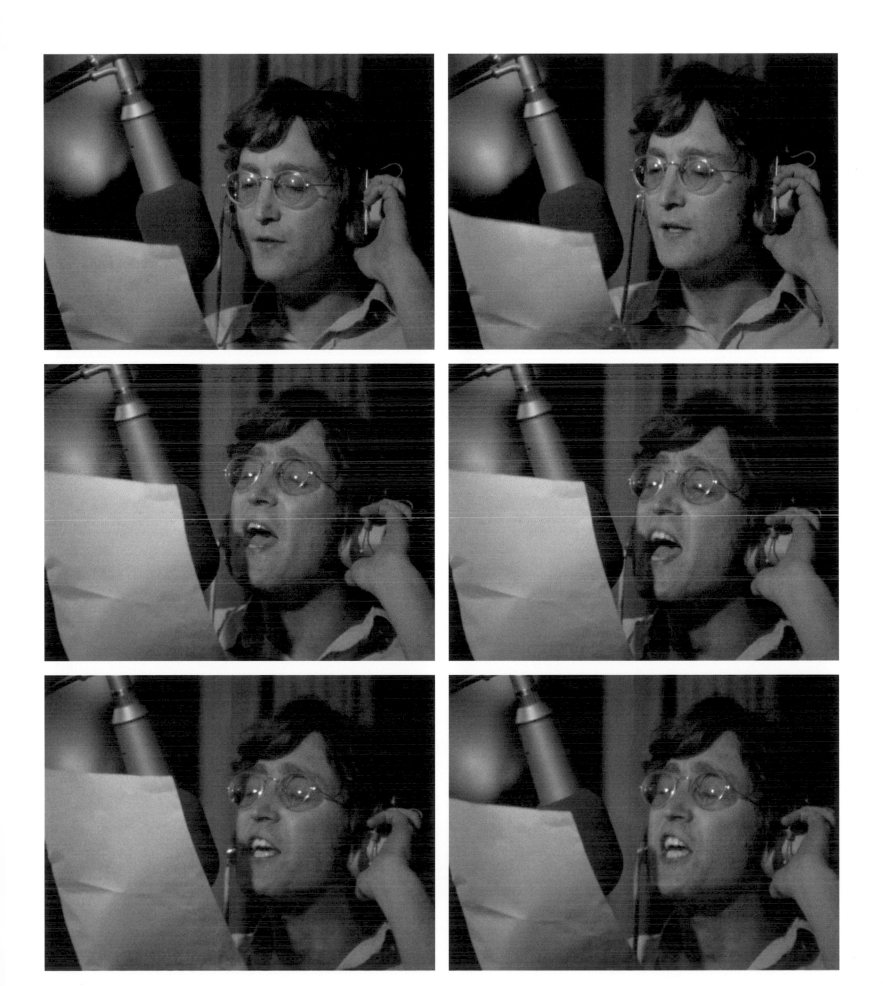

'Gimme Some Truth'? It's about politicians, newspaper men and all the hypocrites of the world. And male chauvinists, it's about them too. I think that music reflects the state that the society is in.

John, 1971

John photographed recording the master vocal for 'Gimme Some Truth'; Ascot Sound Studios, 28 May 1971.

Good morning, love.

I'm sorry - Eternally, Yoko

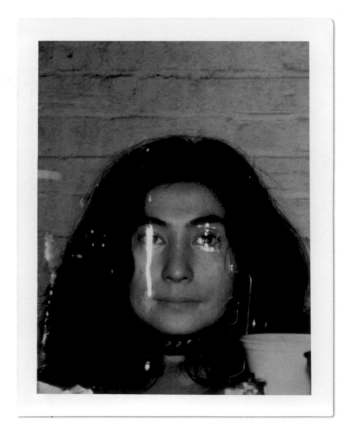

album artwork

imagine
front and back album cover art
by yoko ono

John: My album front and back is taken by Yoko as a Polaroid. It's a new one called a Polaroid close-up. It's fantastic. She took a photo of me, and then we had this painting off a guy called Geoff Hendricks who only paints sky. And I was standing in front of it, in the hotel room and she superimposed the picture of it on me after, so I was in the cloud with my head. And then I lay down on the window sill to get a lying down picture for the back side, which she wanted with the cloud above my head. And I'm sort of 'imagining'.

imagine the clouds dripping. dig a hole in your garden to put them in. yoko '63

sw 3379

imagine
john
lennon

Imagine front and back cover polaroid photography by Yoko Ono, July 1971.
Previous pages: polaroids by John & Yoko; 29 June and July 1971.

geoffrey hendricks
artist – clouds

24 June 1971 was our tenth wedding anniversary and because by then Bici and I had both realized we were gay and in very different relations, we organized a Flux Divorce event. The house got divided in all kinds of funny ways. It was a great event. Many of our Fluxus friends attended and to the delight of the neighbours, John & Yoko arrived in their limousine. They had a card that they gave us – Yoko signed her half to Bici and John signed his half to me.

The next day, somebody from their office called up and said that they would like to purchase a Cloud Painting I had created in 1966 – the one they had seen in the dining room. So we agreed on a price, and they came and picked it up, and I signed the back 'For John & Yoko with love Geoff, 25 June 1971'. I had no idea my painting would end up being used as part of the *Imagine* album cover. I love painting skies and have been painting them since the mid-Sixties. I had a sky bundle in a show in the

Bianchini Gallery in '65, sky on sky on sky, all tied together with rope and pages with overlapping skies. That whole show was all sky. There was a stretch when I was doing acrylics of sky over and beyond those sky bundles and I've painted a lot of watercolours of sky over the years. I just had a show in Blois in France – a wall of 113 watercolours of skies, all about 11x18 inches in size, interspersed with roof slates, along with a couple of environments and some letter pieces and stair pieces.

When John & Yoko were working with Allen Klein at ABKCO, they wanted me to paint a Sky Ceiling for their conference room, but unfortunately the project never got realized in time. There are some good memories from all of that time. Fluxus is the latin for Flux. And it's about change, it's about purging, so that you have Flux as abnormal discharge but it's also like welding and bringing two different pieces of metal together. And I think all of

these qualities are part of what are incorporated into the idea of Fluxus as a group of artists working together. It's wanting to break with tradition, be revolutionary, working as a group, challenging traditional ideas and breaking open one's thinking so that you move into a different realm of perception and ideas.

Left and above right: Geoffrey and Bici Hendricks' *Invitation for Fluxdivorce*, 331 West 20th Street, New York, June 24, 1971 (offset lithograph on two sheets, designed by George Maciunas); Geoffrey Hendricks' *Flux Divorce Box* with *Flux Divorce Album* (cut version), 24 June 1971. Opposite and below right: *Untitled (Sky)*, 1966, by Geoffrey Hendricks, dedicated to John & Yoko by the artist: 'To John and Yoko with love Geoff, 25 June 1971'.

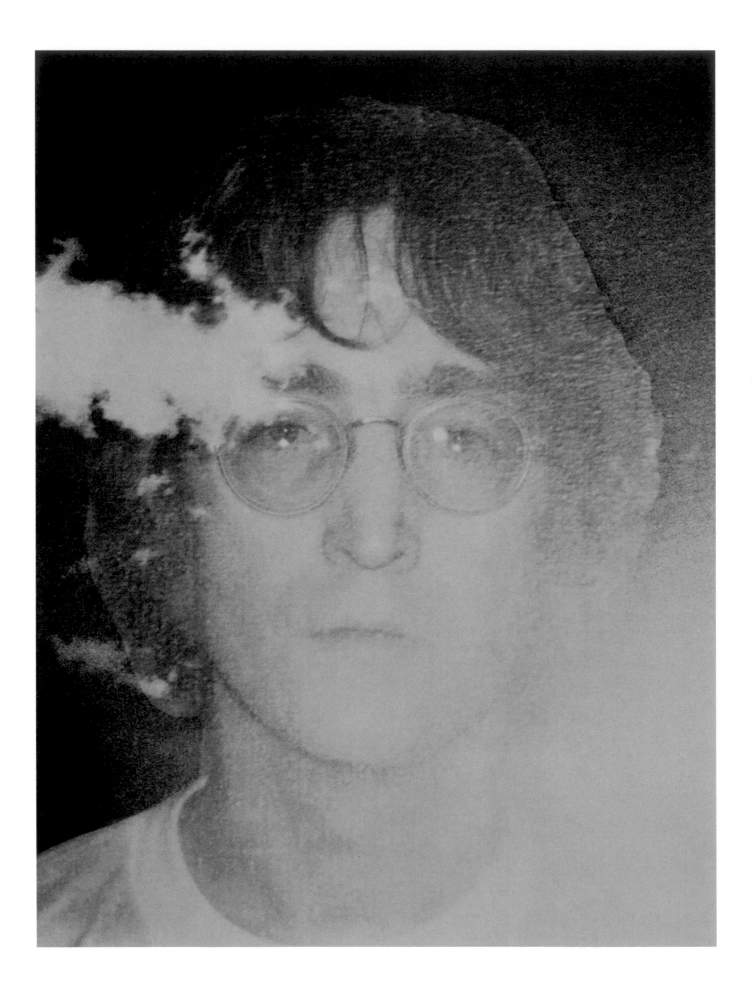

imagine
inner sleeve artwork by john lennon

01	John Lennon Pianos, Vocals, Guitars, Harmonica, Co-Producer	23	Klaus Voormann Bass, Upright Bass
02	Phil Spector Co-Producer	24	Klaus Voormann Bass, Upright Bass
03	Steve Brendell General Assistant, Upright Bass	25	George Harrison Electric Guitars, Dobro
04	Dan Richter Personal Assistant	26	Paul Prestopino Engineer, Record Plant
05	Eddie Klein Engineer, Ascot Sound Studios	27	Mal Evans Road Manager
06	King Curtis Saxophone	28	Phil McDonald Engineer, Ascot Sound Studios
07	John Barham Harmonium, Vibraphone	29	Nicky Hopkins Piano, Keyboards
08	Allen Klein Owner, ABKCO	30	Phil Spector Co-Producer
09	Rev. T. J. Bower*	31	Alan White Drums, Upright Bass, Tibetan Cymbals, Good Vibes
10	Shelly Yakus Engineer, Record Plant	32	Diana Robertson Secretary
11	Eddie Veale Engineer, Ascot Sound Studios	33	Joey Molland Acoustic Guitars
12	Roy Cicala Engineer, Record Plant	34	Val Wilde Housekeeper & Cook
13	Joe Marcini Chauffeur, Apple UK	35	Arlene Reckson Night Manager, Record Plant
14	Les Anthony Chauffeur to John & Yoko	36	Diana Robertson Secretary
15	Prof. J. H. Kurzenknabe*	37	Rod Lynton Acoustic Guitars
16	Dan Richter Personal Assistant	38	Ted Turner Acoustic Guitar
17	Jim Gordon Drums	39	Yoko Ono Co-Producer
18	Jack Douglas Engineer, Record Plant	40	Harry Ritz Comic Actor (Kentucky Moonshine, 1938)
19	Rev. J. M. Runkle*		
20	Richie Appuzo Engineer, Record Plant		
21	Tom Evans Guitar		
22	Al Steckler A&R, Apple NY		

* denotes portraits taken from a photographic composite of members of the Eastern Synod, Williamsport, PA, October 1905.

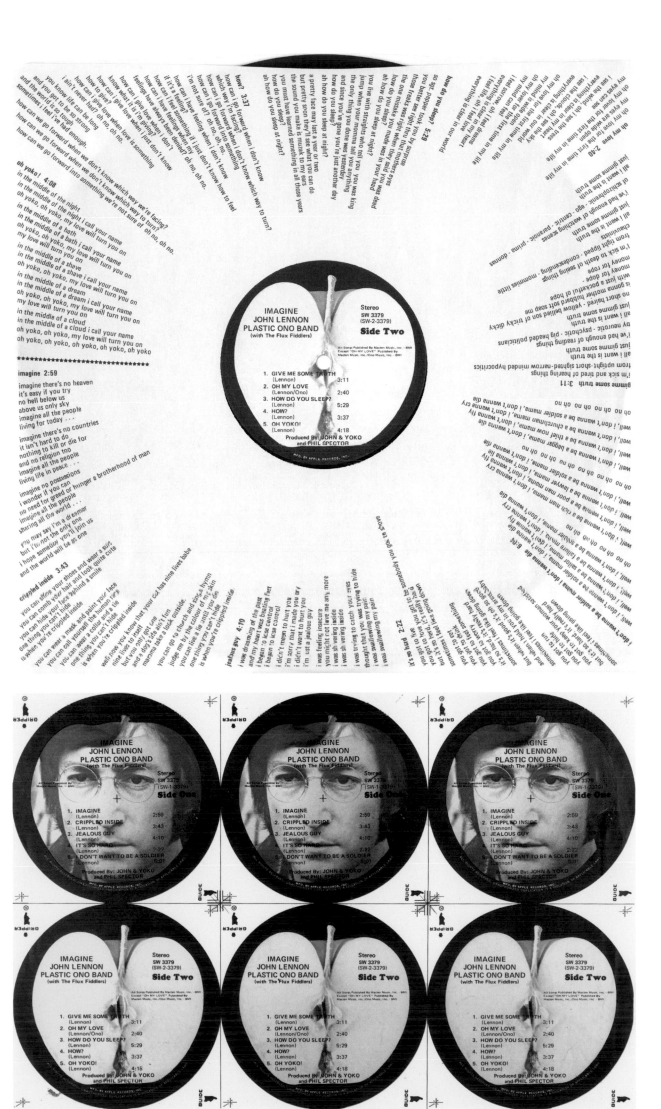

Clockwise from top left: Yoko seated beside *Painting to See in the Dark (Version 1)*, 1961, installation view at 'Paintings and Drawings by Yoko Ono', AG Gallery, New York, photo by George Maciunas, 16 June 1961; polaroid of George Maciunas by John Lennon, Fluxhouse Cooperative, 80 Wooster St, New York, 29 June 1971; in front of George Maciunas's poster, *U.S.A. Surpasses All the Genocide Records*, 1966, Tittenhurst UK, 22 July 1971.

george maciunas
typography

Jonas Mekas: In 1957, I was editing *Film Culture* magazine and I needed somebody to help me with the design. George Maciunas was a student and it was the beginning of a very long friendship. Sometimes he designed just a little bit to help me out; he also designed a number of issues totally – from beginning to end.

Yoko: By 1961, the concerts that I was hosting at my Chambers Street loft were getting very popular. First it had only been ten people coming, but soon there were hundreds, including John Cage, David Tudor, Peggy Guggenheim, Marcel Duchamp, Max Ernst, George Brecht, George Segal, Richard Maxfield, Beate Gordon, Robert Rauschenberg, Jasper Johns, Isamu Noguchi, and La Monte Young. And a young George Maciunas, although I didn't know it at the time.

Later that summer, George opened the AG Gallery on Madison Avenue in midtown, hosting exactly the same kind of events as I had been doing in my Chambers Street loft. All the artists from my Chambers Street Series then started lining up in front of his gallery. George had seen one of my accordion-shaped calligraphy books at Richard Maxfield's house and offered me the last show at his gallery. This was my first show of Instruction Paintings. The instructions gave me the freedom to do all sorts of things that you can't do in the material world, for instance, to 'mix three paintings in your head'.

George said we had to have a name for this movement that was happening. 'You think of the name,' he told me. I said, 'I don't think this is a movement. I think it's wrong to make it into a movement.' To me, 'movement' had a dirty sound – like we were going to be some kind of an establishment. I didn't like that. So I didn't think of any name. The next day, George said

'Yoko, look.' He showed me the word 'Fluxus' in a huge dictionary. It had many meanings, but he pointed to 'flushing'. 'Like toilet flushing!', he said laughing, thinking it was a good name for the movement. 'This is the name,' he said. I just shrugged my shoulders in my mind.

George Maciunas: <u>Purge</u> the world of bourgeois sickness, 'intellectual', professional & commercialized culture, PURGE the world of dead art, imitation, artificial art, abstract art, illusionistic art, mathematical art, — PURGE THE WORLD OF 'EUROPANISM'! PROMOTE A REVOLUTIONARY FLOOD AND TIDE IN ART. Promote living art, anti-art, promote <u>NON ART REALITY</u> to be grasped by all peoples, not only critics, dilettantes and professionals. <u>FUSE</u> the cadres of cultural, social & political revolutionaries into united front & action. (*Fluxus Manifesto*, 1963)

Jon Hendricks. In a way, George Maciunas was the Marinetti or the André Breton of the Fluxus movement. He knitted it together, shaped the earliest concerts, wrote the manifestos, and oversaw the publications and editions, through his editing, design, production and advertising. But it would be a mistake to think of Fluxus as a one-man show. Fluxus artists recognized Maciunas's role but remained fiercely independent, at times embracing the ideals of the movement and at other times going their own way. Ultimately, Maciunas' vision of a collective 'united front' proved impossible to realize except within his production of Fluxus anthologies, editions and occasionally in Fluxfests and environments.

Jonas Mekas: In 1966, I was running film screenings and needed a place. George created the first artist cooperative at 80 Wooster Street in SoHo and we did a lot of work together.

I bought in. I took the first floor and basement and gave the basement to George for him to live and work in because he was so poor. George was laughing at it all, and creating in its place his own fragile life, a totally inconsequential unimportant world, a world of games, little boxes, puzzles, jokes, all in praise of nothingness. His art had no value at the time, and he gave so many of his works away, or sold them for just enough to survive. He lived very economically. He worked day and night. He was an insomniac. He was the one who made SoHo. He created the first twenty-five or so cooperative buildings. He risked jail, he was badly beaten up. In the summer of 1971, George held that famous dumpling party with very badly cooked dumplings! John had just acquired a Polaroid camera that day, I think, and he wanted to test it. He brought it with him and he took snaps. He gave them away to some of the people who were there but seven of them he gave to me because they involved George and me. Andy Warhol was also there. He respected George very much and although George critiqued what Andy was doing, we were all friendly and got along very well.

John: He has pancake parties in his bomb shelter which has a nice little stone garden at the back, and that was filmed too. I took a great picture of Yoko, double exposed with a Polaroid camera, close up, and that's going to be her LP cover.

Yoko: From June to October 1971, George constructed many pieces for my Everson Museum show. In general, if I said I wanted to do something, he would immediately say, 'Okay let's do it.' He was someone who materialized things for me. He was good at that. But he did it in his own way and I sometimes had to say that I didn't want it like that. And this happened at the Everson Museum.

John Lennon 1971   Spring evening 1879. *National Museum of Fine Arts, Budapest.*

Dear Raver,

We never did talk to Miles about working with him – so there. anyway the idea was for Miles and Yoko to do a track together – i mean she worked with Ornette Coleman in 1967-8 at Albert Hall – it's on her last album. Having met Miles at Kleins party – i know damn well he wouldn't be as snidy as you cunts

lots of Rave,

John + Yoko. (remember?)

FARMER J. wrestling with

Dear Julian,
thanx for pic.etc here is the telephone number (again).
—212.595.4457.
we've been home about a week, hope you had a good summer,
love
Dad, Yoko, Sean

JULIAN LENNON
BRON-Y-GOF
Llanfwrog,
Ruthin,
NORTH WALES,
U. Kingdom (come!)

SPECIAL DELIVERY
SPECIAL DELIVERY
EXPRESS
AIRMAIL EXPRESS.

This page, left: the pig postcard came with initial pressings of the *Imagine* album and was John's parody of Paul and Linda McCartney's *Ram* album front cover (1971). This one (of 'Farmer J wrestling with an agricultural problem etc etc') was posted to Julian Lennon from John, Yoko and Sean, and is included with Julian's kind permission. Photographed at Tittenhurst, 23 July 1971.
This page, above: photocollage by John Lennon based on *Spring Evening* (1879) by Arnold Böcklin. Included as a postcard with the *Imagine* album, this one is addressed to the Dear Raver column in *Melody Maker*, 1971.
Opposite: poster included with the *Imagine* alblum. John photographed while recording 'Imagine' on Yoko's white piano in the White Room, Tittenhurst, 27 May 1971.

① oh my love for the first time in my life
my eyes are wide opened
oh my lover for the first time in my life
my eyes can see,

② oh my love for the first time in my life
my ears are wide opene
oh my lover for the first time in my life
my ears can hear

③ I see the wind, oh I see the tree
everything is clear in my ~~mind~~ heart
I see the clouds, oh I see the sky
everything is clear in our world

② I hear the rain, oh hear the grass
everything is clear in my heart
I hear the wind, oh hear the river
everything is clear in our world.

③ Oh my love for the first time in my life
my mind is wide open
oh my lover for the first time in my life
my mind can feel.

③ I feel sorrow, oh I feel dream
everything is clear in my soul.
feel like, oh I feel clear
everything is clear in our world.

oh my love

Oh my love for the first time in my life
My eyes are wide open
Oh my lover for the first time in my life
My eyes can see

I see the wind, oh I see the trees
Everything is clear in my heart
I see the clouds, oh I see the sky
Everything is clear in our world

Oh my love for the first time in my life
My mind is wide open
Oh my lover for the first time in my life
My mind can feel

I feel sorrow, oh I feel dreams
Everything is clear in my heart
I feel life, oh I feel love
Everything is clear in our world

oh my love

John: A joy to write and a joy to sing and record! Written with Yoko – based on her original lyric – we finished it very quickly one late night together, the beginning of the melody being started last year. Writing songs is like writing books – you store little melodies/words/ideas etc in your mind library and fish them out when you need them. The oriental-sounding note in the 'heart' bit is not Yoko's influence! I used the same kind of 'flats' in an old song I recorded with the Beatles – 'Girl'. But everything else, yes! You hear Yoko's classical influence. She was trained as a classical musician all her life, and she only went mad, avant-garde, later in life, you know, [laughs] like a lot of people do. She went bananas before she met me. [laughs] We're both bananas, that's why we fell in love. But in this song, you can hear the classical influence of Yoko has influenced me on this. And this is 80% her lyric and 50% her tune.

Yoko: In most love songs you're making people feel hot or whatever about each other. But instead of that, he's saying, 'I see it clearly for the first time.' It's not so much about sexual interest or 'I miss you' – it's more to do with true love. What is love then? Love is when you understand each other so well that you finally relax.

John: One thing we've found out is that love is a great gift, like a precious flower or something. You have to feed it and look after it and it has storms to go through, and snow, but you have to protect it. It's like a pet cat. You know, people get a cat and they don't want to feed it, or they get a dog and they won't want to walk it. But love has to be nurtured like a very sensitive animal because that's what it is. And you have to work at love. You don't just sit round with it and it doesn't just do it for you. You've got to be very careful with it. It's the most delicate thing you can be given.

When two of you are together, man and wife, there's nothing that can touch you. You have the power of two people, you have the protection – you don't need the society or the room or the uniform or the gun because you have the power of two minds, which is a pretty powerful thing.

Yoko: He was incredibly shy. I know you're not going to believe this, but he was. And that made me feel like we were two of a kind.

John: There's nothing I like more than to get home at the end of the day and sit next to Yoko and say, 'Well, we're together at last.' Although we may have been holding hands all day, it's not the same when we're working or talking to the press. We feel a hundred miles apart by comparison.

Yoko: I was a very lonely person before I met him. Most people in the world are very lonely, that's the biggest problem, and because of their loneliness they become suspicious. The reason we're lonely is because we can't communicate enough from the various complexes we have and from the various social habits we've created. We become very inhibited. When I met John, I started to open up a little through love and that's the greatest thing that happened to me yet. There are various facets to my life and my personality, and I never met anybody else who could understand me. We understand each other so well, and I'm not lonely any more, which is a shocking experience, really. Also, through loneliness or something, I was starting to become a very firm and strong ego…but that's melting away, and it's very nice.

John: I was lonely, and didn't have full communication with anybody, and it took a bit of adjusting. She rediscovered or cultivated the thing that existed in me before I left Liverpool, maybe, and re-cultivated the natural John Lennon that had been lost in the Beatles thing, and the worldwide thing. She encouraged me to be myself, because it was me that she fell in love with, not the Beatles or whatever I was. When you get sidetracked, you believe it, and when you're in the dark, you believe it. She came and reminded me that there was light, and when you remember there's light, you don't want to get back in the dark again. That's what she did for me.

Yoko: But I didn't do it intentionally or anything. It's the falling in love bit. You start to see all sorts of things that you don't see if you're not in love. I found that he has all these qualities that he was hiding away. Music-wise, he was doing all sorts of freaky things at home, just recording it on a cassette, but not really showing it publicly. Publicly he was doing the Beatles things. But he showed me all these cassettes and things and I said: 'Why don't you produce these as records?' I performed the role of a mirror in a way. He was doing all those things anyway. I didn't suggest them. It was there and that goes for his drawing, paintings and poetry too, especially his drawings. I think he's better than Picasso.

fly
yoko
ono

FLY
front and back album cover
photography by john lennon

FLY front and back cover photographs – polaroids taken
by John Lennon at George Maciunas's dumpling party at the
Fluxhouse Cooperative, 80 Wooster St, New York, 29 June 1971.

Yoko: 'Fly' is the last track of the record but it has been
made the first just when my last album was finished and
was out in the street. It was made in our bedroom in the
Regency Hotel in New York on Xmas 1970 on a Nagra
operated by John. I was thinking that I must make a
soundtrack for my film *FLY* which was just near completion.
Then John suggested maybe we should knock it off before
the ten o'clock news that night. It was that casual. We
did it in one take, as most of my things are done. I don't
believe in doing things over, and unless it is a really bad
take, I believe in the first take.

I asked Joe Jones, an old friend from the avant-garde,
to make me instruments which were unlike any in the world.
Making strange instruments was his thing. Joe came up
with instruments which played themselves without any
musicians. 'Don't Count The Waves', 'You' and 'Airmale'
were made that way.

fly
yoko
ono

love is having to say you're sorry every five minutes. john '71

John: We did a fantastic session for her album. There's this guy who is an old friend of hers as well who gets things like music stands with toy violins and different things hanging off them, and they all play when he plugs them in, and he brought along about forty pieces, so we did about eight tracks of them and eight tracks of Yoko, and then a live thing of them all playing and Yoko improvising – it's just fantastic. And then again me and him were playing, putting on the switches and then we did a jam session with her and the stuff – it was beautiful. They're called Joe Jones and the Tone Deaf Music Company.

Yoko: I was always fascinated by the idea of making special instruments for special emotions – instruments that lead us to emotions arrived by their own motions rather than by our control. With those instruments, I wanted to explore emotions and vibrations which have not been explored as yet in music. I thought of building a house on the hill which

makes different sounds by the wind that goes through different windows, doors and holes.

Ten years ago I met Joe Jones who's been making such instruments almost unnoticed. This time, Joe built me eight new instruments specially for this album which can play by themselves with minimum manipulation. (Turning switches only.) I'm very happy about what happened with 'Airmale' and 'You' as a result of my session with Tone Deaf Co. 'Airmale' is Yang and 'You' is Yin. 'Don't Count The Waves' is the water that connects the two islands. 'Airmale' expresses the delicateness of Male. 'You' expresses the aggressiveness of Female. 'You' has all the feminine resentment, moan and animal satisfaction in it. Finally, there is just a wind blowing over a sand hill over white dried female bones, but still, with emotion. The wind created by tape feedback is what I always wanted to do a rock number with a tape loop of feedback as a riff. But this will do for now.

When I was in Sarah Lawrence, which was before I joined the avant-garde, and in London around 1967–68, which was when I was feeling very miserable, I composed many songs. 'Mrs Lennon' is in that category of songs, but unlike 'Remember Love' and 'Who Has Seen The Wind', I felt it was recorded very well. It's an extension of my last album. More far out, so I don't expect it to sell.

John: It's even further out than her last one...so this one's for the birds! [laughs]

Yoko: I've expressed pain and human emotions in my works. Even in *FLY* it was expressed pretty realistically. But it was expressed in an abstract form. The screaming, people didn't think of it as anything but music. Well, some people didn't even think it was music!

FLY inner sleeve photocollage by George Maciunas, featuring instruments designed by Yoko and built by Joe Jones, 1971.
Opposite: Yoko Ono – *A Hole To See The Sky Through*, 1971.
Postcard included with the *FLY* album.

FLY
inner sleeve
dot drawings by yoko ono

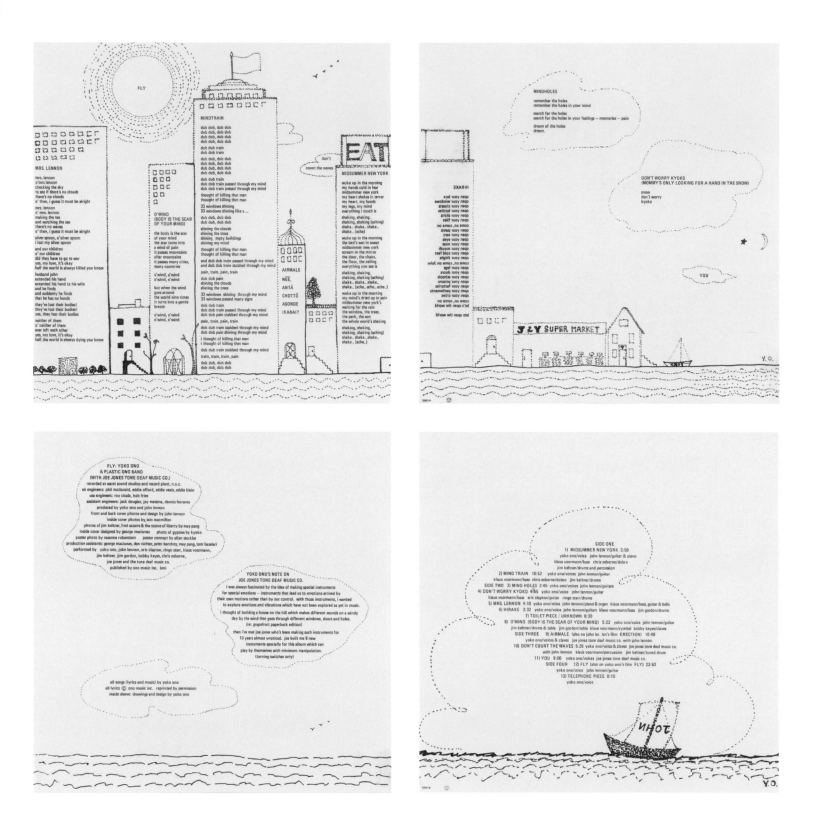

FLY inner sleeves – dot drawings by Yoko Ono,
typography by George Maciunas, 1971.
Opposite: *FLY* album fold-out poster (above), record labels for
FLY (below), both photographed by Raeanne Rubenstein.

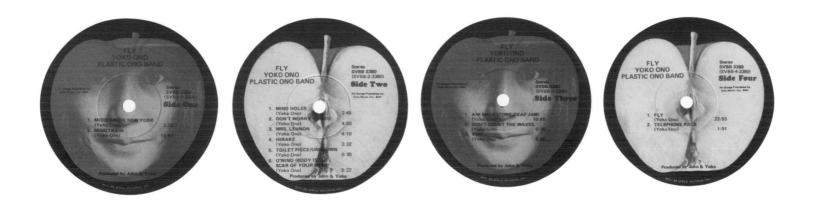

How do you sleep?

So Sgt Pepper took you by suprise
You better see right thru that mothers eyes
Those freaks was right when they said you was dead
The one mistake you made was in your head.

How do you sleep?

You live with straights who tell you you was king
Jump! when you wanna tell you anything.
The only thing you done was yesterday.
~~And I tell you fucked that bitch from somebody~~
~~and since~~ gone you just another ~~day~~
glue.   How do you ~~spill~~ sleep?

~~(Atook any live to make a rolling band)~~
          a
~~you~~ pretty face may last a year or two
but pretty soon they'll see what you can do
the sound you make is muzak to my ears
~~what did teach~~
you must have learned something in all those years

how do you sleep?

So Sgt. Pepper took you by surprise
You better see right through that mother's eyes
Those freaks was right when they said you was dead
The one mistake you made was in your head

Oh, how do you sleep
Oh, how do you sleep at night

You live with straights who tell you you was king
Jump when your momma tell you anything
The only thing you done was yesterday
And since you're gone you're just another day

Oh, how do you sleep
Oh, how do you sleep at night
Oh, how do you sleep
Oh, how do you sleep at night

A pretty face may last a year or two
But pretty soon they'll see what you can do
The sound you make is muzak to my ears
You must have learned something in all those years

Oh, how do you sleep
Oh, how do you sleep at night

how do you sleep?

John: I know you'll all be wondering about this one! It's been around since late '69 in a similar form to this – but not quite (i.e. more abstract). I'd always envisioned that heavy kind of beat for it and wanted to record it whatever the lyrics turned out to be. George Harrison's best guitar solo to date on this cut – as good as anything I've heard from anyone – anywhere. Nice piano from Nicky – I'm singing sharp again – but the rhythm guitar makes up for it! A good 'live' session from all the band (strings added as usual in Record Plant).

Most of you, because he [Paul] didn't hand out a lyric sheet, don't know what he was saying. It starts off with 'too many people going underground' ['Too Many People'], 'that was your first mistake', and the 'first mistake' bit is referring to us and/or the others about 'you took your lucky break and broke it in two'. Now if that doesn't mean what it says, I don't know what. Also the song ['The Back Seat Of My Car'] ends 'we believe that we can't be wrong'. Documentary my dear Datsun can't be wrong huh! I mean Yoko, me and other friends can't all be hearing things.

So I wrote a reciprocal song. And I think that some of the funniest lines on the album are 'The only thing you done was "Yesterday".' I think it's the funniest thing I ever heard. And to have some fun I must thank Mr Allen Klein publicly for the line 'just "Another Day"', a real poet! That was some single he had out at the time and I was falling all over the floor laughing at that line. Some people don't see the funny side of it at all. Too bad. What am I supposed to do, make you laugh? It's what you might call an 'angry letter' only sung. Get it?

Yoko: John really respected Paul and he felt that he was not getting the same kind of feeling from Paul.

John: I felt resentment so I used that situation the same as I used withdrawing from heroin to write 'Cold Turkey'. I used my resentment against Paul (that I have – a kind of sibling rivalry resentment from youth) and withdrawing from Paul and the Beatles, and the relationship with Paul, to write 'How Do You Sleep?' It was like Dylan doing 'Like A Rolling Stone', one of his nasty songs. It's using somebody as an object to create something, in a way. I wasn't really feeling that vicious at the time, but I was using my resentment toward Paul to create a song.

He saw that it pointedly refers to him, and people kept hounding him about it. But, you know, there were a few digs on his album before mine. He's so obscure other people didn't notice them, but I heard them. I thought, well, I'm not obscure, I just get right down to the nitty-gritty. So he'd done it his way and I did it mine. I don't really go around with those thoughts in my head all the time. I wanted to make a funky track and this is a good way to make it.

Paul personally doesn't feel as though I insulted him or anything because I had dinner with him last week; he's quite happy. If I can't have a fight with my best friend I don't know who I can have a fight with. I think it's quite funny and I was laughing when we were making it and listening to it. I was laughing at his later, but first I was saying, 'Oh, I see, that's what he thinks', huffing and puffing.

Yoko: John and Paul are very close to each other and when they're doing a session, they used to kid each other with words that may sound harsh to other people. I think it would have sounded very different to Paul.

John: Somebody said the other day 'It's about me'. You know, there's two things I regret. One is that there was so much talk about Paul on it, they missed the song. It was a good track. And I should've kept me mouth shut – not on the song, it could've been about anybody, you know? And when you look at them back, Dylan said it about his stuff, you know, most of it's about him.

The only thing that matters is how he and I feel about those things and not what the writer or the commentator thinks about it, you know? Him and me are OK. So I don't care what they say about that, you know? I've always been a little, you know, loose. And I hope it'll change because I'm fed up of waking up in the papers. But if it doesn't, my friends are my friends whatever way.

I think there's none of us that wouldn't say that the other three are their best friends. I blab me mouth off more than any of them, 'cause I'm an emotional freak. So I was the one that did all the screaming, y'know, but they know me better. They say, 'Sure he screams, but that's his problem.' I got a letter from George yesterday: 'Hi. What's going on?' Just to say hello. Even between pals, when it comes down to making a business deal, even when we played Monopoly we got serious. But we just walk out and leave the lawyers to it sometimes and we have a laugh and then we go back in and play Monopoly, it's down to that. It was an emotional thing to split with people after you've practically lived in each other's pockets for a long time.

Original film footage of the recording of 'How Do You Sleep?' John & Yoko are pictured with George Harrison, Nicky Hopkins, Phil McDonald and Eddie Klein; Ascot Sound Studios, Tittenhurst, 26 May 1971.

'How Do You Sleep?' started off in a more abstract form about a year-and-a-half ago. And then it just sort of formed itself through anger and sadness. It's really like an outburst, you know? And my outbursts are in song, not in any other media at the moment.

John, 1971

Bag Productions Inc.
Tittenhurst Park,
Ascot, Berkshire.
Ascot 23022

Dear Linda and Paul,

I was reading your letter and wondering what middle aged
cranky Beatle fan wrote it. I resisted looking at the last
page to find out- I kept thinking who is it - Queenie?
Stuart's mother? - Clive Epstein's wife? - Alan Williams?
- What the hell - it's Linda!

You really think the press are beneath me/you? Do you think
that? Who do you think we/you are? The "self-indulgent
- doesn't realize who he is hurting" bit- I hope you realize
what shit you and the rest of my kind and unselfish laid on
Yoko and me, since we've been together, it might have sometimes
been a bit more subtle or should I say "middle class" - but
not often. We both "rose above it" quite a few times +forgave
you two - so it's the least you can do for us - you noble
people. Linda - if you don't care what I say - shut up! - let
Paul write- or whatever.

When asked about what I thought originally concerning MBE, etc.
- I told them as best as I can remember - and I do remember
squirming a little - don't you, Paul? - or do you - as I suspect -
still believe it all? I'll forgive Paul for encouraging the
Beatles - if he forgives me for the same - for being- "honest with
me and caring too much"! Fucking hell, Linda, you're not writing
for Beatle book!!!

I'm not ashamed of the Beatles -(I did start it all)- but of
some of the shit we took to make them so big - I thought we all
felt that way in varying degrees - obviously not.

Do you really think most of today's art came about because of
the Beatles? - I don't believe you're that insane -- Paul - do
you believe that? When you stop believing it you might wake up!
Didn't we always say we were part of the movement - not all of
it? - Of course, we changed the world - but try and follow it
through - GET OFF YOUR GOLD DISC AND FLY!

                                    - continued

friends

Bag Productions Inc.
Tittenhurst Park,
Ascot, Berkshire.
Ascot 23022

Don't give me that ~~Auty Gin~~ shit about "in five years I'll look
back as a different person" - don't you see that's what's
happening NOW! - If I only knew THEN what I know NOW - you seemed
to have missed that point....

Excuse me if I use "Beatle Space" to talk about whatever I want -
obviously if they keep asking Beatle questions - I'll answer
them - and get as much John and Yoko Space as I can - they ask
me about Paul and I answer - I know some of it gets personal-
but whether you believe it or not I try and answer straight -
and the bits they use are obviously the juicy bits - I don't
resent your husband - I'm sorry for him. I know the Beatles are
"quite nice people" - I'm one of them - they're also just as
big bastards as anyone else.- so get off your high horse!
— by the way - we've had more intelligent interest in our new activities ~~than~~ in
one year than we had throughout the Beatle era; ~~unbeated even~~..

Finally, about not telling anyone that I left the Beatles - PAUL
and Klein both spent the day persuading me it was better not to
say anything - asking me not to say anything because it would
'hurt the Beatles'- and "let's just let it petre out" - remember?
So get that into your petty little perversion of a mind, Mrs.
McCartney - the cunts asked me to keep quiet about it. Of course,
the money angle is important - to all of us - especially after
all the petty shit that came from your insane family/in laws-and
GOD HELP YOU OUT, PAUL - see you in two years - I reckon you'll
be out then -

                    inspite of it all

                              love to you both,

                              from us two

P.S. about addressing your letter just to ~~~~ me
— STILL ϟ...!!!

filming imagine

VAUGHAN FILMS PRESENTS A JOKO FILMS PRODUCTION

IMAGINE

STARRING AND DIRECTED BY JOHN & YOKO

GUEST STARS

FRED ASTAIRE	DICK CAVETT
GEORGE HARRISON	JONAS MEKAS
JACK PALANCE	ANDY WARHOL

MUSIC FROM 'IMAGINE' BY JOHN LENNON & 'FLY' BY YOKO ONO
ON APPLE RECORDS

ON THE RANK CIRCUIT   IN EASTMAN COLOR

john & yoko
directors

Yoko: We tried to make the film after the music was there already. So I wanted that kind of rhythm and beat, and music – that music visual. I was influenced by the avant-garde underground films, vaguely thinking in terms of directors like Jean-Luc Godard.

Movement – camerawork and editing – had always been done so slowly in movies. John and I were used to watching TV, especially the adverts and that fantastic way of doing things. Kids are used to information all the time. And our age, the time is accelerating so much that we started to develop a sense to grasp things more instantly. When we were watching news reporters, I noticed that people are now so used to films and they're such experts, that there's almost a solid understanding between the editor and the audience, that it's alright to edit in a place that they would never have thought of editing.

In editing a film, they would do it in such a way so the editing is not shown so much, or if it's going from one scene to another, then it's alright   it shows the editing. But if there's a continuous scene, like you and I am talking and there's some parts that's sort of like dragging, so you want to cut that part out. Then they would do fine editing, so that people would notice the editing. But these days in news, they don't care about that. Probably because they don't have enough time to do fine editing, but they just do a 'butcher cut', I call it. And I love that butcher cut, because that really gives a pulsation that is very contemporary. And the fine-cut age has got something else. The fine cut is almost like trying to deceive the audience….Whereas in the butcher cut, you're being honest and you respect the audience more because you're saying, 'Well look, you don't need this draggy part; I'm just giving you the essence of the thing.'

The eyes are incredible. For instance, when I watch a very, very old film, like a Chaplin or Buster Keaton, I find that butcher-cut element of it, and it's incredible, it's beautiful. And then when you go to the 1940s, and American film, it's very interesting, they do butcher cuts, but in those days that was supposed to be a fine cut, they weren't meant to be butcher cuts. Now these days our eyes are so sensitive, that the fine cut of 1940s, you can see it as a butcher cut…. The fine cut of today is really, really fine cut, and I respect that kind of movie too. I like to do that too in certain cases. But I'm more interested in the butcher cut now.

The way you make a film is you get the utmost out of everybody you are using. And to get the utmost out of them is not to control them and kill them by controlling them but by opening them up so that they can free themselves and they can get the utmost limit out of themselves.

I wanted to just do what came into the head that day. Day by day. And I believe in that because, for instance, if I want to eat a chocolate cake now, that probably has a lot of meaning. More than I think. But if I planned it so that I would eat a chocolate cake tomorrow, then that's something else again. So it was done very instantaneously. You'd be surprised. Like in the evening I was saying, 'Let's hire a helicopter tomorrow.' By the way that was John's idea and I thought it was beautiful, but 'Helicopter tomorrow, okay!' And we tried to do something with the helicopter, but we weren't sure what we were going to do. In other words, just the idea, not much, just a vague idea – and that worked.

John: This one we're making now [*Imagine*] is very loose; they just bring the camera every day and we just decide what to do that day, almost. We're just making it up as we go along. It will show some of the recording sessions, but I'm not going to do a lot of that like *Let It Be* because they're all boring, those things. But there is one song that we can show bits of all the way through, which is 'How?' from nothing to the finished thing.

And there might be one I'll sing all the way through, which is 'Give Me Some Truth', because they've taped it at the right speed. Others I'll use as background songs – I don't know how many to put in yet – backgrounds to Yoko's artworks downstairs, and there'll be some shots of us in the house, and the garden, and then the contrast with some of the New York stuff which was shot by other people – and the guy [Jonas Mekas] that always shoots very fast with stills and single-frame stuff. There's scenes of the party and on the boat, and some from Yoko's session.

Imagine film press kit cover image, as issued by JOKO Films, 1972.
Previous pages: filming 'Imagine'; Tittenhurst, 21 July 1971.

imagine

Yoko: 'Imagine' is a complete vision. A succinct bible of truth. It will start to unfold as you believe in it. The film? Well, it just happened naturally. I was well aware of the symbolism of everything – closing and then opening the shutters to let the light in. It's rather personal, but I had a definite reason why I smiled at the end, in addition to loving being next to John.
John: Yoko's quite adept in filmmaking and she'd made quite a few films before I'd met her. I used to make 8mm films at home and superimpose and do tricks with it and just play arbitrary records with it. But when I met Yoko she said, 'Well why don't you do it seriously?' So she sort of helped me to develop in that area and I find it's very similar to recording, just visual. And it's beautiful to work with. When we did *Imagine*, we felt great about it, and were saying, 'This is going to widen the field of film! This is it! This is the Seventies! We started off…we were going to do a few clips and we ended up filming every song on the album and a few from Yoko's album too, and we ended up with a seventy-minute film.

John plays Yoko's white Steinway 'O' piano and sings 'Imagine' as Yoko opens the shutters and lets the light into the White Room, Tittenhurst, 21 July 1971.

nic knowland
cameraman

I first met John & Yoko in 1969. They had asked for me to help them make a film called "*RAPE*" that was to reflect their own experience of being chased, hounded and as it were 'raped' by the press and paparazzi. They were both very nice, very straightforward and coherent artists.

At the time I was an up-and-coming freelance cinematographer living in Notting Hill Gate, London. I was working in documentaries for the likes of *World in Action* on what was then Granada TV. This was before music videos had taken off.

After "*RAPE*" I found myself working with John & Yoko on quite a few of their projects: *Apotheosis*, 'The Ballad of John & Yoko', *Bed Peace* and of course 'Imagine' the music video and *Imagine*, the long-form movie.

When we started filming the *Imagine* sessions in the studio, it was really to capture the musicians' performances. I wasn't the only camera person to work on this as it was quite an on/off affair so both the late, great John Metcalfe and Richard Stanley both put time in when I was not free. Most of the footage from this period ended up in the *Gimme Some Truth* film. After that, John & Yoko went to New York to finish mixing the album and when they came back, we started to film the more conceptual footage for their *Imagine* film.

I stayed in one of the cottages at their Ascot estate for a few days and we had a lot of fun filming with a helicopter, a golf buggy and rowing boats and finished up capturing the nice cinematic material that was used in the film.

For the 'Jealous Guy' sequence I had to hang out of the helicopter to get what actually turned out to be a one-take-wonder of a surprisingly smooth, seamless take, as John & Yoko travel by hearse from the mansion down to the lake to play chess on the island. I remember the filming of that chess game later where Yoko did everything she could to distract John's concentration from the rather surreal game they were playing!

John particularly was very keen to get on with all this, so our work schedule was quite hectic. I recall that at that time I didn't try to impose any strong sense of style to the images as such, but was very happy to improvise in a sort of 'verité' style. I was just there to do what I could – pick up a camera and film something when it seemed right, or when John or Yoko asked me to. I don't remember having any problems with this mode of operation. Mostly they had very clear ideas of what they wanted to do, how they wanted to do it, and we got on with it and did it. It was kind of one long 'Happening' and it was always great fun. Well, that's my memory of that time.

John, of course, was a very famous, important and interesting musician. Yoko a little bit less well-known, but I could see that she had really interesting ideas. I don't think I thought of it in terms of capturing history or anything, partly because I was something of a 'present-moment' person. Still am. Yoko always referred to me as 'the cloud person'. I think

she saw me as a bit of a dreamer but that also referred to the filming of *Apotheosis* when I filmed them from gas balloon in Lavenham market square in Suffolk one snowy morning. From their position in the ground I did literally disappear into the clouds! I do remember how simply we made the 'Imagine' video, it was all so straightforward and easy. It really was. We started with the hand-held shot following John & Yoko from behind on the misty pathway, and then we did the locked-off shot at the front door and then went in and ran through the song on a wide shot, a mid and a close-up, and off we went home again.

Well, the secret of course was Yoko's idea for her to walk slowly round the lovely white room opening the shutters and letting in the light in both physically and, probably more importantly, emotionally. That was her genius.

I seem to remember I was paid my daily rate of £16 for it. I guess if I had a penny for every time it has been watched, I'd be pretty rich by now. Oh well, no regrets there!

When I first heard the song I thought, 'This is just wonderful.' And it's still wonderful and I feel the same way about the 'Imagine' video and it seemed perfectly natural that they became as successful as they did.

The impulse from it has been enormous for me. In a sense it's powered my whole life in so many ways. It's a song of no religion and hopefully the time of religion is passing and has certainly passed for me. I see it as a song for human beings living our lives on the planet Earth now. And what is so wonderful about the words and concept 'Imagine' is that it's not a doctrine. It can never be quoted as the words of some prophet. It has to live in our hearts and our thoughts. It's just common sense, isn't it?

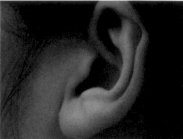

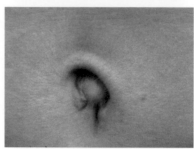

crippled inside

John: Allen Klein was having a party for his wife's birthday, and he had fifty straights going, like his business friends and old friends and relatives. He invited us, so we thought we'd hot it up a bit. Yoko got a list out of all her old friends and they all came, including some mutual friends like Miles Davis and Viva, and Andy brought his whole mob. It was a very interesting party, which we filmed. There were fifty straights and fifty freaks all at one party – they didn't mix much, they all stayed in their own groups.

Photoshoot at Tittenhurst, 28 May 1971; Betty Klein's birthday party filmed by Jonas Mekas at the Klein residence in Riverdale, Bronx, New York, 12 June 1971.

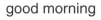

good morning

John: We made an album called *Imagine* and then we made Yoko's album *FLY*, and we were going to make a short film clip and it just went on. We went on filming and filming 'til we had a seventy-minute movie. And it only has two words in it: 'Good morning'. And all the rest is music. So it's like a musical. It's fairly wild and we made it up as we went along.
Yoko: The idea of not saying anything during the film – except in the beginning to just say 'Good morning' to each other – was John's.

In the master bedroom, bathroom and balcony at Tittenhurst, 16 July 1971.

jealous guy

Yoko: We enjoyed make films together. John came up with big ideas, or ideas that seemed big to me at the time. He thought of using a helicopter, which added a new dimension to our film. When John first said, 'Let's use a helicopter', I – who was supposed to have sold out in a big way – thought, 'Oh dear, aren't we getting a bit Hollywood?' The result was that beautiful scene in 'Jealous Guy'. There was nothing so-called 'Hollywood' about that.

John & Yoko ride their black 1956 Austin 'Princess Hearse' limousine down to the lake, driven by Dan Richter, while being filmed by Nic Knowland aboard a helicopter; Tittenhurst Park, 20 July 1971.

don't count the waves

Yoko: It's called *Play It by Trust*. Because the chess pieces on both sides are white, you always have to be aware of which are your pieces. There comes a moment when you feel like maybe you want to cheat, or you want to convince your opponent which pieces were yours. Then there's a moment when you feel like it really doesn't matter which pieces are yours or the opponent's. Actually it's the same. And we are all one. Life is not that defined. It's not black and white. You are not there to be an observer; you have to participate. But it's a participation that hits a very delicate chord in you. The board goes through many quiet changes, which correspond to the changes within you. It immediately dispenses with the idea of war and a battle, because if you are the same, you don't have a war. Who are we fighting? And why?

John & Yoko playing Yoko's White Chess Set, *1966, underneath John's artwork* You Are Here, *1968; Tittenhurst Park, 20 July 1971.*

steve gebhardt
producer

When I got my master's degree in 1968, I thought, 'I'm really unhappy not doing what I want to do,' so I quit doing architecture and hooked up with this buddy of mine, Bob Fries, and started making films.

I got this call from my friend Jonas Mekas. He was about to open this film museum, Anthology Film Archives in New York. He called and asked, 'Do you want to come and manage this place?' Jonas brought me there because I'd brought him to Cincinnati as well as all of the avant-garde film and music movement. Everybody he recommended. We had filmmakers in from all over the world presenting films and running workshops. It was a hot environment. There was a lot of activity here in that period in the mid-1960s as culture sort of matured. It was a very energised time.

Anthology Film Archives was frequented by famous filmmakers and artists on a daily basis. Before I knew it, John Lennon & Yoko Ono showed up. They were patrons of the Archives. I had admired Yoko's work for a few years by then. Lennon was my favourite Beatle. Look, I'm from Ohio and in New York to make films and what an opportunity. They wanted a cameraman who was not too far out to do some projects they had in mind, which were *FLY* and *Up Your Legs*

Forever. I realized I needed some backup. John & Yoko had an assistant who was a mime. I called Bob Fries and said, 'Come on up here.' Who wouldn't drop everything?

We got both projects on the screen – really two hours of movies in their first versions in less than two weeks. That impressed John & Yoko and that was the beginning of what turned out to be a three-year deal where I was just busy every day doing things for them. It was without a doubt the most exciting thing I ever did.

They rented half of the seventeenth floor of the St Regis hotel to work on *Imagine*. The Beatles would come by. Bob Dylan would come by. I can't really compare John to Yoko, though, because when I was around them, they were one person – two bodies speaking as one person. John was fantastically smart. I was astounded by his candour, his humanness and his brilliance. He was very open. He didn't have some sneaky hidden agenda. He was a star. He was unique.

I walked away from my time with them with experience I never would have gotten anywhere else. It was an awesome opportunity. I had considerable responsibility, spending their money on creating things in my medium. Yoko would call in the middle of the night from Japan. I did seventeen different pieces for them over the years. Along with that I saw all kinds of other people's works in art, film and music. I went to Frank Zappa's screening of *200 Motels* as their emissary. I went to Elvis's concert at Madison Square Garden with their tickets. So I had opportunities I wouldn't have. And I had the opportunity to work around a major musical talent. In many ways it was the best three years of my life.

Jonas Mekas: He was very good working with other people. Sometimes he did not get credit for it. I think he helped a lot with what John Lennon & Yoko Ono did. And he was dedicated, selfless. He did not work for credit; he just did what he liked to do and was very helpful to many people.

BAGPROD ASCOTMMO
BAGPROD ASCOTMA
BAGPROD ASCOT
RCANY 065 1110
STIGMA 224874

3/4/71

ATT DAN RICHTER

STEVE GEBHARDT LEAVING TONIGHT MARCH 4, 1971, ON TWA FLIGHT 700 ARRIVES IN LONDON 7:35 A.M. HE IS BRINGING ALL FILMS WITH HIM. AS EXCESS BAGGAGE, FILMS ARE PACKED IN SEVEN CARTONS.

REGARDS,

PAUL
BAGPROD ASCOT
STIGMA 224874OOM

Dan: Steve's room is ready at the Berystede whenever he wants it tomorrow.

Making Yoko's film *FLY* with cameramen Bob Fries and Steve Gebhardt;
Dan Seymour's loft, Bowery, New York, 21 December 1970.
Opposite: telex to Dan Richter from Paul Mozian regarding Steve
Gebhardt with annotation by Diana Robertson; 4 March 1971.
Previous pages: filming 'Don't Count The Waves' with Yoko's
White Chess Set, 1966, John's *You Are Here*, 1968, and
two cans of Dr Pepper; Tittenhurst, 20 July 1971.

it's so hard

John: We've got some great footage in our film we're just making with a man in a bag wandering all over London. And most people don't take any notice of him. He's just walking around. It's fantastic.

Yoko: From the white sneakers, it looks like John in the bag!

John: We're all in a bag, you know? I was in this pop bag in my little clique, and she was in her little avant-garde clique. We all intellectualize about how there is no barrier between art, music and poetry but I'm a rock and roller, she's a poet, so we just came up with the word so you would ask us what Bagism is, and we'd say 'We're all in a bag, baby!' We get out of one bag and into the next.

Yoko: John is doing my *Cleaning Piece for A.P., 1966*. It goes on forever.

John in a bag in Chelsea, London; John cleaning Yoko's Cleaning Piece for A.P., *1966, and Yoko striking a pose in the upstairs hallway, Tittenhurst, 21 July 1971.*

mrs lennon

Yoko: 'Mrs. Lennon' was meant to be an ironic joke on me, by me, and an anti-war song. The lyrics were made in 1969, the music was finished in New York during the recording sessions. John: Before this one press conference, one assistant in the upper echelon of Beatle assistants leaned over to Yoko and said, 'You know, you don't have to work. You've got enough money now that you're Mrs Lennon.' And when she complained to me about it, I couldn't understand what she was talking about. The same kind of thing happened in the studio. She would say to an engineer, 'I'd like a little more bass', and they'd look at me and say, 'What did you say, John?' Those days I didn't even notice it myself. Now I know what she's talking about. In Japan, when I ask for a cup of tea in Japanese, they look at Yoko and ask, 'He wants a cup of tea?' in Japanese.

Yoko walks down the staircase; in Salvador Dali style dress; John & Yoko perform Whisper Piece, *1961; in the woods, Tittenhurst, 21 July; South Beach, Staten Island, 10 September 1971.*

bob fries
cameraman, film editor

Steve Gebhardt called me up. Jonas Mekas had got him a job shooting for Yoko Ono in New York and he wanted to borrow my camera. So I drove up from Cincinnati to help him out with *Up Your Legs Forever* and *FLY*.

Historically, Cincinnati is a very old television and radio town because of Crosley Broadcasting and WLW Radio – which at one point was a 500,000 Watt station called The Nation Station. You could hear it all over the nation. I had attended the College-Conservatory of Music in Cincinnati, which had this little tiny broadcast radio and television department where the faculty were essentially people working in the industry. I was a musician. I wrote a lot of songs, played in a band and recorded a couple of albums. I was really immersed in music. I was also making lots of local commercials and underground films in Cincinnati, which is where Steve had worked for me.

Yoko did a lot of the talking, because they were her films. John was there to make sure everything went well and also to help inspire her – which he did. He was impressively quick and intelligent. I was also really impressed with everybody's ability to laugh so long, because it became a very long session. Everything was so interesting that it wasn't too much of a problem. When it came to filming *Imagine*,

it really was guerilla filmmaking. We made do with what we had. To get an 'up' shot in Wall Street, I just lay down in the middle of the street and we got on with it! We were lucky it was Labor Day weekend, so there was no traffic.

Staten Island beach was interesting. There was one little kid that ran up to John and said 'Will you sign my autograph, Ringo?' [laughs] and so John took his paper and signed it 'Ringo'. Cute little kid.

The credits in the sand being washed away by waves was hard. We found some really long, heavy planks of wood and made a little dam, and once the writing was done, we could lift the planks so the sea came in to wash away the writing. We worked a long time on that and it worked really well.

John was used to meeting everybody in the world, but he was like a little kid meeting movie stars like Jack Palance. He was very, very nervous about meeting Fred Astaire. He kept saying things like, 'Now this is a real movie star.' [laughs] He put on a suit to meet him and spent a long time making himself look really good. To meet Fred Astaire.

One night, we started in the front of the St Regis hotel and just went for a walk. It was really dark out on the sidewalk and there's Steve and me and Tom the chauffeur walking down these dark streets and John's there in an old mac and Yoko's there dressed like a hooker and we've got all this equipment. I had a little fold-up dolly with a couple of cameras and a stills camera and we're trying to drag that all down the street while John & Yoko were walking. Now, in New York, you need a permit just to blow your nose, but that didn't bother them. If we ever saw a cop they always left happy with an autograph or something.

We went up to Kykuit – the Rockefeller Estate – to film 'How?' It is absolutely

beautiful. It's so big that it's on both sides of the Hudson River. The rock garden has this wonderful serenity – you can actually feel it there.

For filming, I used an Arriflex BL self-point. And a KEM for editing. I had a bunch of lights which we didn't use too much, but we did with Fred Astaire and that dancing in the room.

I was editing night and day, continuously. It was one long experience. I hardly ever got out. One night, John and I snuck out to a little stand about two blocks away to get a hamburger and a couple of hotdogs and brought them back to the hotel. There wasn't too much trouble but people did recognize him and it was New York.

One night around ten o'clock or so, I was in their hotel suite editing by myself and there was a knock at the door. So I open the door and it's Bob Dylan there, you know, asking for John & Yoko. They had invited him over to see a film. So I made excuses for them, invited him in and showed him 'Crippled Inside'. He watched the whole thing in silence and at the end turned to me and said, 'Umm…what does it mean?' [laughs] So I gave him a long description of what I thought it meant and that seemed to satisfy him, you know? He said, 'Oh yeah…' and I thought I did pretty well because I did sing it back to him and told him what I thought, but it was kinda out there. After he left, and Yoko came flying in from the other room and said, 'What'd he say? What'd he do?' [laughs], so I explained what I had said, and she seemed satisfied with that.

I always thought 'Imagine' was a great song. And it still is. And that's very unusual for a song. You can probably turn on the radio right now and hear it somewhere. It makes me feel a certain way that I want to feel. It's a powerful song. A hymn for everyone.

'The Statue of Liberty said come!' – Bob Fries filming
John & Yoko at Battery Park, New York, 4 September 1971.

Filming on Labor Day weekend at Battery Park with (right) the
Statue of Liberty in the background; New York, 4 September 1971.

in bag

Yoko: This life is speeded up so much and the whole world is getting tenser and tenser because things are just going so fast. So it's nice to slow down the rhythm of the whole world, just to make it peaceful. So, when you get in the bag, you see that it's very peaceful and your movements are sort of limited. You can walk around on the street in a bag. But no-one should fit into anybody else's bag. We should all have our own bags. I stood in Trafalgar Square in London wearing that bag before I met John, and I was thinking that if everybody wore this bag then there wouldn't be any racial war, things like that.

I get obsessive about things like that and think, 'Oh, well I should go in front of the White House and wear a bag, and if I get shot maybe the whole world will become peaceful.'

Five people in bags, St Michael and All Angels church, Sunningdale, 23 July, 1971; Yoko draws flowers in the garden, Tittenhurst, 21 July 1971; War Is Over! billboards, Times Square, New York, 25 December 1969.

i don't wanna be a soldier mama i don't wanna die

John: I was in a German airport. I had an American army mac on and a guy [Sergeant Peter James Reinhardt] came up and said, I just got out of the army [Imjin Scout Regiment, 2nd Infantry Division, South Korea] and if you'd like these clothes, I'd love to give them to you. I said 'all right', and he sent me all these army clothes in the post.

Yoko: Both of us experienced World War II from two opposite sides. We knew what it meant to be in the war. We knew how, suddenly, you could lose everything. We knew that people like us were the ones who really suffered, and the generals and the politicians just kept dishing out lies to keep us pacified. Never in a million years did we think that promoting World Peace could be dangerous.

East Coast Memorial, Battery Park, 4 and 10 September 1971; news footage of Vietnam, the Kent State Massacre and Northern Ireland; outside the St Regis hotel on East 55th St after the Dick Cavett Show on 8 September 1971.

doug ibold
photographer, film editor

It was a very hot day in August 1971 when Bob, Steve and myself went up to the 17th floor of the St Regis hotel. John & Yoko had a beautiful corner suite looking south down Fifth Avenue and they were dressed really nicely. John had a Nagra tape recorder right beside him and said, 'Right lads, give a listen to this…' and out came 'Imagine'. And from the first piano chord, right off the bat, I knew this was something special. I remember it so clearly. I was looking out through the seventeenth-floor hotel windows and could see these big helicopters dropping huge steel beams onto the top of the World Trade Centre as they were building it. It haunts me to this day.

When it was over, John asked us what we thought, and you could have heard a pin drop. We were just stunned by the magnitude of the lyrics and the beauty of the song. And our group decision was 'Whatever you want us to do we're in.' And that's how we got the job on the *Imagine* film. It was the biggest thing we'd ever worked on.

We started by editing the film that Nic Knowland had shot in England and after about three weeks they decided to shoot some more in New York. We didn't have much of an initial plan other than to drive around in two limos and find some interesting locations. We had no permits and no authorization. It was total guerilla filmmaking. Bob was the cameraman, Steve was the producer and I was the production photographer. We started on Pine St and it was so bizarre. It was Labor Day weekend and the streets were totally empty. We started early in the morning, and we shot for a whole day until it got dark.

Bob Fries and I edited the film. Bob sat at a KEM and cut whatever song we were doing at the time and I was on a Steenbeck pulling shots and feeding him material. Yoko sat side by side with Bob, directing the edit, and John would sit at the back, sometimes in the lotus position with his guitar kinda noodling and watching the procedure, generally saying something funny or encouraging. It was a pleasure for me to just sit there and watch these two amazing people work.

The editing took about two-and-a-half months. We had no real narrative other than the songs and the lyrics. We had thousands of feet of footage to choose from, which made it exciting but also frustrating – worrying if we had we missed a shot here or there. It all turned out pretty good in the long run.

I got on the elevator one morning to come to work, and who gets on the elevator with me but Jack Palance. I immediately said to him 'Hey, man, *Shane* is one of the greatest Westerns ever made.' And he turned and looked at me and said, 'Thank you very much.' When he got off, I noticed he was on the tenth floor. And so when John & Yoko came in that day, they sent him a note with Peter Bendrey and May Pang and we got a note back saying he'd love to do it and he would come up at four o'clock that afternoon. It's hilarious the way Jack played it, when he would bend over to listen. We all loved it. We thought it was fantastic. When Jack left, John signed a copy of *Imagine* and gave it to him. And the next day, a messenger from Warner Brothers arrived with a signed copy of *Palance* – an album of him singing country and western songs. So we immediately put it on the turntable and started listening to it. It was pretty funny.

George Harrison and Bob Dylan showed up one day to see John. Bob Fries and I were both working and saying 'Holy shit, there's three icons of rock 'n' roll in the next room.' Pretty soon, John came in and said, 'I'd like to show George and Bob some of the footage, can we do that?' And we said 'Of course we can do that!' So they came in and we ran a couple of songs for them. I ran the chess sequence I'd cut for 'Don't Count The Waves' and Bob Dylan was fascinated by it because you really believe, from the editing, that John is eating the chess pieces.

Then John came in with a Dobro for George, a nice Gibson for Bob and John had another Gibson. Bob Fries was a pretty good guitar player in his own right, and he was noodling on a twelve-string. And I was sitting there with three rock 'n' roll icons and my fellow editor, jammin' and riffing on each other's tunes and imitating each other and laughing and scratching, having the time of their lives.

The whole experience will always be part of my fondest memories. For me as an editor, it was a huge confidence builder, because I'd just done something that nobody was doing in the industry at that time, and it turned out pretty good. When I got my ACE Career Achievement Award, I'm proud to say they used a part of it in my highlights reel.

To John from John on Pancake Day.

I live, therefore I make home movies. Wherever I go, I always film. I keep filming. That's part of my nature; part of what I am. In the Seventies, it was always on a 16mm Bolex camera. They don't make them anymore. I used five Bolexes and each time they issued a new version there were some tiny changes but I don't know which models I had. I still have all five of them but only one works. That's how I filmed the pieces featuring John & Yoko – Bed-In, the Klein party, the dumpling party, the Everson show, John's birthday and all my other films in those days. I did not follow scripts. I was just filming. I didn't work with any preconceived ideas. I just react to life. I film what happens and I never know what is going to happen. My decisions are unconscious. There is no thinking, there is no planning, there is no creativity, there is just doing the right thing the way you feel. Every second is real, right there in front of your eyes. Cinema is not 100 years old. Cinema is young! Cinema is beginning!

George Macunias introduced me to Yoko in 1961. He asked me to help her move house. She had her first New York show at George's AG Gallery in the summer and then she went to Japan. We had a lot of correspondence because she was trying to help some film makers bring their films to New York and I wanted

to show them. Then she went to London, came back with John, settled down here in New York and then we resumed our friendship.

I was forever getting calls from universities to advise them on independent films they could show, so I and a few friends decided we should establish a definitive film collection of three hundred titles or so. That's how Anthology Film Archives was born in 1970. We opened with 110 movies – 'The Essential Cinema Repertory'. Later we expanded to include new films as well, because there were not many places where new film makers could show their work, so we opened our theatre to them as well. Even today we screen those 110 programmes as a 'History of Cinema'. If you come and see them, you will have a good idea about what cinema as an art form has achieved. That was the purpose.

It was December 1970, very late; after midnight. And John wanted to know is there any place where he could get espresso. And it was very difficult to find a place in New York after one o'clock, not even at nine o'clock. But I knew one on Sixth Avenue between Third and Fourth Street. There was a little Italian place called Emilio's,

Jonas + Butch looking. By John.

and that's where they spent their first two hours in New York. And John was like, 'This is the beginning. It's like a new life. Here I begin. And from here, now, I'm free!' At one point, he said, 'How good it is to be in a place where nobody knows you, and you are free!' And then, when we are leaving, the waitress comes with a little piece of paper and said: 'Could you sign an autograph for my daughter?'

I was organizing an end-of-the-year film festival and I thought I would ask Yoko to contribute one or two of her earlier films. She said, 'No, no, no, I will make you a new one.' And she ended up making two new ones, within a week – FLY and Up Your Legs Forever. Steve Gebhardt helped her make those two films and continued to work for them for several years at Joko Films, looking after all of their films and filming needs.

New York in the 1970s was the art capital. All the music, happening, theatre, Andy Warhol….It was all part of Yoko Ono's life and John wanted to be connected to both worlds. At the time I saw a lot of John & Yoko, and I always enjoyed our time together. He was open, relaxed, very spontaneous. It felt like anything could happen, at any moment. Yoko was more controlled, but she was very warm and we remain good friends. She loves New York as much as I do.

Stills from Jonas Mekas's home movie of George Maciunas's dumpling party attended by John & Yoko, George, Jonas, Andy Warhol, Fred Hughes and Peter and Barbara Moore; Fluxhouse Cooperative, 80 Wooster St, New York, 29 June 1971. Opposite: polaroids of Jonas Mekas taken by John at the same party. Following pages: filming the 'Mrs Lennon' and 'Mind Train' sequences for *Imagine*; Tittenhurst, 20 July 1971.

mind train

Yoko: Most of the pieces on the *FLY* album are centred around a dialogue between my voice and John's guitar. John and I crawl, roll and fly together. John brought in musicians that are fine samurais. He pushes them to fly with me. Listen to Jim Keltner's drumming, Klaus Voormann's bass, Chris Osborne's guitar and the intricate conversation that goes between all of us in 'Mind Train'.

Performing Yoko's Whisper Piece, *1961, with Jack Palance, St Regis hotel, 6 September 1971; Jonas Mekas and George Maciunas on the Fluxus Hudson boat trip, Commander Hamilton, New York, 1 July 1971; Yoko with telescope, John & Yoko with shoes, Jill and Sacha Richter with* Danger Box, *1965/1971, Yoko's sister Setsuko Ono with* Eternal Time, *1965,* Forget It, *1966, at dawn on the balcony; all at Tittenhurst, 21 and 22 July 1971.*

whisper piece

Yoko: *Whisper Piece* was originally called a *Telephone Piece*, and was the start of the word-of-mouth pieces. It is usually performed by whispering a word or a note into an audience's ear and asking to have it passed on until it reaches the last audience. One time I did *Whisper Piece* in the Destruction in Art Symposium in 1966 in London. Four or five very hot-blooded Destruction in Art Symposium-type male artists protested that my work was not destructive. But I was not interested in just smashing a piano or a car or something – I was interested in the delicate way that things change – in that kind of destruction which, in a way, is more dangerous. I whispered a word and the word went around and got destroyed.

Performing Yoko's Whisper Piece, *1961, with Dick Cavett in their suite at the St Regis hotel, New York, 6 September 1971.*

sir michael parkinson
interviewer

I met John at Granada Television when I was producing a show called *Scene at 6.30*. The programme was among the first to feature the Beatles before they rocketed to fame.

Then, when I moved to the BBC and started *The Parkinson Show*, John & Yoko were on the first series and helped to establish the fact that this was the show the biggest stars appeared on. I had not met Yoko before and she gave me a silver box entitled *A Box Of Smile*, which remains a treasured possession.

The interview was remarkable in the sense that John insisted if I asked him a question about the Beatles I had to sit inside a black bag, which was then closed before I could speak to him. It was the most bizarre encounter of all the eight hundred *Parkinson* shows I did. He was promoting his *Imagine* album, which made it even more special because the title song is one of the best he ever wrote. If I had to choose another track from the album it would be 'Jealous Guy'.

Looking back at those times Is to understand how rich they were in producing people like Lennon who helped change the face of popular music with songs to last forever. It was an exciting time to be around and John & Yoko did more than most to add to the gaiety of the moment.

. . . . .

Parkinson: Can I put something to both of you, about the sort of crazy phase that you're both going through at present? I think you've got to accept, John, that it's alienated you from the people who originally loved you in this country?

John: When I left Liverpool with the group, a lot of Liverpool people dropped us and said, 'Now you've let us down.' When we left England to go to America, we lost a lot of fans because they began to feel that they own you. So we fell in love and we married and Yoko just happens to be Japanese, which didn't help much and so everybody had the impression that John's just gone crazy. But all I did

was fall in love, like a lot of people do. The British press actually called her ugly. I've never seen that about any woman or man, even if the person is ugly. You don't normally say that in the papers. She's not ugly and if she were, you wouldn't be so mean! They even say 'attractive' about the most awful-looking people, to be kind.

Parkinson: Recently, another reason for people taking a dislike to you is because you're known again through the newspapers, as the woman who broke up the Beatles.

John: But that's not true! Listen, I tell you, people on the streets and kids do not dislike us. It's the media; I'm telling you. We go on the streets and the lorry drivers wave, 'Hello John, hello Yoko,' all that jazz and I judge it by that.

John & Yoko interviewed by Michael Parkinson from inside Yoko's bag; BBC TV Centre, London, 17 July 1971.
Opposite: John & Yoko on *The Dick Cavett Show*; ABC Studios, New York, 8 September 1971.

dick cavett
interviewer

6 September 1971 was a rainy day in New York. I was thrilled that John & Yoko might appear on my TV show, so I went over to the St Regis Hotel to discuss how we could make it work. They had a really spacious room and had set up office on a huge bed with notebooks and pads and folders all around them. They seemed to be working on a lot of projects.

John opened with: 'You know, you have the only half-way intelligent show on US television.' So I said, 'Well, why would you want to go on a half-way intelligent show?' He thought that was funny.

We liked each other right away. He was a great word and language man and he sure could make me laugh. He was such an accessible person – it sounds funny to say, but I immediately felt like I had known him for quite a while. He was very good at making people feel that way.

Yoko was very sweet and pleasant and fun to talk to. I have learned a lot of Japanese since then and I wish I had had more of it then. I often remind

people that Yoko was a highly regarded artist before meeting John.

John told me that they had just finished filming a dream sequence with Yoko and Fred Astaire, who they had collared in the lobby. John pulled out his 16mm camera and asked me if I would mind appearing in their film too, so we filmed the whispering and the door opening sequences from *Imagine*, which was fun. It was a wonderful day. And of course, as we know, they did do the TV show.

One of my favourite moments in the show is when John suddenly said (in a funny accent), 'Dick, what's your definition of loooove?' That was Frosty's favourite game to spring upon people. Some were mystified by it. It is fair to say that my opinion of David Frost made me laugh heartily.

There was a blossoming of personality in John. Harpo Marx had a quality that when he was in a room full of people, children and animals came over to him when they didn't to anybody else. It may not be the precise quality of John's, but

there was something inviting about his look and his personality was just terrific.

The film for the song 'Imagine' (where John sings and plays piano and Yoko opens the shutters to let the light in) premiered on our show on 11 September 1971. The style of the film is very Yoko. It sure works for me. It's very calming to watch and has a nice lyrical quality that I really enjoy. The lyrics for 'Imagine' often run through my head at different times. It has a kind of haunting quality that sticks with you.

Shirley MacLaine said on the show, 'These two have done more to promote peace and love than any other artists in the past few years.' I think that was true. The impact they had was deep and broad. They were right about the Vietnam War. I don't see anything to criticize them on that. And they weren't graduates of a university specializing in politics and world affairs, as far as I know.

John & Yoko's interviews are still some of the most popular of all our shows. When we taped them, the audience didn't want to leave.

what's that in the sky?

Yoko: Fred Astaire was so meticulous. He made us do five takes because he didn't like the way he was moving. John just loved this kind of thing. When I was very young, I started to learn that very little things can really make your heart dance, like looking at the sky and knowing that the sky has a little shine or looking at the park when all the trees are still frozen, but then you see that some trees are budding and you almost sense spring coming. There's something marvellous about it, because it's the sign of life, that life is continuing. And that's the kind of thing that my heart dances for. When you are feeling bad, do one thing a day to make your heart dance. It could be a simple thing like looking up at the sky. The blue of the sky is the colour that is always in my mind. I guess that's my favourite.

George Harrison, Dick Cavett, Jack Palance, Jonas Mekas, Fred Astaire and John Lennon all perform with Yoko for her film; St Regis hotel, 2 and 6 September 1971.

gimme some truth

Yoko: On our way back from installing at *Art Spectrum* in Alexandra Palace we saw a march at Marble Arch and joined in. Someone handed John a megaphone and he led a chant of 'Power To The People'. We marched down Oxford Street, Shaftesbury Avenue, along Piccadilly and up to Grosvenor Square where the US Embassy was sealed off by police.

John: Did you hear what it said about Selfridges in the *New York Post*? 'John Lennon and his wife Yoko Ono were chased through Selfridges by a gang of screaming fans.

A thousand fans, most seen to be holding copies of the book, Beatles records and photographs, set upon the couple as they sat in the book department.' It wasn't like that at all. It says also that they bought a thousand copies. In fact, four hundred were knocked off!

Protesting on the Northern Ireland / Oz march, London 11 August 1971; John recording the master vocal of Gimme Some Truth, *28 May, 1971; Michael Parkinson in Yoko's bag on the Parkinson TV show, 17 July 1971;* Grapefruit *book signing at Claude Gill, 16 July 1971.*

Filming *Imagine* – John & Yoko sitting at one of five plinths of George Adamy's plexiglas artwork *Month of June*, 1970, at 77 Water Street on the corner of Front St and Old Slip, New York, 4 September 1971.

Following pages: filming *Imagine* – John & Yoko outside the Equitable Building, 120 Broadway, on Pine St, New York, 4 September 1971.

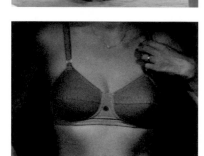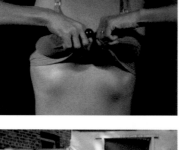

midsummer new york

Yoko: I always wanted to make a song that uses the word 'shaking' with a double meaning, since I discovered the usage of the word in rock songs in 1968. In '71, John and I made a brief visit to New York mainly to finish bits and pieces of *Imagine*. In the middle of the night, after long hours of recording, when the musicians looked totally exhausted, John suddenly said, 'Yoko says she's got something. Let's try.' I was surprised that he remembered the song I had shown him just briefly that morning. That's how 'Midsummer New York' was made. The musicians found a second wind and they played well. We did two takes with no rehearsal. I sang normally in one and for fun I did a take-off of Elvis on the other. John selected the Elvis one to be on the record.

Sitting at George Adamy's sculpture Month of June, 1970, at 77 Water Street; Pine Street; excerpt from Yoko's feminist film Freedom, *1971; performing* Whisper Piece, *1961, Emilio's Restaurant, 309 6th Ave; waltzing down Pine St, New York, 4 September 1971.*

oh my love

Yoko: This was filmed at the beautiful shoin-style tea house designed by Junzo Yoshimura in the Japanese Garden of the Kykuit Rockefeller Mansion and Estate in Sleepy Hollow in upstate New York. We did the filming on the sly because we didn't have any permits and then pretended we had filmed it in Japan. [laughs] I think it's OK to admit this now. I hope they don't mind! Have you seen an evening light lately? If you have, watch it for a while, for you never know, it may not be the same. They say the evening light is sacred. Well, in my book, every moment in our lives is sacred, and incredibly enjoyable.

Kissing at 79th St, Boat Basin, New York, 4 September 1971; the Japanese Garden at Kykuit, Rockefeller Estate, Sleepy Hollow, New York, 7 September 1971; Pointedness, *1964, and* Painting To Let The Evening Light Go Through, *1961/1966, Tittenhurst, 22 July 1971.*

Painting To Let The Evening Light Go Through, 1961/1966, by Yoko Ono; plexiglas with engraved text, 83.5 × 68.6 cm. Photographed through the window at Yoko's home, 25 Hanover Gate Mansions, London, 26 July 1968. Opposite: *Pointedness*, 1964, by Yoko Ono (above), *Forget It*, 1966, by Yoko Ono (below); both installation views, *This Is Not Here* exhibition, Everson Museum of Art, Syracuse, New York, 9 – 27 October 1971.

PAINTING TO LET THE EVENING LIGHT GO THROUGH YOKO ONO 1961

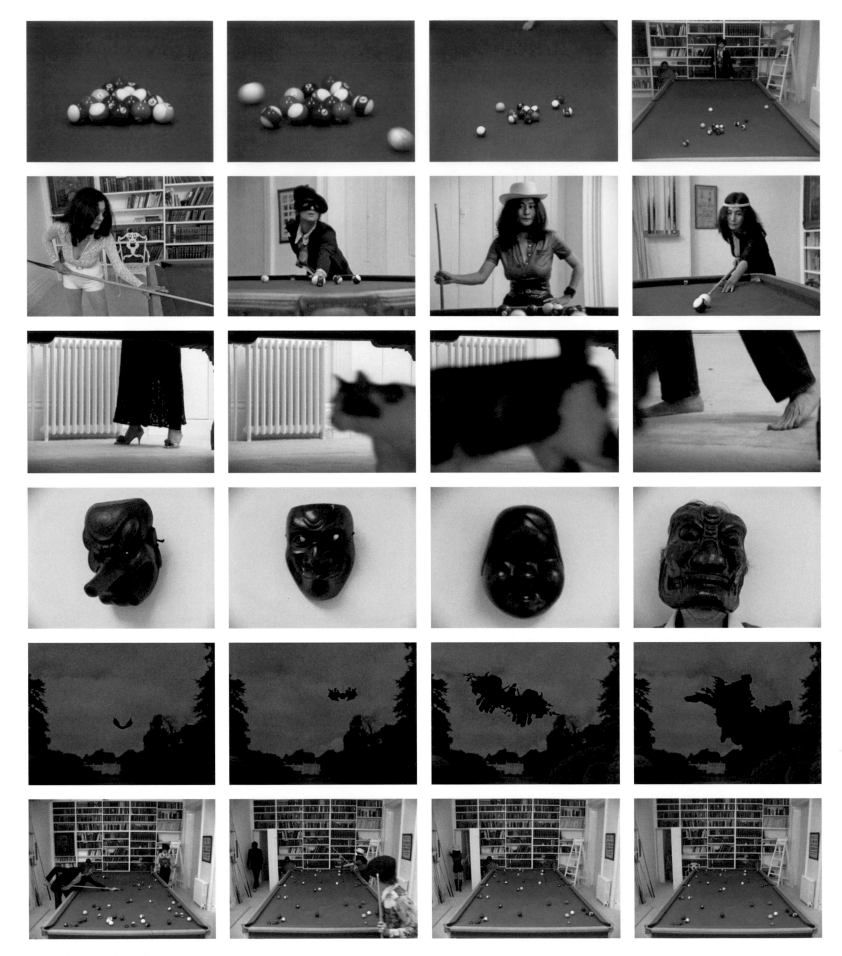

how do you sleep?

John: When I met Yoko is when you meet your first woman and you leave the guys at the bar, and you don't go play snooker and billiards. Once I found the woman, the boys became of no interest whatsoever, other than they were like old friends. You know the song: 'Those wedding bells are breaking up that old gang of mine.' It didn't hit me until whatever age I was when I met Yoko, twenty-six. That was it. That old gang of mine was over the moment I met her. I didn't consciously know it at the time, but that's what was going on. Yoko really woke me up to myself. She didn't fall in love with the Beatle, she didn't fall in love with my fame. She fell in love with me for myself, and through that, brought out the best in me. She was the ultimate trip. She said to me, 'You've got no clothes on.' Nobody had dared tell me that before.

Playing snooker in the billiards room; Japanese Noh masks on the upstairs landing; bat animation by Carmen D'Avino over the house; all at Tittenhurst, 22, 23 and 26 May 1971.

how?

John: It's a romantic song, and we're filming on a lake and I'm rowing and it's meant to be very romantic but the boat wouldn't leave the shore. It's going 'How can I go forward?' The boat won't go, I got the oars on and the oar comes off and in the end I finally make it, half-way through the second verse!

Yoko: I thought it was so funny that it goes 'da da daa' [motions climbing the ladder]; it's like a detective story, and she goes on and on and then the end is that she comes across this sculpture that's mine, where you just put a little drop of water on

[*Water Piece*, 1962/1966 – water every day]. And that's all she does. And life is like that. You go on a heroic trip and at the end, what you do is not very much.

John & Yoko rowing and walking; Diana Robertson climbing up ladders and onto the roof to reach Yoko's artwork Water Piece (Painting to be watered), *1962/1966 – water every day; all at Tittenhurst Park, 21 and 22 July 1971.*

david bailey
photographer

I first met John Lennon at the Ad Lib Club in London in the Sixties. He was in his early twenties. When I first photographed the Beatles, they were still a boy band. There were some talks of us doing the Paris Collections together with the Beatles, but the English folk turned it down.

I always liked John because he was an arsehole like me. I like arseholes because they get things done. He was cool. The one I liked the best. He didn't intimidate me. I'd lived with the Krays for two weeks. Do you think I was going to be scared of John Lennon?

I preferred it when he was with Yoko. As 'John & Yoko', things got much more interesting. They appealed to me more. They were as much about ideas as making music. There was a message in what they were doing. Pop music was a way of getting that message across. And with him doing it, it was quicker, because people listened to what he had to say.

I wasn't into that Maharishi nonsense and all that Hare Krishna bit, but I thought John & Yoko were great when they did 'Give Peace A Chance'. It made it more acceptable to the public because the way they presented it appealed to everyone and it wasn't such an underground thing any more.

John phoned me in the summer of 1971 and said, 'We're doing a documentary and we'd like you to be in it and film a photo session.' So I said, 'That sounds great!' and that's how the shoot came about. It had nothing to do with *Vogue* or Condé Nast. They came in much later when they asked to use my pictures for their December issue. The shoot was created just between us as friends. We knew each other, it wasn't like a business thing, it was, 'Yeah! Let's do it.'

I shot it at my home in Primrose Hill on 10 × 8-inch plate film. I use it a lot, because you can still talk to the person and you don't have to look through the camera. We also had to slow it all down because of the film crew.

I didn't really know Yoko that well. In the photo shoot I was joking with her, asking her to say the word 'lesbian'. I'd just directed a documentary about Cecil Beaton [*Beaton by Bailey*, for ATV], and in it, Beaton says [on how to get a good smile for a photograph] 'Oh, don't say "smile"; nowadays, one says "lesbian".' It was a joke on Cecil Beaton, really.

I did a book on Sudan for charity and called it *Imagine*. I thought it was such a great name for anything, just 'Imagine'....

'Imagine' always gets played when they need a song for peace. If there's an apocalypse, they always play the Stones!

Has 'Imagine' affected me? You mean as much as W. H. Auden or T. S. Eliot? No, but I was with the ambassador of Sweden one day and he said, 'John Lennon made us rethink everything.' He told me he was going to bring it up at the United Nations, 'Give Peace A Chance'.

. . . . .

Bailey: Do you remember when I first met you, John?

John: Yeah, with Paul. We were nervous because you were the great David Bailey. We thought it was life or death whether you came out all right or not. Photo sessions were really nerve-wracking because you always felt so phony.

Bailey: Now that's good. Now relax.

John. Don't kiss her. Just get closer to her. OK. And Yoko, bend your knee a bit more that way, otherwise it is going to distort. Good. Now you're blocking all the light. Good. OK. Stay still, John. Now this camera makes everything look so sort of mundane. That's why I like it. You can't do anything with it. Sorts out the boys from the men. It's much easier in the end to take pictures with this camera because you have to make a decision.

Bailey: Put your chin down a wee bit. OK. Think about it. Good. Stay, John. Good. OK. Alright. It's over.

John: Oh, is it? Very nice. I'll go put your 18th-century jodhpur outfit on. Yeah. Nice, isn't it? It was a nice build-up.

Bailey: Just lift up your skirt. Good. Say 'lesbian'.

Yoko: Lesbian.

Bailey: Say it again.

Yoko: Lesbian.

Bailey: You look much nicer like that.

John: Than with the beard and Jesus....

Bailey: Yeah.

John: I feel better. I was hiding.

Bailey: I want to cut all my hair off.

John: I cut it like a skinhead last year. It was great because you don't have to fucking touch it and you just go 'umhhh' and it's done. That was the good thing about that.

John drawing romantic grafitti for Yoko; Field 5 Lane 12,
South Beach, Staten Island New York, 10 September 1971.
Opposite: list of footage in the can and proposed filming
schedule for 'Your Show', the working title for the *Imagine* film;
Tittenhurst, 13 – 23 July 1971.

"YOUR SHOW"

FOOTAGE IN THE CAN

1.   MUSIC RECORDING OF (1) JEALOUS GUY
                          (2) HOW
                          (3) CRIPPLED INSIDE
                          (4) HOW DO YOU SLEEP

2.   HEAD SHOTS OF JOHN   SINCE CHILDHOOD

3   CLAUDIO SEQUENCE

4.   CHILDREN/"WORKING CLASS HEROES" (MANCHESTER)

5.   IN THE KITCHEN

6.   YOKO'S SCULPTURES   "THIS IS NOT HERE"

7.   BBC RADIO "WOMANS HOUS" INTERVIEW - ABOUT MORALITY
       AND PERMISSIVENESS

8.   CONVERSATION WITH TARIQ ALI, BLACKBURN AND DEBRAY

9.   JOE WATCHING TV

10   PHIL SPECTOR

11   GARDEN AT NIGHT AND EARLY MORNING

"YOUR SHOW"   13TH JULY 1971

PROPOSED SCHEDULE FOR TEN DAYS FILMING TO SHOW JOHN
AND YOKO ON THEIR RETURN FROM U.S.A.

WED. 14TH JULY   P.M. DISCUSSION WITH JOHN AND YOKO
                              OF THIS SCHEDULE

THURS. 15TH JULY   9.00A.M. SHOOT JOHN AND YOKO GETTING
                              UP - BREAKFAST - PREPARE TO
(GENERAL ACTIVITIES DAY)   LEAVE HOUSE - JOURNEY TO LONDON
                              (WITH NIC IN MERDEDES) -
                        11.00A.M. ARRIVAL AT SPHERE BOOKS
                              GRAYS INN ROAD - MEETING WITH
                              BRIAN LEVEY
                        12.00 A.M. ARRIVAL AT SELFRIDGES -
                              DRINKS WITH P.R. UPSTAIRS -
                              DOWNSTAIRS TO SIGN COPIES OF
                              "GRAPEFRUIT"
                        P.M. TO APPLE TO SHOOT BUSINESS SCENE -
                              PETER HOWARD - DISCUSS"YOUR SHOW"
                              - NEIL SHOWS JOHN THE BEATLES
                              MOVIE.
                        LATER   SHOOT REHEARSAL AND POSSIBLY
                              LIVE SHOW OF BBC RADIO PROGRAMME
                              "LATE NIGHT EXTRA". INTERVIEW
                              RE GRAPEFRUIT.

TUESDAY 20TH JULY   TONY CASH INTERVIEW (BBC TV)
                        ABOUT JOHN'S MUSIC

WED. 21ST JULY   ALAN MURGATROYD INTERVIEW
                        SOUND TAPES "WORKING CLASS HERO"
                        P.M. TRIP TO PARIS WITH ROBIN
                        TALK TO RADICALS - AIRPORT HASSLES

THURS. 22ND JULY   AN APPEARANCE OUTSIDE COURT
                        "OZ OBSCENITY TRIAL" - BAG STUNTS

                        P.M. PAUL LOWE (QUAESITOR) - JANOV
                        - PRIMAL SCREAM THERAPY

FRIDAY 23RD JULY   A.M. JOHN AND YOKO TALK ABOUT THEIR
                        OWN FILMS - AND ABOUT MOVIES
                        GENERALLY

                        P.M. SUPER JAM SESSION - IN TEMPLE-
                        INVITED GUESTS - IN AID OF"OZ
                        DEFENCE FUND".

FRI. 16TH JULY   1.00 PM ARRIVAL AT CLAUDE GILL
                        BOOKS - FOOTAGE OF DISPLAY
(YOKO'S DAY)   "GRAPEFRUIT"T SHIRTS - YOKO
                        AUTOGRAPHING COPIES

                        LATER P.M. YOKO WITH HER SCULPTURES
                        - ARRANGING THE EXHIBITION - FILMING
                        THEM AND HERSELF BEING FILMED

            MEANWHILE: MICHAEL WHALE OF "THE TIMES" TALKS
                        TO JOHN ABOUT MUSIC, BEATLES, ETC.
                        THE MUSIC INTERVIEW

SATURDAY 17TH JULY   P.M. JOHN TALKS TO CAMERA ABOUT HIS
                        POLITICAL BELIEFS - ATTITUDES -
(POLITICS DAY)   HOPES

                        TEATIME: TARIQ AND ROBIN ARRIVE -
                        FURTHER CONVERSATION

                        LATER PM : POSSIBLE APPEARANCE
                        ON "PARKINSON" (BBC TALK SHOW) WITH
                        TARIQ AND ROBIN

SUNDAY 18TH JULY   JOHN PLAYS "IMAGINE" TO PLAYBACK -
                        THINGS HAPPENING AROUND THE HOUSE
(MUSIC DAY)   - GARDEN - LAKE - DONKEYS -
                        "I DON'T WANT TO BE A SOLDIER MAMA"

MONDAY 19TH JULY   FRANCO OFF TO SEE AUNT MIMI - SOUND
                        ONLY IF NECESSARY - JOHN'S
REST DAY)   CHILDHOOD

oh yoko!

Yoko: When I think of Ascot I think of making the *Imagine* album and also just being together, strolling around in the gardens. We together declared to the world that we were a working partnership. It was a very intense and beautiful time for us. Both of us were activists already. So we spoke about it and said, 'Hey, that's what we can do together!' World Peace is definitely attainable. We are working on that now. You included.

David Bailey photoshoot, Primrose Hill, London, 19 July 1971; Apple, *1966; walking on the front lawn at Tittenhurst, 21 July 1971;* Look At Me I'm Only Small, *1971, and John's artwork over the Henry Wills organ pipes, installation views, Art Spectrum, Alexandra Palace, London, 11 August 1971; running and writing on the sand at South Beach, Staten Island with the Verrazano-Narrows bridge in the background, 10 September 1971.*

beach / end credits

Yoko: John was the most romantic man I ever encountered. He said you have to water your love every day. John used to make me laugh, and I, him. We were great partners in that sense. In the world's eye we were Laurel and Hardy. In our minds we were Heathcliff and Cathy. In a moment of wisdom we were a wizard and a witch. In a moment of freedom, we were Don Quixote and Sancho. In reality, we were just a boy and a girl who never looked back. We were on South Beach on Staten Island. 'Let's really upset them and end the film with us walking on water.' (I'll let you guess whose idea that was!) We tried – that is, I know it looked a bit awkward, but it was a windy day and the waves were rough.

Kissing and walking on the water at the pier opposite Fountain of the Dolphins *with Hoffman Island in the background, South Beach, Staten Island, 10 September 1971.*

① How can I go forward when I don't
know which way I'm facing?
how can I go forward when I don't
know which way to turn?
how can I go forward into something
I'm not sure of? an oh no, oh, no.
② How can I have feeling when I don't know
if it's a feeling?
How can I feel something if I just don't know
how to feel?
how can I have feelings when my
feelings have always been denied?
③ How can I give love when I don't
know what it's I'm giving?
How can I give love when I just don't know
how give?
how can I give love when love is something
I have never had?

how?

How can I go forward when I don't know which way I'm facing?
How can I go forward when I don't know which way to turn?
How can I go forward into something I'm not sure of?
Oh no, oh no

How can I have feeling when I don't know if it's a feeling?
How can I feel something if I just don't know how to feel?
How can I have feelings when my feelings have always been denied?
Oh no, oh no

You know life can be long
And you got to be so strong
And the world is so tough
Sometimes I feel I've had enough

How can I give love when I don't know what it is I'm giving?
How can I give love when I just don't know how to give?
How can I give love when love is something I ain't never had?
Oh no, oh no

You know life can be long
And you got to be so strong
And the world she is tough
Sometimes I feel I've had enough

How can we go forward when we don't know which way we're facing?
How can we go forward when we don't know which way to turn?
How can we go forward into something we're not sure of?
Oh no, oh no

John: I started 'How?' at the same time as I was doing the last album and I finished it off this time with the middle eight. It's just a nice ballad. 'How?' is George's favourite song, I'm proud to say. (He also digs the strings on 'It's So Hard' – maybe a few of his fans will follow his taste heh! heh!) The verses were written last year. Middle eight was written during the recording session (my favourite bit, it's new, you see). Wish I'd sung it better, but it's a nice tune, it was hard doing those breaks. Mellow.

I think the more relationships you have, the more you learn about other people. I think whatever love is (and it's many, many things) it is constant. It's been the same forever. I don't think it'll ever change. It's a sort of abstract concept that comes and goes whether you like it or not. It's whatever legislation or whatever philosophies people have put out about it it exists without words or without philosophy or without discussion. Everybody's continually searching for love and it manifests itself in many different ways. Like for Ted Heath it manifests itself in being number one. But to me, all he really wants is to be loved by everyone. That's why he's in that position and that's why I'm doing what I'm doing basically because I want love from all those people. That's just the way it goes.

Yoko: John was raised by Aunt Mimi and because of his loyalty to Mimi, he decided not to see his mother so much because it would hurt Mimi.

Young kids are trying to ignore love. That's very natural because they don't get it and they're bitter about it, so they'd rather not want it. You know that feeling that you're not going to get it and if you try to get it, it's so much pain, so you'd rather pretend you don't want it and you start to believe in that – 'Oh I'm glad I'm not the type to fall in love' and 'I'm so glad about it because I dont have to get hurt.'

John: I always write music to do with my feelings – not to describe that hedge or that situation down there, but to write about me. All I was doing is stripping myself mentally and singing about it. All poets have done that throughout the ages. 'Help!' it's the same kind of song. 'I'm A Loser' is the same. So is 'In My Life'. Those songs are just the same style. Simple lyrics. They're all personal songs. My songs have always been like personalised diaries.

Yoko: My mother once told me this interesting story. In the big earthquake in the Thirties, there was this woman friend of hers, and this woman with her very young daughter looked around after the earthquake and there was not one place in the sky that was not red, because it was all on fire. The Japanese houses were all wood so it was very easy to quickly burn. There was just one little blue spot in the sky, and she thought, 'I'm going to get there.' And that's how she was saved. She saved herself and her daughter. That's how I feel about ourselves, that we're going to follow that one blue spot.

John: My philosophy is 'You Are Here'. All the bibles, Jesuses, gurus, poets and artists have ever said to people is that this minute is the one that counts; not tomorrow or yesterday. That's the whole game. There's no other time but the present. Anything else is a waste of time. When you run fast, which is usually what you do as a youth, you think you have to run fast to stay ahead of the game. But all you're really doing is running fast, which is fun, you know, but you're running fast, that's all. But the fastest movement is no movement. Because it's really going so fast that it's, you know, when something is going so fast it appears to be still, like the Earth or the Moon or something. There's no apparent movement. It's apparent by the change, but there's no zooming going on around us. The things that are really, really moving, are apparently still.

Yoko: The Japanese poet Matsuo Bashō was an influence for me. Bashō is minimal and very Zen and embodies the kind of Romanticism that I pursue in my work. There is one beautiful poem by him: 'Sick on my journey | only my dreams will wander | these desolate moors.' The sense is that he can't move but his dreams are running wild. I just love that. His poems are almost like a travelogue and are very relevant to the journey of life. And he was a traveller, he loved to travel. He ended up falling ill at an inn and he wrote about his dreams running wild. It is the height of Romanticism.

John: I like autobiographies, usually about famous people. But it is the little decisions that are made, those sort of cosmic decisions, that change the whole person's direction. And who knows whether they make the decision or it's made for them or what it was that just made that move. So I don't regret any of it, the suffering or the happiness.

Yoko: For women or men, the first step to help the world improve is to love oneself.

John: If one just spends time concentrating on a problem, that's all you do. But if one puts one's mind on the solution, the problem tends to go away.

DAN — if we don't wake up.

[a] take a polaroid photo — a close up of the full length telescope and 'tri-pod' →

please look at me
i'm only small

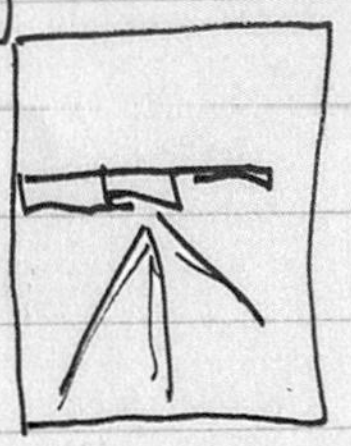

then cut it out

glue it on some wood or cardboard and make the model thus —

title: 'minature sculpture for john.' 4.0.71.

clear plastic.

cut out man.

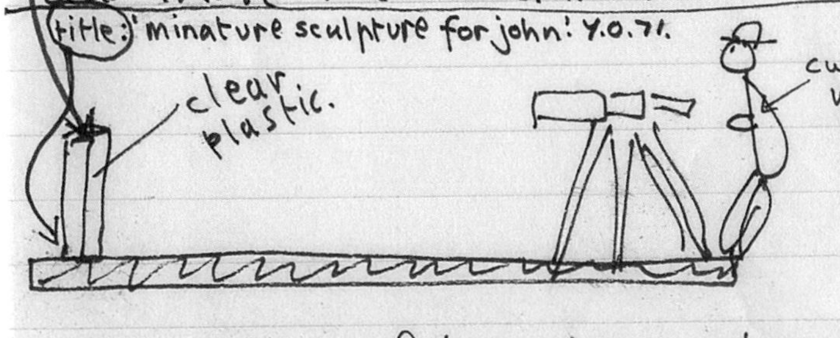

something like this. also give proper measurements etc

[b] the letter about the gloves should mention how little space is needed etc.

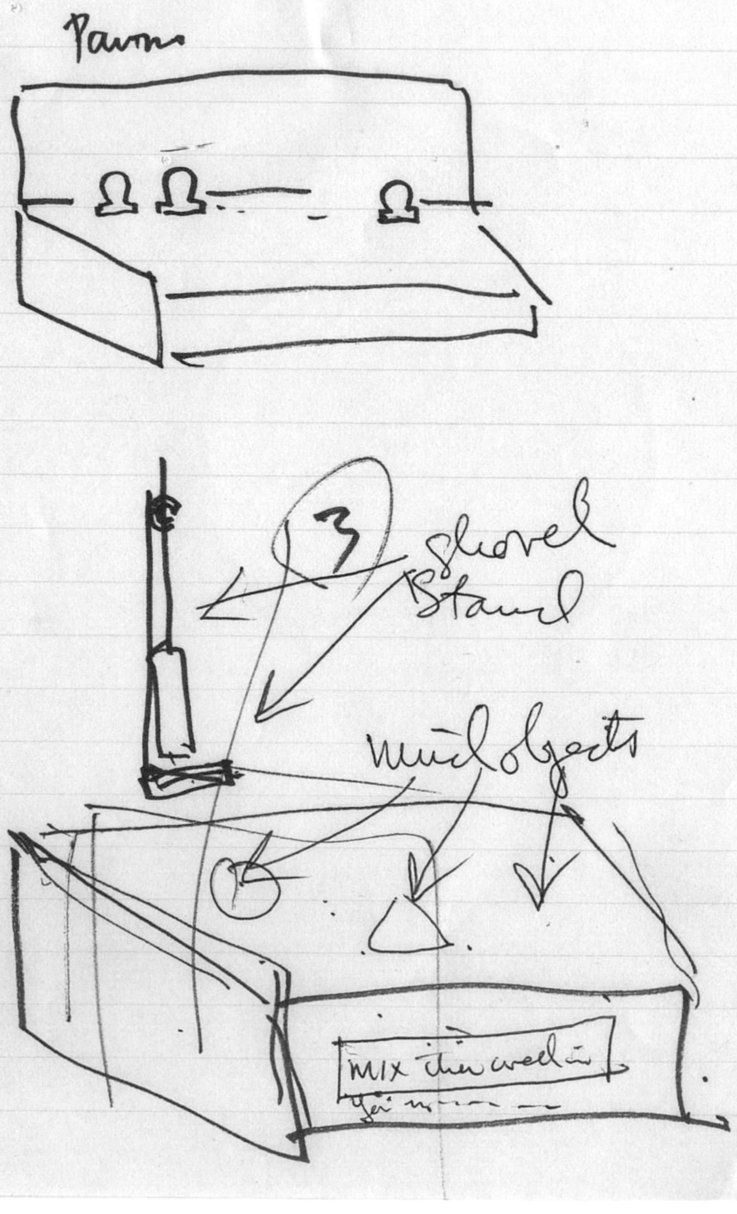

Pavros

3 shovel stand

mud objects

MIX then weed in

this is not here

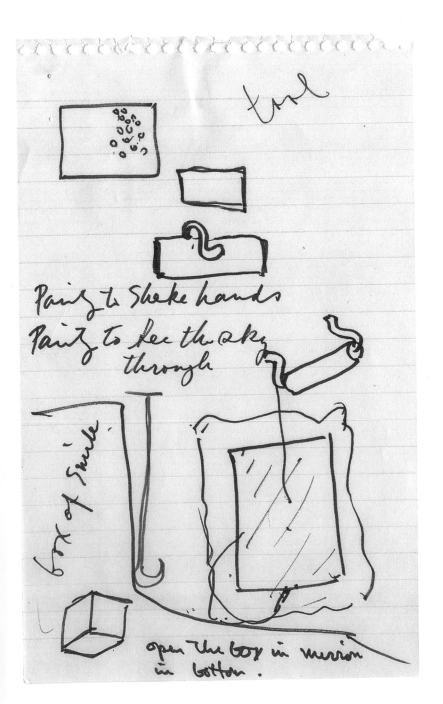

BY YOKO ONO · JOHN LENNON-GUEST ARTIST · AT EVE

ON MUSEUM OF ART, SYRACUSE, N.Y. · OCTOBER 9-27

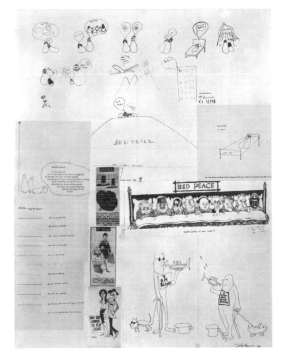

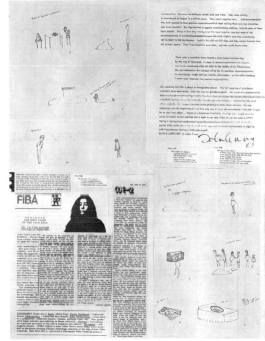

Pages 278–279: plans for *Look At Me I'm Only Small* in John's handwriting, and *Pawns*, *Cloud Shovel*, *Mind Objects*, *Painting To Shake Hands*, *Painting To See The Sky Through*, *Box Of Smile*, *Danger Box* and *Object To Be Seen In The Dark* in Yoko's handwriting, 1971. Pages 280–281 and 282–283: *This is Not Here* poster, concept by Yoko Ono, photos by Iain MacMillan, realized by George Maciunas, *This is Not Here* newspaper designed by John Lennon; both for *This Is Not Here* exhibition, Everson Museum of Art, Syracuse New York, 9 – 27 October 1971.

this is not here

Thank-you note from John to Yoko for dedicating her Everson art show to him, Hotel Syracuse, New York, October 1971. Opposite: at the opening of the *This Is Not Here* exhibition, Everson Museum of Art, Syracuse, New York, 9 October 1971.

Yoko: The reason we called the exhibition *This Is Not Here* was because I was trying to get across the idea that the art is in the people who come to see it. It's like saying, 'You're important, not the objects.' I'm not saying 'Come and look at these beautiful things on pedestals.' I'm saying that whatever is important is in your head. It's your reactions that count.

This was the first time that somebody really took a chance on me in the sense that he's risking other things and also he's giving me all the freedom that I can have to set up the show and I'm very thankful. Jim Harithas [director of the Everson Museum] is a very remarkable guy to do that.

John: I'll have a little corner with some work that has been inspired by Yoko's work that I've produced. You can't live with a woman like Yoko and not start to be inspired in her direction…some of the pieces I've done are dialogues with Yoko's work, and some are just independent ideas that came through working with her.

Yoko: In this show I'd like to prove the fact that you don't need talent to be an artist. 'Artist' is just a frame of mind. Anybody can be an artist and anybody can communicate, if they're desperate enough.

There's no such thing as the imagination of an artist. Imagination, if you're desperate enough, will come out of necessity. Even the best artists if they don't have the necessity, will dry up and they won't have any imagination. So there's no talent, no professionalism, there's no nothing, there are only people. Billions of people in this world.

Every person in the world is desperate for communication. The kind who still don't know – the minute they learn how desperate they are to communicate, they're going to start communicating.

In this show, I'd like to show how easy it is to communicate and also that there is no other way to communicate but to communicate in your own way. And that you can do. Don't feel that you don't have something that we have, or that some privileged people have, who can communicate.

Everybody has one mouth. Don't feel that some people are unique because everybody in the world has a different mouth. So you are unique. Don't worry about that. You're unique without trying. All you have to do is to be yourself.

These are things that I'm sort of telling myself, more or less, and this museum show is a show, as you will see, of a very untalented artist who is just desperate for communication and who's been communicating for years.

And I hope after seeing this show, you will realize your own bag, and start communicating.

Total communication equals peace. And that's what I think that artists can still do in this world – to change the value of the world.

The communication media is getting more and more developed but it's not enough yet. There's a certain kind of privileged class who are controlling the communication media. Don't rely on TV and radio only. There are many other ways of communication and we can do it.

Anything is art if you can influence people by it. And if you can communicate yourself with it. Yes. We're all audience and we're all artists.

When you go through this, you'll see that you're going to be not just watching it, but you're going to be involved in it. I don't believe in just showing a lump of stone and saying, 'This is an artwork, so applaud.' That's like a narcissism of an artist. I believe in allowing people to have a direct experience and communication with the piece. I don't believe in only communication on a conscious level because subconsciously everybody is communicating whether you like it or not. It's a total meeting.

This Is Not Here, a show of unfinished paintings and sculpture is dedicated to John Lennon on his 31st birthday, together with wind, rain, sky, sunshine and smile – everything beautiful and funny that is related to the show. Happy birthday, John. I love you. Yoko Ono Lennon, Everson Museum, Syracuse, New York, 9 October 1971.

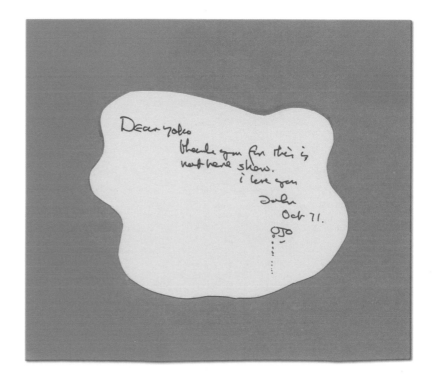

jim harithas
director, everson museum

During the summer of '71, I ran into John & Yoko at Richard Bellamy's gallery on Madison Avenue. I was aware of her New York work with Fluxus and I knew she'd shown a bit in England. I thought her work was extraordinary. I also thought that she and John were two of the finest people in the world and their commitment to peace was truly important. I introduced myself and told them as director of the Everson Museum in Syracuse, I would love to show her work.

I brought my new assistant David Ross down to meet them at their hotel. He was completely star-struck. John was playing guitar and John being John, brought another out so they could play together. David knew all the Beatles' songs. At one point John said, 'Oh my God, you remember these songs better than I do!' In the meantime, Yoko and I discussed the show. I said to her, 'Look, the whole museum is yours. You can expand the show in any direction and we'll accommodate it.'

In those days, women were marginalized and weren't expected to be artists. I think we were the first museum to dedicate the whole museum to a woman. It happened right at that moment where the women's movement was gathering strength in the early Seventies, so it was a really important show from a political and sociological standpoint. Some of my male colleagues in the museum profession were really irritated about it.

The mainstream then was Pop Art. Commercial-looking art made by white men. If you went to museums to see art, you rarely saw a South American artist, for example. I went to Texas in the mid-Seventies and found out there'd never been any Mexican artists shown in Texas museums and Texas is practically a Mexican state.

Yoko was strongly pushing the ideology that 'everyone is an artist'. It's important to consider how radical that was, not just on an individual level but in a much broader sense. With the exception of what we were doing at the Everson, in those days you never saw exhibitions by women or non-white people. Opening up these possibilities to everyone and being so inclusive was revolutionary. That was the power of that show.

'This Is Not Here' was a really mysterious title. What it meant to me was that it was not simply the pieces; you had to recognize your own self being there. Only your personal participation could complete this exhibition full of unfinished paintings and objects.

Practically every piece was an invitation. The instructions encouraged interaction – physically by adding to an object or performing in an event – or mentally by inspiring you to complete the artwork using the theatre of your imagination, where everything is possible, everything is more vivid and you can become a powerful artist by exercising your ability to imagine.

There were white *Add Color* canvasses where the visitors were encouraged to paint with the brushes and colours supplied. They filled up really quickly. There was a 'Weight Event' room where you had large heavy-looking objects that were very light and very small objects that were very heavy, so people would lift them up and experience differences in weight that challenged their perceptions. There was a '6th Dimension' room where visitors had to wear rubber masks with distorted eyes to experience a different world – a surrealist and very rare interaction. There were live music performances, film screenings and even a soundproof room. The show was incredibly imaginative. For *Add Water Event*, Yoko invited over 120 artists to participate with her by bringing an object for her

to add water to. I thought this was incredibly generous for an artist – that she wasn't taking all the credit for herself and encouraged them to participate in this moment as well. Bob Watts brought a Volkswagen that got filled with water. Andy Warhol had a great videotape piece of a water cooler with audio of chat around it. All the Fluxus artists contributed something. The sense of collaboration was wonderful.

John & Yoko had a 'Dialogue Room' in which the artworks acted as a conversation between one another. Yoko's *3 Spoons* with John's *4 Spoons*. Yoko's *Forget It* with John's *Needle*. Yoko's *This Is Not Here* with John's *You Are Here*.

AMAZE was a Plexiglas maze with a toilet in the centre. I think it was the same expression of taking a common everyday object that you use in a certain way and, like Duchamp, raising it to a work of art. He did the urinal, she did the toilet. It was the first answer to the Duchamp that I've ever seen.

There were thousands of people parked and camping outside the museum. They came in from all over the country. It helped having John & Yoko there for the opening, which was a thrill for everyone, and the show continued to be popular throughout its run. It was one of the most spectacular, inspiring and imaginative shows of that decade.

I still believe that everyone is an artist, but in the roughly fifty years that I've been doing museum work, there's still only a handful of artists that are really great. That is also true with musicians, don't you think? John had a great spirit and Yoko has a great spirit and I think together they were dynamite.

Museum Director Jim Harithas being interviewed at the opening of the *This is Not Here* exhibition, Everson Museum of Art, Syracuse, New York, 9 October 1971.

this is not here

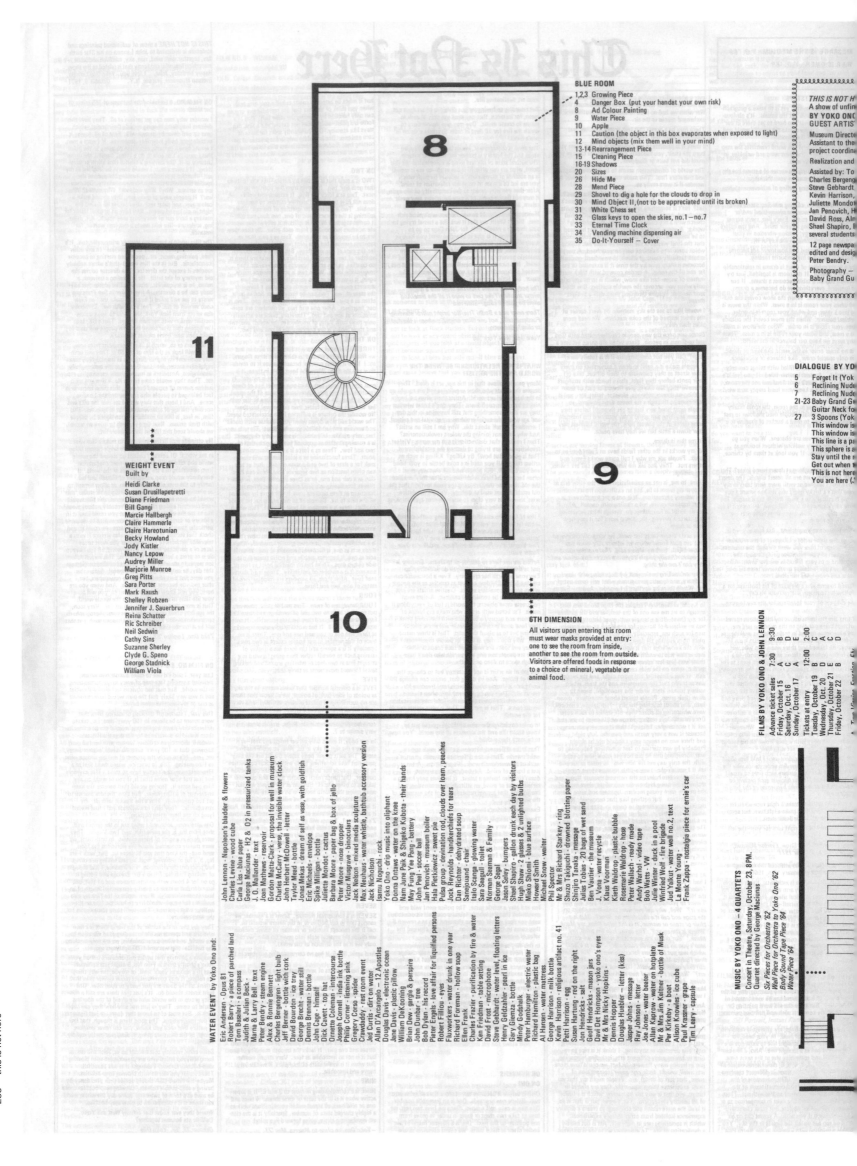

This Is Not Here

BLUE ROOM

1,2,3 Growing Piece
4 Danger Box (put your hand at your own risk)
8 Ad Colour Painting
9 Water Piece
10 Apple
11 Caution (the object in this box evaporates when exposed to light)
12 Mind objects (mix them well in your mind)
13-14 Rearrangement Piece
15 Cleaning Piece
16-19 Shadows
20 Sizes
26 Hide Me
28 Mend Piece
29 Shovel to dig a hole for the clouds to drop in
30 Mind Object II, (not to be appreciated until its broken)
31 White Chess set
32 Glass keys to open the skies, no.1 – no.7
33 Eternal Time Clock
34 Vending machine dispensing air
35 Do-It-Yourself — Cover

THIS IS NOT H...
A show of unfin...
BY YOKO ONO
GUEST ARTIS...
Museum Directe...
Assistant to the...
project coordina...

Realization and...

Assisted by: To o...
Charles Bergeng...
Steve Gebhardt...
Kevin Harrison,...
Juliette Mondot...
Jan Penovich, H...
David Ross, Alm...
Shael Shapiro,...
several students...

12 page newspa...
edited and desig...
Peter Bendry.

Photography —
Baby Grand Gu...

DIALOGUE BY YO...
5 Forget It (Yok...
6 Reclining Nude...
7 Reclining Nude...
21-23 Baby Grand Ge...
Guitar Neck fo...
27 3 Spoons (Yok...
This window is...
This window is...
This line is a pa...
This sphere is a...
Stay until the...
Get out when...
This is not here...
You are here (...

6TH DIMENSION

All visitors upon entering this room
must wear masks provided at entry:
one to see the room from inside,
another to see the room from outside.
Visitors are offered foods in response
to a choice of mineral, vegetable or
animal food.

WEIGHT EVENT
Built by

Heidi Clarke
Susan Drusillapetretti
Diane Friedman
Bill Gangi
Marcie Hallbergh
Claire Hammerle
Claire Hareotunian
Becky Howland
Jody Kistler
Nancy Lepow
Audrey Miller
Marjorie Munroe
Greg Pitts
Sara Porter
Mark Raush
Shelley Robzen
Jennifer J. Sauerbrun
Reina Schatter
Ric Schreiber
Neil Sedwin
Cathy Sins
Suzanne Sherley
Clyde G. Speno
George Stadnick
William Viola

FILMS BY YOKO ONO & JOHN LENNON

Advance ticket sales
Friday, October 15
Saturday, Oct. 16
Sunday, October 17

Tickets at entry
Tuesday, October 19
Wednesday, Oct. 20
Thursday, October 21
Friday, October 22

WATER EVENT by Yoko Ono and:

Eric Andersen - Opus 81
Robert Barry - a piece of parched land
Tom Basolari - a compass
Judith & Julian Beck -
Marnia & Larry Bell - text
Peter Bendry - steam engine
Alex & Ronnie Bennett
Charles Bergengren - light bulb
Jeff Berner - bottle with cork
David Bourdon - ice tray
George Brecht - water still
Dennis Brennan - bottle
John Cage - himself
Dick Cavett - top hat
Ornette Coleman - intercourse
Joseph Cornell - India ink bottle
Philip Corner - listening sink
Gregory Corso - spider
Crawdaddy - dirt on water
Jed Curtis - dirt on water
Allan D'Arcangelo – 12 Apostles
Douglas Davis - electronic ocean
Jane Davis - plastic pillow
William DeKooning
Brian Dew - gargle & perspire
John Dunbar - tree
Bob Dylan - his record
Pieter Engels - love affair for liquified persons
Robert Filliou - eyes
Fluxworkers - water drunk in one year
Richard Foreman - hollow soap
Ellen Frank
Charles Frazier - purification by fire & water
Ken Friedman - table setting
David Frost - microphone
Henry Geldzahler - pearl in ice
Gary Giemza - bottle
Mindy Godshalk
Peter Hamburger - electric water
Richard Hamilton - plastic bag
Al Hansen - water mattress
George Harrison - milk bottle
Patti Harrison - egg
Kevin Harrison - religious artifact no. 41
Susan Hartung - red on the right
Jon Hendricks - salt
Geoff Hendricks - mason jars
Davi Det Hompson - yoko ono's eyes
Mr & Mrs Nicky Hopkins -
Dennis Hopper
Douglas Huebler - message
Jasper Johns - letter
Ray Johnson - letter
Joe Jones - water beater
Allan Kaprow - water on hotplate
Mr & Mrs Jim Kaltner - bottle of Musk
Per Kirkeby - a boat
Alison Knowles - ice cube
Paul Krasner - grape
Tim Leary - capsule

John Lennon - Napoleon's bladder & flowers
Charles Levine - wood cube
Carla Liss - blue paper
George Maciunas - H2 & O2 in pressurized tanks
J. O. Mallander - reservoir
Joan Mathews
Gordon Matta-Clark - proposal for well in museum
Charles McCarry - verse, the invisible water clock
John Herbert McDowell - letter
Taylor Mead - bottle
Jonas Mekas - dream of self as vase, with goldfish
Eric Michaels - envelope
Spike Milligan - bottle
Juliette Mondot - cactus
Barbara Moore - paper bag & box of jello
Peter Moore - nose dropper
Victor Musgrave - binoculars
Max Neuhaus - mixed media sculpture
Jack Nelson - mixed media accessory version
Jack Nicholson
Isamu Noguchi - rock
Yoko Ono - drip music into oliphant
Donna Ontaws - water on the knee
Nam June Paik & Shigeko Kubota - their hands
May Fung Yee Pang - battery
Jan Penovich - museum boiler
Hala Pietkiewicz - eyes
Pulsa group - devination rod, clouds over loam, peaches
Jock Reynolds - handkerchiefs for tears
Dan Richter - dehydrated soup
Sanejouand - chair
Italo Scanga - glowing water
Sara Seagull - toilet
Norman Seaman & Family -
George Segal
Shael Shapiro - gallon drunk each day by visitors
Hugh Shaw - 2 glasses & 2 unlighted bulbs
Mieko Shiomi - blue surface
Howard Smith
Michael Snow - water
Phil Spector
Mr & Mrs Richard Starkey - ring
Shozo Takiguchi - drowned blotting paper
Shinjiro Tanaka - message
Julias Tobias - 20 bags of wet sand
Ben Vautier - the museum
J. Vona - water recycle
Klaus Voorman
Kieth Waldrop - plastic bubble
Rosemarie Waldrop - hose
Peter Wallach - ready made
Andy Warhol - VW
Bob Watts - VW
Julia Winter - duck in a pool
Winfried Wolf - fire brigade
Jud Yalkut - water well no.2, text
La Monte Young -
Frank Zappa - nostalgia piece for ernie's car

MUSIC BY YOKO ONO – 4 QUARTETS

Concert in Theatre, Saturday, October 23, 8 PM.
Quartet directed by George Maciunas

Six Pieces for Orchestra '62
Wall Piece for Orchestra to Yoko Ono '62
Body Sound Tape Piece '64
Water Piece '64

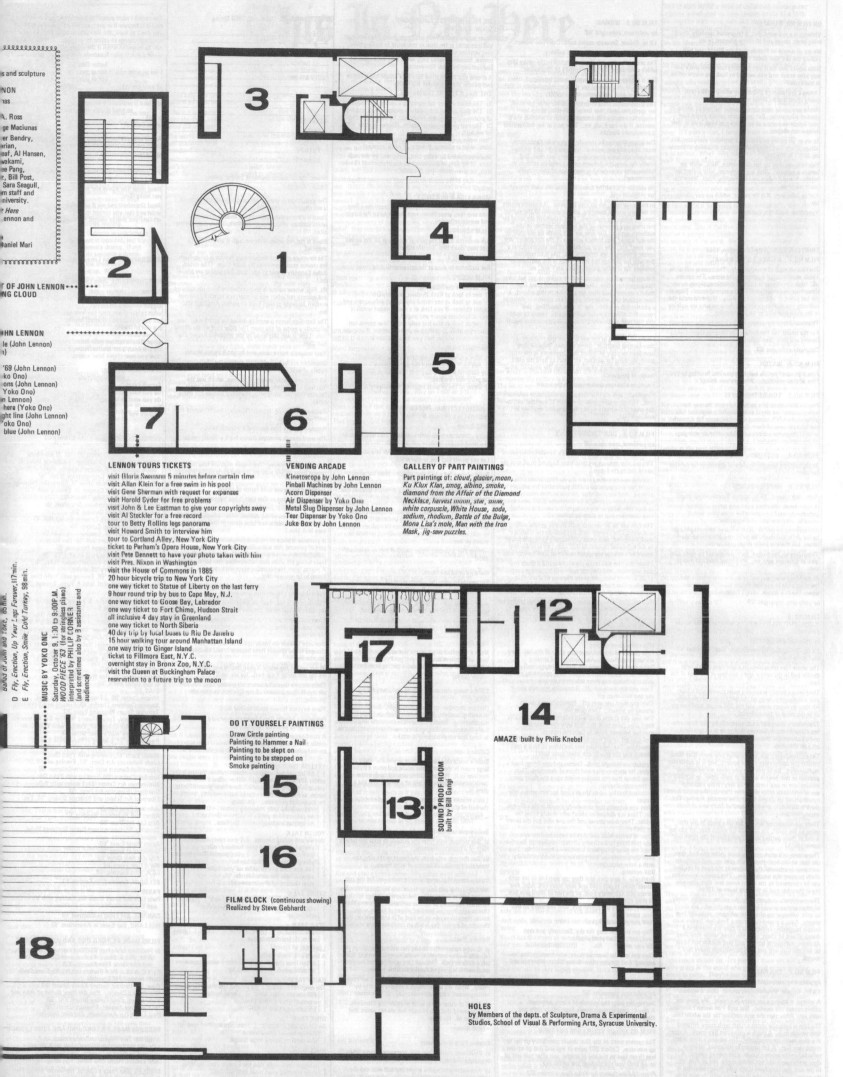

This Is Not Here

...is and sculpture

...NNON
...has

...A. Ross
...ge Maciunas
...er Bendry,
...erian,
...eaf, Al Hansen,
...wakami,
...ee Pang,
...e, Bill Post,
...Sara Seagull,
...m staff and
...niversity.
...Here
...ennon and

...aniel Mari

...OF JOHN LENNON
...NG CLOUD

...HN LENNON
...le (John Lennon)
...n)
...'69 (John Lennon)
...ko Ono)
...ons (John Lennon)
...Yoko Ono)
...n Lennon)
...here (Yoko Ono)
...ght line (John Lennon)
...oko Ono)
...blue (John Lennon)

Band of John and Yoko, 65 min.
D Fly, Erection, Up Your Legs Forever, 117 min.
E Fly, Erection, Smile Cold Turkey, 98 min.

MUSIC BY YOKO ONO
Saturday, October 9, 1:30 to 9:00 P.M.
WOOD PIECE '63 (for stringless piano)
interpreted by PHILIP CORNER
(and sometimes also by 3 assistants and audience)

LENNON TOURS TICKETS
visit Gloria Swanson 5 minutes before curtain time
visit Allan Klein for a free swim in his pool
visit Gene Sherman with request for expenses
visit Harold Syder for free problems
visit John & Lee Eastman to give your copyrights away
visit Al Steckler for a free record
tour to Betty Rollins legs panorama
visit Howard Smith to interview him
tour to Cortland Alley, New York City
ticket to Perham's Opera House, New York City
visit Pete Dennett to have your photo taken with him
visit Pres. Nixon in Washington
visit the House of Commons in 1885
20 hour bicycle trip to New York City
one way ticket to Statue of Liberty on the last ferry
9 hour round trip by bus to Cape May, N.J.
one way ticket to Goose Bay, Labrador
one way ticket to Fort Chimo, Hudson Strait
all inclusive 4 day stay in Greenland
one way ticket to North Siberia
40 day trip by local buses to Rio De Janeiro
15 hour walking tour around Manhattan Island
one way trip to Ginger Island
ticket to Fillmore East, N.Y.C.
overnight stay in Bronx Zoo, N.Y.C.
visit the Queen at Buckingham Palace
reservation to a future trip to the moon

VENDING ARCADE
Kinetoscope by John Lennon
Pinball Machines by John Lennon
Acorn Dispenser
Air Dispenser by Yoko Ono
Metal Slug Dispenser by John Lennon
Tear Dispenser by Yoko Ono
Juke Box by John Lennon

GALLERY OF PART PAINTINGS
Part paintings of: *cloud, glacier, moon, Ku Klux Klan, smog, albino, smoke, diamond from the Affair of the Diamond Necklace, harvest moon, star, snow, white corpuscle, White House, soda, sodium, rhodium, Battle of the Bulge, Mona Lisa's mole, Man with the Iron Mask, jig-saw puzzles.*

DO IT YOURSELF PAINTINGS
Draw Circle painting
Painting to Hammer a Nail
Painting to be slept on
Painting to be stepped on
Smoke painting

AMAZE built by Philis Knebel

SOUND PROOF ROOM built by Bill Gangi

FILM CLOCK (continuous showing)
Realized by Steve Gebhardt

HOLES
by Members of the depts. of Sculpture, Drama & Experimental Studios, School of Visual & Performing Arts, Syracuse University.

david a ross
director's assistant, everson museum

Jim Harithas had just given me a job as his assistant and and we drove down to the city to meet John & Yoko about Yoko's upcoming show. Jim knew I played guitar and he said, 'Your job is to take John and play guitar with him in another room while I work with Yoko.' And I thought to myself, 'I'm being paid a hundred dollars a week and my first job is to play guitar with John Lennon? Shit! Why was I thinking about being a journalist?' And I did get to spend a few days in a smoke-filled hotel suite with John Lennon playing guitar and that was a wonderful time, but what it really meant for me was the beginning of learning about artists, about art from artists, about the history of art, and more importantly, the purpose of art from artists.

Everything about the *This Is Not Here* show was beautifully put together. I still have the invitation – it was an unfixed photograph. You only had

a few seconds to look at it before it turned completely black and illegible. 'This Is Not Here'. This Is Not – what? What? What was the date? Where was it? Syracuse? What?

For the night of the opening as a birthday present for John, Yoko wanted a secret midnight jam session in our little two-hundred-seat theatre. Nicky Hopkins, Klaus Voormann, Ringo and some other musicians would be there. I didn't have the time to do it, so I said to a friend, 'Listen, I need you to set up these amps on stage in advance, and, you know, you can be there, but don't tell anyone.' Soon enough the word on the street was that there was going to be a Beatles reunion and thousands of people were camped outside the museum.

The night before the opening, a meeting was called at the Hotel Syracuse. The chief of police was

saying to Allen Klein, 'We're really concerned about the number of people and what might happen tomorrow and we're going to have to put some extra police on duty to take care of this.' Allen Klein reaches into his pocket and takes out a fat envelope, slides it across to the chief of police who puts it in his pocket and says, 'I think you can rest assured that there'll be no trouble tomorrow and no one will be harassed or busted.' That was a big insight. People everywhere were constantly trying to hustle them, or simply steal from them.

On the first night of the show, hordes of fans literally broke down the door. The entire museum filled up with people who were not going to be denied seeing the Beatles reunite. They were smoking pot, freaking out, so excited and then when word started filtering out that this wasn't going to happen, the mood started turning really dark. People

were angry and upset. Some artworks got broken. Then a miracle happened.

Allen Ginsberg and Peter Orlovsky were sat in the lower gallery where the Plexiglas maze was. Allen had his harmonium with him and he just started chanting, 'Om Shanti, Om Shanti Om' and within a half-hour it slowly spread throughout the gallery and throughout the whole museum. People were just sitting with their arms around each other, rocking back and forth, chanting with Allen Ginsberg. He completely turned the mood into something transcendent. It was the power of that chanting, the power of Allen's humanity that turned it all around.

A little birthday jam session did happen later, but only at the Hotel Syracuse, with just a few acoustic guitars.

But my fanboy experiences with John aside, what really mattered here was

that I had the opportunity to work with and learn from an artist as extraordinary as Yoko. Oddly enough, *This Is Not Here* seemed quite normal to me at the time, but in retrospect it has to be seen as a radically important event in American museum history.

Something that took me a long time to recognize and understand was the role that Yoko's genius played in the continuing evolution of John's artistic output, both as a musician and as a visual artist. For John, having a woman with a business sense like Yoko's on your team, finally someone that you could completely trust, who was brilliant at business and still is, was an incredible asset. Her father was one of the most important business leaders in the banking industry in post-war Japan, and she grew up with that mentality too. Yoko had two very important Russian aunts who were mentors – Anna Bubnova who was a world-class violinist and

Varvara Bubnova who was a very respected artist. These were the people who made her who she is.

Yoko was raised and educated to a very high standard and has a sense of the world that very few people of her generation have. She experienced first-hand what war means and what peace means. A lot of people understand that what happened to Japan should never happen again, but very few people have devoted their lives to it.

AMAZE, 1971, by Yoko Ono; *This Is Not Here* exhibition, Everson Museum of Art, Syracuse, New York, 9 – 27 October, 1971.
Previous pages: *This Is Not Here* exhibition map annotated by George Maciunas, 1971.
Following pages: stills of footage from the opening of *This Is Not Here* exhibition, Everson Museum of Art, Syracuse, New York, 9 October 1971.

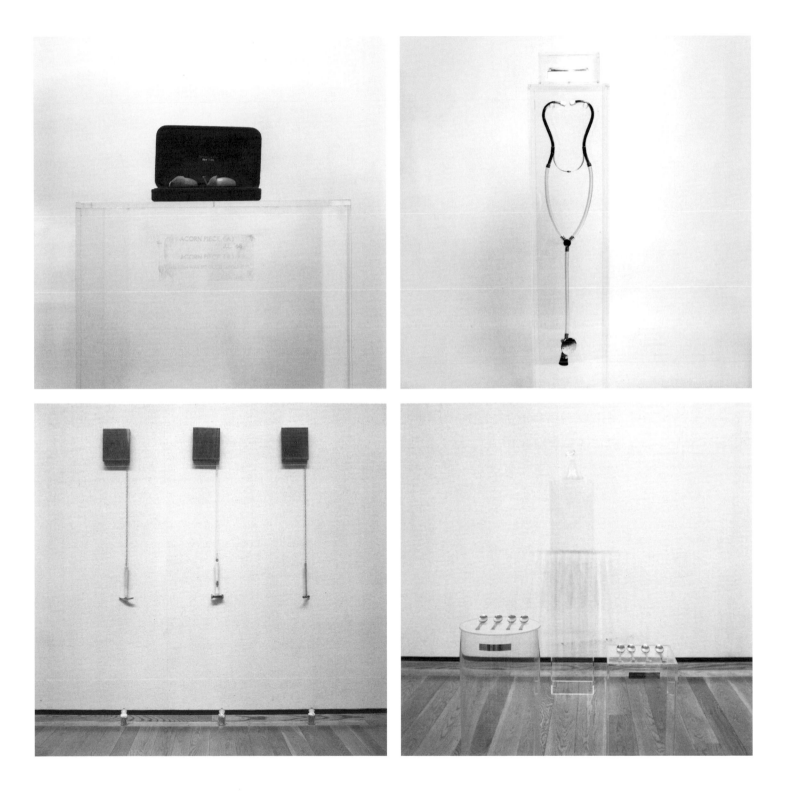

This page and opposite: artworks displayed at *This Is Not Here* exhibition, Everson Museum of Art, Syracuse, New York, 9 – 27 October 1971. This page, clockwise from top left: *Acorns* 1968 (John Lennon & Yoko Ono), *Eternal Time*, 1965 (Yoko Ono), *Four Spoons*, 1971 (John Lennon), alongside *Three Spoons*, 1967 (Yoko Ono), *Painting to Hammer A Nail* (3), 1961/1966 (Yoko Ono). Opposite: *White Chess Set,* 1966 (Yoko Ono) with *You Are Here*, 1968 (John Lennon).

O, YOKO

IN THE MIDDLE OF A BATH
IN THE MIDDLE OF A BATH I CALL YOUR NAME
O, YOKO

IN THE MIDDLE OF A SHAVE
IN THE MIDDLE OF A SHAVE I CALL YOUR NAME
O, YOKO   MY LOVE WILL TURN YOU ON
             "   "   "   "   "   "

IN THE MIDDLE OF THE SEA
IN THE MIDDLE OF THE SEA I CALL YOUR NAME
O, YOKO

IN THE MIDDLE OF THE NIGHT
IN THE MIDDLE OF THE NIGHT I CALL YOUR NAME
O, YOKO MY LOVE WILL TURN YOU ON
            "   "   " "   "   ""

                              cloud
IN THE MIDDLE OF A ~~WIND~~
IN THE MIDDLE OF A ~~WIND~~ I CALL YOUR NAME
O, YOKO   cloud

IN THE MIDDLE OF A DREAM
IN THE MIDDLE OF A DREAM I CALL YOUR NAME
O' YOKO   MY LOVE WILL TURN YOU ON

oh yoko!

In the middle of the night
In the middle of the night I call your name

Oh Yoko, oh Yoko
My love will turn you on

In the middle of a bath
In the middle of a bath I call your name

Oh Yoko, oh Yoko
My love will turn you on
My love will turn you on

In the middle of a shave
in the middle of a shave I call your name

Oh Yoko, oh Yoko
My love will turn you on

In the middle of a dream
In the middle of a dream I call your name

Oh Yoko, oh Yoko
My love will turn you on
My love will turn you on

In the middle of a cloud
In the middle of a cloud I call your name

Oh Yoko, oh Yoko
My love will turn you on

Oh Yoko, oh Yoko
Oh Yoko, oh Yoko
Oh Yoko, oh Yoko

oh yoko!

John: There's a song I wrote in 1968 called 'Oh Yoko!' An easy come, easy go song – like whistling down the lane to meet your lover: 'She's mine and I'm always singing/thinking/being/about her.' It came naturally. We did one take and enjoyed it.

Phil and me worked on the backing chorus later. I always do the wrong songs first, so when it's time to sing softly, I've wrecked my throat rocking!! I'll never learn. 'Twist And Shout' was recorded at the end of a twelve-hour session! Jeezus, what torture. (Old man reminiscence.)

My most happy moments are since I met Yoko. The simplest way of saying what Yoko is to me is that before we met, we were half a person. There is a myth about people being half and the other half being in the sky or in heaven or something, or the other side of the universe, or the mirror image bit. We are two halves and together we are a whole. Half the way I'm thinking – musically, philosophically and every other way – is her influence both as a woman and an artist.

My biography now reads: 'Born, lived and met Yoko.' Whatever I went through was worth it to meet Yoko. So, if I had to do all the things I did in my life – which is have a troubled childhood, a troubled teenage life and an amazing whirlwind life with the Beatles, and then finally coming to land meeting Yoko – it was worth it. Yoko is the beginning of life for me.

Yoko: Between us, we were very psychic. We knew all the time what the other was thinking, what was going to be said by the other, our responses, everything. It was sometimes unnerving.

John: We both think alike. We've both been alone. And we seem to have had the same kind of dreams when we were alone. I can see now that I always dreamed of a woman like this one coming into my life. You can't go out looking for this kind of relationship. It's like somebody was planning it from above.

Yoko: Yes, it was hard, but he and I had no doubt we would get through. John's excitement at doing things together with me as an artist was so obvious that he didn't have that much time to get upset about what people were thinking.

John: We'd like to be remembered as the Romeo and Juliet of the 1970s.

Yoko: When people get cynical about love, they should look at us and see that it is possible.

John: There is nothing more important than our relationship, nothing. We dig being together all the time, and both of us could survive apart, but what for? I'm not going to sacrifice love, real love, for any fuckin' whore, or any friend, or any business, because in the end, you're alone at night. Neither of us want to be, and you can't fill the bed with groupies. I don't want to be a swinger. Like I said in the song, I've been through it all, and nothing works better than to have somebody you love hold you.

I'm completely positive, and when I'm negative I've got Yoko who is just as strong as me. And it helps. And this is only the beginning. The Sixties were just waking up in the morning and we haven't even got to dinner time yet and I can't wait. I'm so glad to be around and it's just going to be great and there's going to be more and more of us, and whatever you're thinking there, Mrs Grundy of South Birmingham on toast, you don't stand a chance: (a) you're not going to be there when we're running it and (b) you're gonna like it when you get less frightened of it.

Jann Wenner: Do you have a picture of 'When I'm 64'?

John: I hope we're a nice old couple living off the coast of Ireland or something like that – looking at our scrapbook of madness.

My ultimate goal is for Yoko and I to be happy and try and make other people happy through our happiness. I'd like everyone to remember us with a smile. But, if possible, just as John & Yoko who created world peace forever.

The whole of life is a preparation for death. I'm not worried about dying. When we go, we'd like to leave behind a better place.

Yoko: It was such an incredible loss when I think about it. Every day was different because he made it well for me. Because he knew what I was going through, being a certain race and being a woman as well, all that, he had an incredible concern about it. See, most people think, 'Well, he's a rocker and just kind of rough, maybe,' but no. At home he was a very gentle person and extremely concerned about me but also concerned about the world too. I still miss him, especially now because the world is not quite right and everybody seems to be suffering. And if he was here it would have been different, I think.

I think that in many ways John was a simple Liverpool man right to the end. He was a chameleon, a bit of a chauvinist, but so human. In our fourteen years together he never stopped trying to improve himself from within. We were best friends. To me, he is still alive. Death alone doesn't extinguish a flame and a spirit like John.

Polaroid multi-exposure portrait by John Lennon, inscribed on verso:
'Portrait of my flower girl – Yoko. XMAS DAY Sunday with love to Yoko from John xxx'.
Following pages: filming *Imagine*: searching for one another in the fog;
Tittenhurst grounds, 21 July 1971.

legacy

strawberry fields, new york

Yoko: In memory of John Lennon, New York City has designated a beautiful triangular island in Central Park to be known as Strawberry Fields. It happens to be where John and I took our last walk together. John would have been very proud that this was given to him, an island named after his song, rather than a statue or monument.

During his career with the Beatles and in his solo work, John's music gave hope and inspiration to people around the world. His campaign for peace lives on, symbolized here at Strawberry Fields.

This tranquil section of Central Park was named after one of the Beatles' best-known songs, 'Strawberry Fields Forever'. Recorded in 1966, the song's title comes from an orphanage in Liverpool, England, where John used to go to play. His aunt, who raised him, disapproved but he insisted it was 'nothing to get hung about'. Hence the song's famous lyric.

Strawberry Fields was officially dedicated on 9 October 1985 – the forty-fifth anniversary of John's birth. I worked with landscape architect Bruce Kelly and the Central Park Conservancy to create a 2.5-acre meditative spot. The iconic black-and-white mosaic was created by Italian craftsmen and given as a gift by the city of Naples.

Based on a Greco-Roman design, it bears the word: 'Imagine'.

That song was John's plea for us all to envision a world without conflict or division, and imagine instead a world of peace. He wrote those lyrics from a place of incredibly deep love and immense hope for our future.

A designated 'Quiet Zone' in the Park, the memorial is shaded by stately American elms and lined with benches. In the warmer months, flowers bloom all around the area. Along the path near the mosaic, you'll find a bronze plaque that lists the 121 countries that endorse Strawberry Fields as a Garden of Peace.

Yoko Ono Lennon with Julian Lennon and Sean Lennon at the groundbreaking ceremony for a $1-million, 2.5-acre garden memorial to John Lennon: Strawberry Fields, 21 March 1984. Plaque: 'The restoration of this part of Central Park as a Garden of Peace, endorsed by the nations listed on the plaque, was made possible through the generosity of Yoko Ono Lennon.' Previous pages and opposite: the iconic black-and-white *Imagine* mosaic was created by Italian craftsmen based on a Greco-Roman design and given as a gift by the city of Naples to John's memorial garden, Strawberry Fields, Central Park, New York, for its inauguration by Yoko Ono Lennon, Julian Lennon and Sean Lennon on 9 October 1985.

IMAGINA A PAZ

رویای صلح   IMMAGINA LA PACE   חלום שלום

ཞི་བདེ་སྐྱིད་མས།   წარმოიდგინეთ მშვიდობა

BARIŞI DÜŞLE   ILARAWAN ANG MUNDONG MAPAYAPA

평화를 꿈꾸자   IMAGINA LA PAZ

ᓴᐃᒻᒪᖃᑎᒌᓐᓂᖅ   IMAGINE PEACE   احلم سلام

KUVITTELE RAUHA   想像世界有了和平

STELL DIR VOR ES IST FRIEDEN   HUGSA SÉR FRIÐ

TUFIKIRIENI AMANI   KÉPZELD EL A BÉKÉT

IMAGINEZ LA PAIX   சமாதானத்தை நினையுங்கள்

ПРЕДСТАВЬТЕ СЕБЕ МИР   शान्ति की कल्पना करें

平和な世界を想像してごらん

love, yoko

IMAGINE PEACE

by yoko ono

Yoko: What is wrong with war, is, as Gandhi said, 'an eye for
an eye makes all of us blind'. I'd like to see the human race
wake up to the danger and futility of war as soon as
possible. At the time, in the Sixties, we thought we could
change the world just like that! But it's taking a little bit more time!

IMAGINE PEACE is a powerful, universal mantra that we
should all meditate on. With it, we will achieve the impossible.
Hopefully, without bloodshed. Look at all the courageous people
who are now being hurt in marches andthrown in prisons for
no other reason except for carrying 'Peace, Love and Freedom'
in their hearts and voicing it.

I don't want you to get hurt. You shouldn't have to. Seven billion
of us, people of the world, have the birthright to live with a healthy
mind and body at all times. You should not even get one scratch
on you, and you won't, if you don't allow it.

So keep IMAGINE PEACE in your head. Have a clear picture
of where we stand, what we are doing, and where we want
to be. Know that we are connected in our hearts and minds.

Thoughts are infectious. Send it out.
The message will circulate faster than you think.

Remember:
A dream you dream alone is only a dream;
A dream you dream together is reality.

So stand up, speak out, and come together.

Our land is still whole with wisdom and wealth;
It brings with energy beauty and health.
Seven billion of us dreaming together.
It's Time for Action, the Action is PEACE.

Think PEACE, Act PEACE, Spread PEACE.
Shed light in darkness.

IMAGINE PEACE.

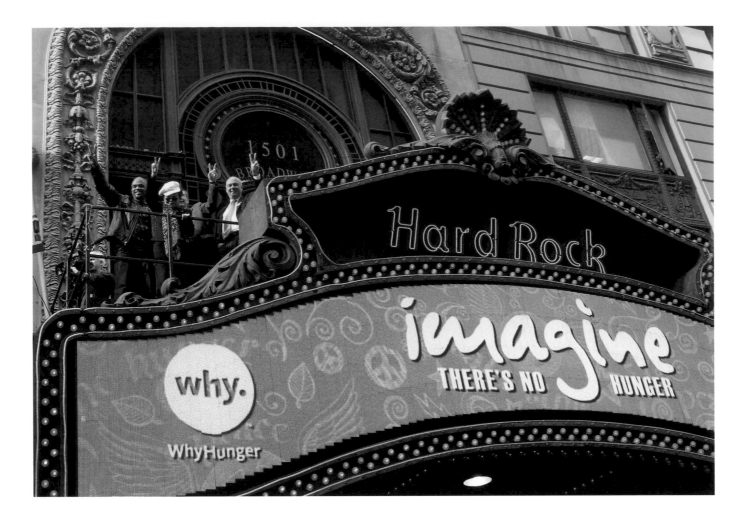

imagine there's no hunger

Today, there are 815 million people in the world — one in every nine – who experience hunger. A startling one in every four children around the globe doesn't have enough to eat. In the face of the obscenity of those statistics, it may seem difficult to imagine John Lennon & Yoko Ono Lennon's vision of world with no hunger.

For decades, Yoko Ono Lennon has worked with WhyHunger on a global campaign called 'Imagine There's No Hunger' to end childhood hunger and address its root causes. By harnessing the power of John & Yoko's iconic song 'Imagine', WhyHunger has been able to build awareness, activate the public and engage celebrity ambassadors to raise more than $6.8 million to support community-led efforts to end hunger around the globe. Together, we are making John & Yoko's vision a reality.

WhyHunger's 'Imagine There's No Hunger' campaign works with grassroots partners around the world to grow nutritious food for children and their families, teach sustainable farming for a future free from hunger and support social movements. To fuel the campaign, WhyHunger teams up with corporate partners, like Hard Rock International, to raise funds and awareness from hundreds of thousands of individual donors. Through nearly a decade of traditional

and social media, the tremendous support of Yoko Ono Lennon and the involvement of key celebrity influencers, like Ringo Starr, Forest Whitaker, Joss Stone, Darryl 'DMC' McDaniels and OAR, #ImagineNoHunger has also educated and activated hundreds of thousands of supporters across the globe. Through an ongoing media and messaging campaign, WhyHunger is raising awareness on the issues of childhood hunger and challenging the traditional charitable approach to end hunger to instead focus on solutions that are community-led, environmentally sustainable and long-term.

Funds raised through the 'Imagine There's No Hunger' campaign have supported forty-eight grassroots initiatives in thirty-one countries to implement sustainable food solutions to nourish people, empower individuals and transform communities. Through these community-led food production and social justice projects, more than 10 million nutritious meals were provided to children and more than 45,728 farmers were trained to grow healthy food using agro-ecological practices that work in harmony with the Earth. Today, tens of thousands of families are growing healthy food and sharing their knowledge with others, multiplying the impact of the 'Imagine There's No Hunger' campaign and improving the future for children and their communities.

Inspired by John & Yoko's vision of a world at peace and free from hunger, WhyHunger calls for the rights to land, water, seeds and training to ensure all children, and their families, have access to healthy food and a dignified life without hunger. WhyHunger believes that nutritious food is a human right, and works to protect the right for all people to live in dignity, free from hunger, food insecurity and malnutrition.

WhyHunger believes its critical to support communities' initiatives and creative power to change their lives by not just meeting their immediate nutritional needs each day, but by supporting grassroots-led efforts as well as engaging others across geographical boundaries to create a chain of solidarity and mutual learning.

WhyHunger's strategy of partnering with grassroots organizations and providing resources to support community-based solutions has proven radically successful both in the efficiency of the investments and the scope of our results. Through strategic partnerships across the US and around the world, WhyHunger has been able to make a substantial impact in alleviating hunger in dozens of communities through long-term, systems-level change. In our forty-year history, WhyHunger has built relationships with thousands of grassroots organizations and social movements in the

US and abroad and we are poised to significantly scale up this effective strategy.

Imagine There's No Hunger's Impact on Building a Better World:

- $6.8 million raised to fight childhood hunger.
- Communities in thirty-one countries growing food sustainably.
- More than 10 million nutritious meals provided to children.
- 45,728 farmers trained to grow healthy food using agroecological practices that work in harmony with the earth.

Yoko Ono: The IMAGINE THERE'S NO HUNGER campaign challenges us to help change the lives of hungry children and families all across the globe. Together, we can work to create a hunger-free existence for all, and realize the peaceful world my husband, John Lennon, and I envisioned.

Children from Kenya, Haiti, Indonesia, Thailand, South Africa, Venezuela and New Orleans are just some of those benefiting from the campaign. Opposite: Yoko Ono Lennon with Hamish Dodds (Hard Rock) and Bill Ayres (Why Hunger) at the Hard Rock Café as they launch the 'Imagine There's No Hunger' campaign in Times Square, New York, 1 November 2011.

IMAGINE PEACE TOWER

IMAGINE PEACE TOWER is an outdoor work of art
conceived by Yoko Ono in memory of John Lennon.
It is situated on Viðey Island in Reykjavík, Iceland. The
artwork was dedicated to John by Yoko at its unveiling
on 9 October 2007, John Lennon's sixty-seventh birthday.

IMAGINE PEACE TOWER is a tall, shimmering tower
of lights which emanates wisdom, healing and joy.
It communicates awareness to the whole world that peace
and love is what connects all lives on Earth. It symbolizes
Lennon's and Ono's continuing campaign for world peace,
which began in the Sixties, was sealed by their marriage
in 1969 and will continue forever. Inscribed on the walls
of the Wishing Well is the phrase IMAGINE PEACE,
translated into twenty-four different languages.

It appears every year and is visible from 9 October
(John's birthday) until 8 December (the anniversary
of his death). In addition, the Tower will illuminate from
Winter Solstice (21 December) and into the morning of
the New Year (1 January) as well as the first week of spring
(20–27 March) the dates of John & Yoko's wedding and
honeymoon. It is lit from one hour after sunset until midnight,
and until dawn on New Year's Day. On 9 October and from
20–27 March, it lights at 8 p.m. In tribute to Yoko, who
was made an honorary citizen of Reykjavík in 2013, the
City of Reykjavík also lights IMAGINE PEACE TOWER
on her birthday, 18 February, from 7 p.m. until 9 a.m.
the following day.

One of the mesmerizing features of the IMAGINE PEACE
TOWER is that the strength, intensity and brilliance of its
light continually changes with the prevailing weather and
atmospheric conditions unique to Iceland. On a cloudless
night, it creates a clear pillar of light. In rain or snowfall,
you can see the beams iridescing with rainbow refractions.
When cloudy, it dramatically lights up and reflects off any
moving layers of cloud.

Send your wishes to IMAGINE PEACE TOWER by Twitter,
email or post, at any one of Yoko's worldwide Wish Tree
installations, or create your own Wish Tree. Find out more
at www.IMAGINEPEACETOWER.com.

DEDICATION

I dedicate this light tower to John Lennon
my love for you is forever
yoko ono
9 October 2007

UNVEILING SPEECH BY YOKO ONO

All spirits of goodness of this magical land, of the planet,
and of the universe,
thank you, thank you, thank you, for witnessing our humble
gathering for the unveiling of IMAGINE PEACE TOWER.

They say that if all the people in China were to jump up
and down at the same time,
the axis of the globe would shift.

Well, we are here together.
Billions of us.

Standing at the dawn of a new age determined to shift the
axis of the world to health,
peace and joy by loving and caring for all lives on Earth.

Some of us are here physically, some are joining us in spirit.
Some of us are imprisoned, tortured, maimed and silenced,
but they are also here today with us.
Some of us have passed away before being able to enjoy
a new age of love and peace.
But we are all here today standing together with hope.

The light is the light of wisdom, healing and empowerment.
Even in the moments of confusion, fear and the darkness
of your souls, hold the light in your hearts, and you will know
that you are not alone, that we are all together in seeing
the light of peace.

I thank the people of Iceland, for having given so much
love to this tower from its inception.
IMAGINE PEACE TOWER was visualized with love,
and realized by love.
It is a gift from John & Yoko and the people of Iceland
to the world.

I know that John is with us, too, in this land of Nutopia,
happy that the light tower is finally a reality after
forty years.

Let's make a wish as the light goes on.

Let's send light to each other and say I love you!

i ii iii

John, we love you!

Yoko Ono Lennon
9 October 2007
IMAGINE PEACE TOWER, Reykjavík, Iceland

sources of illustrations

a = above, b = below, c = centre, l = left, r = right

Film stills

Stills of footage and outtakes from the 1971 film *Imagine*, directed by John & Yoko: Cameramen: Nic Knowland, John Metcalfe and Richard Stanley (UK), Bob Fries (USA) © Yoko Ono Lennon. Includes footage directed and filmed by Jonas Mekas of the Betty Klein party and Fluxus Hudson trip © Jonas Mekas: 10–11, 30, 37, 42–43, 50–51, 57, 58, 68–69, 76–77, 85, 101, 102–103, 116–117, 121, 129, 133, 134–135, 136r, 141c, 144–145, 146, 179, 185, 215, 220–221, 224–225, 226–227, 228–229, 232–233, 238–239, 244–245, 252–253, 256–257, 262–263, 266–267, 270, 272–273

Stills of George Maciunas' dumpling party from *Three Friends* directed and filmed by Jonas Mekas © Jonas Mekas: 249

Stills from the outtakes of *ONO* (*The Making of FLY*) filmed by Dan Seymour © Yoko Ono Lennon: 236a, 237, 240

Stills from *Clock*, directed by John & Yoko, filmed by Steve Gebhardt © Yoko Ono Lennon: 178, 179

Stills of footage from opening of *This Is Not Here*, Everson Gallery, 1971, filmed by Bob Fries and Doug Ibold © Yoko Ono: 292–293

Illustrations

Illustrations by Planet Illustration © Yoko Ono Lennon: 46–47, 61, 62, 66, 100

Photography

1 Photo by Yoko Ono © Yoko Ono Lennon; 4–5 Photo by Iain MacMillan © Yoko Ono Lennon; 6–7 Photo by Peter Fordham © Yoko Ono Lennon; 8–9 Photos by Iain MacMillan © Yoko Ono Lennon; 12 Photo by Sam Gannon © Yoko Ono Lennon; 14 Photo by Ann Terada © Yoko Ono Lennon; 17 Drawing by John Lennon © Yoko Ono Lennon; 18l, c Photos by Iain MacMillan © Yoko Ono; 18r Photo by Michael Sirriani © Yoko Ono; 19l, c Photos by Iain MacMillan © Yoko Ono; 19r Photo by Sam Gannon © Yoko Ono; 20–21 Kiss of John Lennon and Yoko Ono, The 24th Cannes Film Festival May 1971 © Claude Azoulay; 22l Photo by Leslie Bryce for *The Beatles Book*; 22r Mirrorpix; 23l Design by John Lennon © Yoko Ono Lennon; 23r Photo by Ivor Sharp © Yoko Ono Lennon; 24 Photo by David Behl © Yoko Ono Lennon; 27 © Barrie Wentzell; 28–29 Photos by Michael Sirriani © Yoko Ono Lennon; 33 Photo by Peter Fordham © Yoko Ono Lennon; 34 Photo by Simon Hilton © Yoko Ono Lennon; 35 Photo by Marcia Bassett © Yoko Ono Lennon; 38–39 Photo by Michael Putland/Getty Images; 40 Photo by Yoko Ono © Yoko Ono Lennon; 45 Photo by Peter Fordham © Yoko Ono Lennon; 48 Associated Newspapers/REX/Shutterstock; 49al Tracksimages.com/Alamy Stock Photo; 49ar, cl, cr, bl, br Associated Newspapers/REX/Shutterstock; 53 Photo by Peter Fordham © Yoko Ono Lennon; 54 Photo by Iain MacMillan © Yoko Ono Lennon; 60al Photo by Peter Fordham © Yoko Ono Lennon; 60ar, cl, cr, bl, br Photos by Tom Hanley © Yoko Ono Lennon; 63, 64–65 Photos by Peter Fordham © Yoko Ono; 67al, cl, cr, bl Photos by Tom Hanley © Yoko Ono Lennon; 67ar Photo by Kieron Murphy © Yoko Ono Lennon; 67br Photo by Peter Fordham © Yoko Ono Lennon; 70–71, 72–73 Photos by Kieron Murphy © Yoko Ono Lennon; 74–75, 78–79 Photos by Peter Fordham © Yoko Ono Lennon; 80 Photos by Sam Gannon © Yoko Ono Lennon; 82, 86–87 Photos by Kieron Murphy © Yoko Ono Lennon; 88 Lenono Photo Archive © Yoko Ono Lennon; 91 Photo courtesy Yoko Ono Lennon; 92–93 Photos by Sam Gannon and Beth Walsh © Yoko Ono Lennon; 95 Photo by Tom Hanley © Yoko Ono Lennon; 97 Photo by Peter Fordham © Yoko Ono Lennon; 98 Plans by Eddie Veale © Yoko Ono Lennon; 99 Photos courtesy Veale Associates; 104 Photo by Sam Gannon and Beth Walsh © Yoko Ono Lennon; 106 Photo by Kieron Murphy © Yoko Ono Lennon; 108 Photo by Peter Fordham © Yoko Ono Lennon; 110–111, 112 Photos by Kieron Murphy © Yoko Ono Lennon; 115 Photo by Peter Fordham © Yoko Ono Lennon; 118–119 Photos by Kieron Murphy © Yoko Ono Lennon; 120 Photo by John Lennon © Yoko Ono Lennon; 122–123 Drawings © Klaus Voormann; 126 Lenono Photo Archive © Yoko Ono Lennon; 131 Photo by Peter Fordham © Yoko Ono Lennon; 132 © Ethan Russell; 136l © Bob Gruen / www.bobgruen.com; 137 Photos courtesy Yoko Ono Lennon; 138–139 Photo by Kieron Murphy © Yoko Ono Lennon; 140l, c Photos courtesy Yoko Ono Lennon; 140r Photo courtesy Mike Pinder; 141l Photo by Michael Ochs Archives/Getty Images; 141r Photo by Jorgen Angel/Redferns; 142–143 Lyric sheets © Yoko Ono Lennon. Photos © Christie's Images / Bridgeman Images; 147l Photo © Roger Dean 1974; 147r Photo by Dick Barnatt/Redferns; 148 Lenono Photo Archive © Yoko Ono Lennon; 150 © Barrie Wentzell; 151 Photo by Peter Fordham © Yoko Ono Lennon; 152–153 Photo © 1993 Christie's Images Limited; 154–155 Letter © Yoko Ono Lennon. Photos courtesy Bonhams; 156–157 © Bob Gruen/www.bobgruen.com; 158 Photo by John Lennon © Yoko Ono Lennon; 159l Photo courtesy Jay Messina; 159r © Bob Gruen/www.bobgruen.com; 160 Photo by John Lennon © Yoko Ono Lennon; 161 Photos courtesy Gilbert Pictorial Enterprise; 162 Photo courtesy Lisa Zito and Helen Merrill Zito; 163, 164 Lenono Photo Archive © Yoko Ono Lennon; 167, 168 Photos by Iain MacMillan © Yoko Ono Lennon; 170 Photo by Janet Goodman, courtesy of ABKCO Archives; 171 Photo by Kieron Murphy © Yoko Ono Lennon; 172 Photos by Stanley E. Michels © The Estate of Stanley Michels (2008), used with kind permission; 173al, bl Photo by John Lennon © Yoko Ono Lennon; 173ar, br Photo by Jonas Mekas © Yoko Ono Lennon. From the personal archives of Jonas Mekas; 174 Apple Corps. Photo courtesy Paddle 8; 175 Pictorial Press Ltd/AlamyStock Photo; 176 Postcard © Yoko Ono Lennon. Photo courtesy Record Mecca; 177 Photo courtesy Allan Steckler; 180 Photos courtesy Yoko Ono Lennon; 181 Photos courtesy Allan Steckler; 182 Lenono Photo Archive © Yoko Ono Lennon; 187 Photo by Peter Fordham © Yoko Ono Lennon; 188 Photos by John Lennon © Yoko Ono Lennon; 189, 190–191 Photos by Yoko Ono © Yoko Ono Lennon; 192 Artwork © Geoffrey Hendricks. Photo © Yoko Ono Lennon; 193l Artwork © Geoffrey Hendricks. Hendricks Geoffrey (b.1931): Invitation for Fluxdivorce, 331 West 20th Street, New York, June 24, 1971. Offset lithograph on two sheets. The Gilbert and Lila Silverman Fluxus Collection Gift. Digital Image © 2018 The Museum of Modern Art, New York/Scala, Florence; 193ar Artwork © Geoffrey Hendricks. Geoffrey Hendricks Flux Divorce Box with Flux Divorce Album (cut version), 1972–1973 Mixed technique, Mixed media; box: 36.83 x 50.8 x 10.16 cm (14 1/2 x 20 x 4 in.) Harvard Art Museums/Fogg Museum, Barbara and Peter Moore Fluxus Collection, Margaret Fisher Fund and gift of Barbara Moore/Bound & Unbound, M26410 Photo: Imaging Department © President and Fellows of Harvard College; 193br Artwork © Geoffrey Hendricks. Photo © Yoko Ono Lennon; 194–195 Artwork © Yoko Ono Lennon. Photo © Christie's Images / Bridgeman Images; 196, 197a Design by John Lennon, typography by George Maciunas © Yoko Ono Lennon; 197b Design by John Lennon, photo by Peter Fordham © Yoko Ono Lennon; 198al Photo by George Maciunas, courtesy Yoko Ono; 198ar Photo by John Lennon © Yoko Ono Lennon. From the personal archives of Jonas Mekas; 198b © Barrie Wentzell; 200 Design by John Lennon, photo by Peter Fordham © Yoko Ono Lennon; 201cl, bl Design by John Lennon, photo by Peter Fordham © Yoko Ono Lennon. From the collection of Julian Lennon; 201ar, cr Photocollage and text by John Lennon © Yoko Ono Lennon. Photos courtesy iCollector; 202 Lenono Photo Archive © Yoko Ono Lennon; 205 © Matthew Lewis, *The Washington Post*, Reprinted with Permission; 206–207 Photos by John Lennon © Yoko Ono; 208–209b Design by Yoko Ono, photocollage by George Maciunas © Yoko Ono; 209al, ar Artwork by Yoko Ono © Yoko Ono; 210 Artwork by Yoko Ono © Yoko Ono; 211a, bl, bcr Concept by Yoko Ono, Photo by Raeanne Rubenstein © Yoko Ono; 211bcl, br Design by Yoko Ono © Yoko Ono; 212 Lenono Photo Archive © Yoko Ono Lennon; 217 Photo by Kieron Murphy © Yoko Ono Lennon; 218–219 © Yoko Ono Lennon; 222 Concept by Yoko Ono, Photo by Iain MacMillan © Yoko Ono Lennon; 230–231, 234–235 Photos by Peter Fordham © Yoko Ono Lennon; 236b Photo by Marcia Bassett © Yoko Ono Lennon; 241, 242–243, 246 Photos by Iain MacMillan © Yoko Ono Lennon; 247 Photo by Iain MacMillan, courtesy Doug Ibold; 248 Photos by John Lennon © Yoko Ono Lennon. From the personal archives of Jonas Mekas; 250–251 Photo by Peter Fordham © Yoko Ono Lennon; 254 © BBC; 255 Photo by ABC Photo Archives/ABC via Getty Images; 258–259 Photo by Iain MacMillan © Yoko Ono Lennon; 260–261 Photo by Iain MacMillan © Yoko Ono Lennon; 264 Photos by Iain MacMillan © Yoko Ono Lennon; 265 Photo by John Reader, Courtesy of Yoko Ono; 269 © David Bailey; 271 Photo by Marcia Bassett © Yoko Ono Lennon; 274 Lenono Photo Archive © Yoko Ono Lennon; 277 Photo by Peter Fordham © Yoko Ono Lennon; 278l Note by John Lennon © Yoko Ono Lennon; 278r, 279 Notes by Yoko Ono © Yoko Ono; 280–281 Concept by Yoko Ono, design by George Maciunas © Yoko Ono; 282–283 Design by John Lennon © Yoko Ono Lennon; 284 Photo by Iain MacMillan © Yoko Ono Lennon; 285 Note by John Lennon © Yoko Ono Lennon; 287 Photo by Iain MacMillan © Yoko Ono; 288–289 Design by George Maciunas © Yoko Ono; 290–291, 294–295 Photos by Iain MacMillan © Yoko Ono; 296 Lyric sheet © Yoko Ono Lennon. Photo © Christie's Images/Bridgeman Images; 299 Photo by John Lennon © Yoko Ono Lennon; 300–301 Photos by Peter Fordham © Yoko Ono Lennon; 302–303, 304al Photos by Simon Hilton © Yoko Ono Lennon; 304ar, bl Photos by Harry Hamburg/NY Daily News Archive via Getty Images; 304br © Bob Gruen/www.bobgruen.com; 305 Michele Falzone/ Alamy Stock Photo; 306 © Yoko Ono; 308 Photo by Laura Cavanaugh/FilmMagic; 309al, ac WhyHunger courtesy of Roots and Shoots; 309ar Hazel Thompson; 309bl WhyHunger courtesy of Project Bona Fide; 309bc WhyHunger courtesy of The Learning Farm; 309br WhyHunger courtesy of Common Ground; 311–312 Photos by Earthcam © Yoko Ono; 313 Photo by TetsuRo Hamada © Yoko Ono; 320 © Yoko Ono Lennon

references

15 Yoko Ono Lennon, 2018

16 John Lennon, 1968 published in *Skywriting By Word Of Mouth*, Pan Books, 1986

18–23 Audio interview: Andy Peebles, BBC Radio, 6 December 1980; Dave Sholin,
RKO, 8 December 1980; David Scheff, 10–28 September 1980
Book: Ray Coleman, *John Ono Lennon*, 1986
Essay: Yoko Ono, *John Lennon Anthology*, 1998
Film interview: Abram de Swaan, *Rood Wit Blau*, Vara TV, 12 December 1968
Print interviews: Jonathan Cott, *Rolling Stone*, 18 March 1971 and 5 December
1980; Peter McCabe and Robert Schonfeld, *Penthouse* magazine,
5 September 1971; Roy Carr, *New Musical Express*, 7 Oct. 1972
TV interview: Mike Douglas Show, CBS TV, 31 January – 7 February 1972;
Tom Cottle, 1986

24–25 Lyrics: 'Imagine'. Written by John Lennon & Yoko Ono © 1971 Lenono Music.

26–36 Audio interview: Andy Peebles, BBC Radio, 6 December 1980; Dave Sholin,
RKO, 8 December 1980; David Scheff, 10–28 September 1980;
Jody Denburg, 1 February 2002
Book: John Lennon, *Skywriting By Word Of Mouth*, 1986; Ray Coleman,
John Ono Lennon, 1986
Essay: John Lennon – 'Lennon on Imagine', *Crawdaddy*, 5 December 1971
Interview: Ray Coleman
Letter: John Lennon, *Melody Maker*, 13 December 1971; John Lennon,
to cousin Leila, January 1979
Online: Yoko Ono, Facebook and Twitter Q&As, imaginepeace.com, 2009–2016
Press Conference: Yoko Ono, Seoul, 2003
Print interview: Andrew Smith, *The Observer*, 4 November 2001, Jonathan
Cott, *Rolling Stone*, 5 December 1980; Peter McCabe and Robert Schonfeld,
Penthouse magazine, 5 September 1971
Radio interview: Howard Cosell, 'Speaking of Everything', WABC, 6 October 1974
TV interview: Jane Middlemiss, ITV Orange Playlist, 9 November 2006;
Michael Parkinson, BBC TV, 1971; Mike Douglas Show, CBS TV,
31 January–7 February 1972; Tom Cottle, 1986

26–7 Dedication written by Yoko Ono, 1967
Poems: 'Cloud Piece', 1963, *Grapefruit*, Wunternaum Press, 1964;
'Drinking Piece For Orchestra', 1963, *Grapefruit*, Wunternaum Press, 1964;
'Tunafish Sandwich Piece', 1964, *Grapefruit*, Wunternaum Press, 1964
Written response by John Lennon, 1967

32 Print interview: Jonathan Cott, *Rolling Stone*, 5 December 1980

41 Audio interview: Andy Peebles, BBC Radio, 6 December 1980

44 Essay: Yoko Ono, *John Lennon Anthology*, 1998

50 Essay: Julian Lennon, 2018
Film interview: Andrew Solt, *Gimme Some Truth*, 1984

52 Audio interviews: Simon Hilton, 2016–2018

53 Audio interview: Simon Hilton, 2016

55 Audio interview: Simon Hilton, 2017–2018

56 Audio interview: Simon Hilton, 2017

59 Audio interviews: Simon Hilton, 2016–2017

70–71 Audio interview: Simon Hilton, 2017

81 Audio recording of Curt Claudio reading aloud the telegrams he wrote
to John & Yoko, Lenono Film Archive, 26 May 1971

83 Radio interview: Alex Bennett, WPLJ, 9 June 1971
Film interview: Andrew Solt, *Gimme Some Truth*, 1984
Audio interviews: Simon Hilton, 2016–2018

84 Audio: Lenono Film Archive, recorded 26 May 1971

88–89 Lyrics: 'Crippled Inside'. Written by John Lennon © 1971 Lenono Music

90 Audio interview: David Scheff, 10–28 September 1980;
Kenji Mizuhara, Apple Tokyo, 2 September 1971
Book: Ray Coleman, *John Ono Lennon*, 1986
Essays: Yoko Ono – 'Feeling The Space' liner notes, 1973;
Yoko Ono – 'When Molecules Rise, They Converge', 1995
Print interview: Jonathan Cott, *Rolling Stone*, 18 March 1971
TV interview: *Mike Douglas Show*, CBS TV, 31 January – 7 February 1972

94 TV interview: *Mike Douglas Show*, CBS TV, 31 January – 7 February 1972
Audio interview: *Kenny Everett Radio Show*, 1971
Print interview: *New Musical Express*, 31 July 1971

96–98 Audio interviews: Simon Hilton, 2016-2018

105 Audio interview: Elliot Mintz 15 October 1971; Kenji Mizuhara, Apple Tokyo,
2 September 1971; Jonathan Cott interview
Book: Barry Miles, *John Lennon In His Own Words*, 1995

Print interviews: Alan Smith, *New Musical Express*, 7 August 1971; *Hit Parader*,
February 1972; Mike Ledgerwood and Roy Shipston, *Disc and Music Echo*,
31 July 1971; *Record Mirror*, 21 August 1971; Steve Peacock, *Sounds*, 17 July 1971
TV interview: Pål Bang-Hansen, NRK, 15 May 1971

107 Print interview: Alan Smith, *Hit Parader* magazine, February 1972

109 Film interview: Courtesy of Vikram Jayanti and Anthony Wall, excerpted from
BBC *Arena*: 'The Agony and the Ecstacy of Phil Spector'
Print interviews: Mick Brown, *The Telegraph*, 4 February 2003. Courtesy
Mick Brown/Telegraph Media Group Limited
Video interview: Mark R. Elsis, 2007

113 Audio interviews: Andy Peebles, BBC Radio, 6 December 1980; Chris Carter,
'A Conversation With George Harrison', Capitol Records, 2001; Yoko Ono,
Simon Hilton, 2017
Books: *Phil Spector Wall of Pain*, Dave Thompson, Sanctuary, 2003;
Richard Williams – *Phil Spector – Out Of His Head*, Sphere, 1975
Film interview: Michael Epstein, LennoNYC, American Masters, 2010
Print interviews: *New Musical Express*, October 1971; *Record Mirror*,
14 August 1971; *Sounds*, July 1971
TV interview: Bob Harris, *Old Grey Whistle Test*, BBCTV, 17 March 1975

114 Audio interviews: Paul Drew, RKO Radio, April 1975; Yoko Ono, Simon Hilton, 2017
Book: John Lennon quoted in *The Beatles* by Hunter Davies, 1967
Film interviews: *Beatles Anthology*, Apple Corps, 1967; *Beatles Anthology*,
Apple Corps, 1990s
Print interviews: *Crawdaddy*, 1971, *Disc and Music Echo*, July 1971, Jann Wenner,
Rolling Stone, 8 December 1970; *Southern Evening Echo*, 29 July 1971
TV interview: *Good Morning America*, ABC TV, 1981; John Fuselgang, VH1, 1997

120 Audio interviews: Simon Hilton, 2016–2018

126–7 Lyrics: 'Jealous Guy'. Written by John Lennon © 1971 Lenono Music

128 Audio interviews: Hilary Henson, *Woman's Hour*, BBC Radio, 28 May 1971;
David Scheff, 10–28 September 1980; Yoko Ono, Simon Hilton, 2017
Essays: Yoko Ono – *John Lennon Anthology*, 1998; John Lennon – 'Lennon
onImagine', *Crawdaddy*, 5 December 1971
Interview: Yoko Ono with Ray Coleman

130 Audio interview: David Scheff, 10–28 September 1980

132 Audio interview: Simon Hilton, 2016
Book: Kevin Howlett and Mark Lewisohn, *In My Life – John Lennon
Remembered*, 1990
Print interviews: Andrew Tyler for *Disc and Music Echo*, 4 December 1971;
Expreso Imaginario magazine, 1977; *Melody Maker*, 11 Dec. 1971;
Stephen P. Wheeler for *Music Connection*, August 1991
TV interview: Merrell Fankhauser, 'California Music', 1991

134 Audio interview: Simon Hilton, 2016

136 Audio interview (Jim Keltner): Simon Hilton, 2016
Audio interview (John Barham): Simon Hilton, 2016

137 Audio interview (Rod Lynton): Simon Hilton, 2016
Audio interview (Ted Turner): Simon Hilton, 2016

140 Audio interview (Joey Molland): Simon Hilton, 2016
Audio interview (Mike Pinder): Simon Hilton, 2016

141 Print interview (Jim Gordon): Scott K. Fish, *Modern Drummer*, January 1983.
Copyright permission of Modern Drummer Publications, January 1983 issue.
Essay (John Tout): Rod Lynton, 2016
Audio interview (Andy Davis): Simon Hilton, 2016

142 Lyrics: 'Imagine'. By John Lennon & Yoko Ono, 1971

142–3 Lyrics for 'Crippled Inside', 'Jealous Guy', 'It's So Hard', 'I Don't Wanna
Be A Soldier Mama I Don't Wanna Die', 'How?' by John Lennon,
1971 with annotations in John's handwriting; lyrics for 'Oh Yoko!'
by John Lennon, 1971 with annotations in Yoko's handwriting

144 Audio interview: Yoko Ono with Simon Hilton, 2018
Radio interviews: Ken Doyle, KCSN-FM 88.5 Northridge CA, December 1975,
Laura Gross, KCSN-FM 88.5 Northridge CA, 29 November 1975, both courtesy
of KCSN\Los Angeles, and Lily Evans, Gary Malcolm Evans and Julie Rossow

146 Essay (Phil McDonald): Phil McDonald, 2016

146–7 Audio interview (Eddie Klein): Simon Hilton, 2018

147 Audio interview (Eddie Offord): Simon Hilton, 2018
Audio interview (Ken Scott): Simon Hilton, 2018

148–9 Lyrics: 'It's So Hard'. Written by John Lennon © 1971 Lenono Music

151 Audio interview: Dick Gregory, *Jet* magazine, 23 October 1972; David Scheff,
10–28 September 1980

Essay: John Lennon, 'Lennon on *Imagine*', *Crawdaddy*, 5 December 1971

152–3   Aunt Mimi Smith, 1950s

154–5   Letter to Craig McGregor, John Lennon, 14 September 1971

156   Audio interviews: Yoko Ono, Shelly Yakus and Jack Douglas, Simon Hilton, 2016–2018

158   Audio interview: Simon Hilton, 2016

159   Audio interview (Jack Douglas): Simon Hilton, 2016
   Audio interview (Arlene Reckson): Simon Hilton, 2016

160   Audio cassette: John Lennon recording with King Curtis, Record Plant, 5 July 1971
   Audio interview: *Great Moments For Young Americans* Interview disc, September 1965; Simon Hilton, 2016
   Print interview: Mike Hennessey, 'The Last Interview', 1971; courtesy Gabriele Hennessey
   All King Curtis' words reproduced with permission of Gera Peoples

162   Interview (Torrie Zito): Torrie Zito with Les Tomkins, 1974, reproduced in *Jazz Professional*. Courtesy of National Jazz Archives, and Lisa Zito and Helen Merrill Zito
   Audio interviews (Torrie Zito): Allan Steckler and Aaron Rosand by Simon Hilton, 2016
   Print interview (Torrie Zito): *Disc and Music Echo*, July 1971
   Audio interview (Flux Fiddlers): Simon Hilton, 2016
   Listing (Flux Fiddlers): Steve Danenberg, *American Federation Of Musicians Local* 802, 2017
   Print interview (Flux Fiddlers): Steve Peacock, *Sounds*, 31 July 1971

164–5   Lyrics: 'I Don't Wanna Be Soldier Mama I Don't Wanna Die'. Written by John Lennon © 1971 Lenono Music, lyrics in John's handwriting

166   Audio interviews: Barry Miles, *Zapple*, 23 September 1969; Hilary Henson, BBC *Woman's Hour*, 28 May 1971; Jerry Levitan, Toronto, Canada, 26 May 1969; David Sheff, 10–28 September 1980; Dave Sholin, RKO, 8 December 1980
   Essay: John Lennon – 'Lennon on *Imagine*', *Crawdaddy*, 5 December 1971
   Press conferences: Hotel Okura, Tokyo, 4 October 1977; Toronto, Canada, 7 February 1969
   Print interviews: David Skan, *Record Mirror* 11 October, 1969; Steve Peacock, *Sounds*, 31 July 1971
   Speech: Yoko Ono, Oxford University, October 2002
   TV interview: *David Frost Show*, Westinghouse (CBS), 14 June 1969

169   TV interview: Karl-Heinz Wocker, *Prisma der Welt*, WDR, 8 December 1969

170   Audio interview: Simon Hilton, 2016
   Archival *Playboy* magazine material. Copyright © 1971 by *Playboy*. Used with permission. All rights reserved. With additional thanks to Jody Klein.
   Print interviews: *Crawdaddy*, November 1973; Lisa Robinson, *Hit Parader*, December 1975
   TV interview: *Weekend World*, LWT, 6 April 1973

174   Books: Keith Badman – *The Beatles: Off The Record 2 – The Dream is Over*, Omnibus Press, 2001; Peter Doggett – *You Never Give Me Your Money: The Battle for the Soul of the Beatles*, Harper, 2010
   Print interview: Tony Lofaro, *The Citizen*, 3 February 2001; material republished with the express permission of: *Ottawa Citizen*, a division of Postmedia Network Inc.
   Radio interviews: Teddy Smith and Bob O'Brien, WPAT, November 2012; *Teddy Smith Show*, WPAT, 16 March 2012

176   Postcard to *Rolling Stone* in John's handwriting, 4 August 1971

177   Audio interviews: Simon Hilton, 2017–2018

178   Essay: Yoko Ono, 2018

182–3   Lyrics: 'Gimme Some Truth'. Written by John Lennon © 1971 Lenono Music

184   Audio interviews: David Sheff, 10–28 September 1980; Hilary Henson, *Woman's Hour*, BBC Radio, 28 May 1971; Kenji Mizuhara, Apple Tokyo, 2 September 1971
   Essays: John Lennon – 'Lennon on *Imagine*', *Crawdaddy*, 5 December 1971; Yoko Ono – 'The Word of a Fabricator', 1962; Yoko Ono, Facebook and Twitter Q&As, imaginepeace.com, 2009–2016
   Interview: Ray Coleman
   Print interview: Steve Peacock, *Sounds*, 31 July 1971; William Jobes, *Washington Star News*, 6 February 1975
   TV interviews: Mike Douglas Show, CBS TV, 31 January – 7 February 1972; Peter Lewis, 'Release', BBC2, 6 June 1968

186   Audio interviews: Kenji Mizuhara, Apple Tokyo, 2 September 1971; Hilary Henson, *Woman's Hour*, BBC Radio, 28 May 1971

190   Audio interview: Elliot Mintz, 1971

193   Audio interview: Simon Hilton, 2018

197   Lyrics from *Imagine* album:
     'Imagine' written by John Lennon & Yoko Ono, 1971 © Lenono Music; 'Oh My Love' written by John Lennon & Yoko Ono, 1971 © Lenono Music / Ono Music; 'Crippled Inside', 'Jealous Guy', 'It's So Hard', 'I Don't Wanna Be A Soldier Mama I Don't Wanna Die', 'Gimme Some Truth', 'How Do You Sleep?', 'How?', 'Oh Yoko!' written by John Lennon, 1971 © Lenono Music

199   *Fluxus Manifesto*, George Maciunas, 1963
   Audio interviews: Jonas Mekas, Simon Hilton, 2017; Yoko Ono, Simon Hilton, 2017
   Essays: Jon Hendricks – 'Fluxus: To George With Love', 2008; Yoko Ono – 'Summer of 1961', 2008

201   Postcard: John Lennon to *Melody Maker*, July 1971
   Postcard: John Lennon to Julian Lennon, 1978

202–3   Lyrics: 'Oh My Love'. Written by John Lennon & Yoko Ono, © 1971 Lenono Music/Ono Music

204   Audio interview: Hilary Henson, *Woman's Hour*, BBC Radio, 28 May 1971
   Film interview: Ursula Macfarlane, 'The Real Yoko Ono', Soul Purpose Productions, 7 January 2001
   Essays: John Lennon – 'Lennon on *Imagine*', *Crawdaddy*, 5 December 1971; John Lennon – 'Lennon on *Imagine*', *Crawdaddy*, 5 December 1971 (draft notes)
   Print interviews: Richard Williams, *Melody Maker*, December 1969; Yoko Ono, 'The Playlist Special', *Rolling Stone* November 2010
   TV Interview: *Mike Douglas Show*, CBS TV, 31 January – 7 February 1972

206–8   Book: Keith Badman – *The Beatles: Off The Record 2 – The Dream is Over*, Omnibus Press, 2001
   Essays: Yoko Ono – '*FLY* – A Double Album', *Crawdaddy*, 1971; Yoko Ono – 'Onobox', box set booklet, 1997
   Print interviews: Barry Dillon, *Southern Evening Echo*, 25 July 1971; Steve Peacock, *Sounds*, 7 August, 1971

210   Lyrics from *FLY* album by Yoko Ono, 1971 © Ono Music

212–3   Lyrics: 'How Do You Sleep'. Written by John Lennon © 1971 Lenono Music

214   Audio interviews: Andy Peebles, BBC Radio One, 6 December 1980; David Sheff, 10–28 September 1980; Howard Smith, 9 September 1971; Yoko Ono with Simon Hilton, 2018
   Essays: John Lennon – 'Lennon on *Imagine*', *Crawdaddy*, 5 December 1971; John Lennon – 'Lennon on *Imagine*', *Crawdaddy*, 5 December 1971 (draft notes)
   Print interview: William Jobes, *Washington Star News*, 6 February 1975
   TV interviews: Bob Harris, *Old Grey Whistle Test*, 17 March 1975; *Mike Douglas Show*, CBS TV, 31 January – 7 February 1972

216   Press conference: Everson Museum of Art, 8 October 1971

218–9   Letter to Paul and Linda McCartney, John Lennon, 1971

223   Audio interview, Yoko Ono, 1973
   Print interview: Steve Peacock, *Sounds*, 7 August, 1971

224   TV interviews: *The Mike Douglas Show*, 20 January 1972; *The Dick Cavett Show*, 8 September 1971
   Essays: Yoko Ono, Facebook and Twitter Q&As, imaginepeace.com, 2009–2016

226   Audio interview: Simon Hilton, 2018

228   Print interview: Steve Peacock, Sounds, 7 August, 1971

229   Essay: Yoko Ono – 'Addendum '88', 1988
   TV interview: *Mike Douglas Show*, CBS TV, 31 January – 7 February 1972

232   Essay: Yoko Ono – 'Addendum '88', 1988

233   Interview: 'Don't Count The Waves', 1989
   Print interview: Michele Robecchi, *Contemporary*, September 2006

236   Print interviews: Greg Schaber, *Cincinnati* magazine – originally published in the October 2001 issue of *Cincinnati* magazine, reprinted by permission; Margaret A McGurk, *The Cincinnati Enquirer*, 4 December 2005; Steven Rosen, *Indiewire*, 11 November 2015; Steven Rosen, *Soapbox Cincinnati*, 14 September 2010

238   Audio interview: Simon Hilton, 2017
   Press conference: Sacher Hotel, Vienna, 31 March 1969
   TV interview: *The Dick Cavett Show*, 8 September 1971

239   Filming *Imagine*: 'Mrs Lennon'
   Audio interviews: Simon Hilton, 2017; David Sheff, 10–28 September 1980

240   Audio interview: Simon Hilton, 2018

244   TV Show: *The David Frost Show*: 14 June 1969
   TV Interview: *The Dick Cavett Show*, 8 September 1971

245   Essay: Yoko Ono – 'Give Peace A Chance', June 2006
   TV interview: *The Dick Cavett Show*, 8 September 1971

acknowledgments

246 Audio interview: Simon Hilton, 2017
248 Audio interview: Simon Hilton, 2018
252 Audio interview: Simon Hilton, 2017
    Essay: Yoko Ono, 'FLY – A Double Album', *Crawdaddy*, 1971
253 Essay: Yoko Ono – *Whisper Piece* (2), *Grapefruit*, 1966
    Interview: Yoko Ono with Hans Ulrich Obrist and Gustav Metzger, June 2009
    Lecture: Yoko Ono to Cranbook Art Academy students, 27 September 1997
254 Essay: Sir Michael Parkinson, 2016
    TV interview: *The Parkinson Show*, BBC TV, 17 July 1971
255 Audio interview: Simon Hilton, 2016
256 Audio interview: Simon Hilton, 2017
    Essays: Yoko Ono, Christmas card, 25 December 2000; Yoko Ono, Facebook
        and Twitter Q&As, imaginepeace.com, 2009–2016
    Press conference: Walker Art Center, 9 March 2001
257 Audio interview: Simon Hilton, 2017
    Audio: *Imagine* film outtake, 21 July 1971
262 Essays: Yoko Ono, 'FLY – A Double Album', *Crawdaddy*, 1971; Yoko Ono,
        'Onobox', 1997
263 Audio interview: Simon Hilton, 2017
    Essays: Yoko Ono, Facebook and Twitter Q&As, imaginepeace.com, 2009–2016
    Lyrics: Yoko Ono, 'Have You Seen A Horizon Lately', © Ono Music, 1972
266 Audio interviews: Barbara Graustark, *Newsweek*, 29 September 1980;
        David Sheff, 10–28 September 1980
267 TV interview: *The Mike Douglas Show*, CBS TV, 31 January – 7 February 1972
268 Audio interview: Simon Hilton, 2016
    Audio recording: Lenono Film Archive, 10 July 1971
272 Interview: Andrew Solt, 'Imagine: John Lennon', 1984
    Essays: Yoko Ono, Facebook and Twitter Q&As, imaginepeace.com, 2009–2016
    TV interview: *The Dick Cavett Show*, 8 September 1971
273 Audio interview: Simon Hilton, 2017
    Essays: Yoko Ono – 'Addendum '88', 1988; Yoko Ono, Facebook and Twitter
    Q&As, imaginepeace.com, 2009–2016
    Lyrics: Yoko Ono, 'You're The One', © Ono Music, 1982
274–5 Lyrics: 'How?'. Written by John Lennon © 1971 Lenono Music
276 Audio interviews: David Sheff, 10–28 September 1980; Hilary Henson,
        Woman's Hour, BBC Radio, 28 May 1971; Kenji Mizuhara, Apple Tokyo,
        2 September 1971
    Essays: John Lennon – 'Lennon on *Imagine*', *Crawdaddy*, 5 December 1971;
        John Lennon – 'Lennon on *Imagine*', *Crawdaddy*, 5 December 1971 (draft
        notes); Yoko Ono, Facebook and Twitter Q&As, imaginepeace.com, 2009–2016
    Print interviews: Daniel Rothbart, *Berliner Kunst* magazine, 2002; Jonathan Cott,
        Rolling Stone, 5 December 1980; print interview: Michael Watts, *Melody
        Maker*, 2 October 1971; TV interview: Pål Bang-Hansen, NRK, 15 May 1971
285 Essay: Yoko Ono – THIS IS NOT HERE dedication, 9 October 1971
    Interview: Ray Connolly, 9 October 1971
    Press conferences: Everson Museum of Art, Syracuse, 8 Oct, 1971; Syracuse,
        5 October 1971
286 Audio interview: Simon Hilton, 2018
290–1 Audio interview: Simon Hilton, 2018
296–7 Written by John Lennon © 1971 Lenono Music, annotations in Yoko's handwriting
298 Audio interview: Kenji Mizuhara, Apple Tokyo, 2 September 1971
    Essay: John Lennon – 'Lennon on *Imagine*', *Crawdaddy*, 5 December 1971
    Film interview: '24 Hours John & Yoko', BBCTV, 2 December 1969
    Interview: Ray Coleman
    'Man Of The Decade', ATV Desmond Morris, 2 December 1969
    Press conferences: Everson Museum of Art, Syracuse NY, 8 October 1971;
        Syracuse NY, 5 October 1971
    Print interviews: Barry Dillon, *Southern Evening Echo*, 25 July 1971;
        Jann Wenner, *Rolling Stone*, 8 December 1970; *New Musical Express*,
        7 October 1972
    TV interview: Tom Bradbury, ITV News, 18 February 2016
304 Essay: Yoko Ono, 1985
307 Essays: Yoko Ono, 2008–2011
308–9 Debbie Grunbaum, WhyHunger, 2018
310 Dedication: Yoko Ono, Engraved on IMAGINE PEACE TOWER, 9 October 2007
    Information from website: imaginepeacetower.com
    Speech: Yoko Ono, IMAGINE PEACE TOWER, Viðey Island, Reykjavík, Iceland,
        9 October 2007

A dream you dream alone is only a dream;
A dream you dream together is reality.
y.o.

Producer and Creative Direction: Yoko Ono Lennon

Editor: Simon Hilton

Publishing Coordinator: Tristan de Lancey

Thames & Hudson: Jane Laing, Phoebe Lindsley and Paul Hammond

Lenono Photo Archive: Karla Merrifield and Sari Henry

Lenono Art Archive: Connor Monahan, Marcia Bassett, Michael Sirianni and Nick Lalla

Lenono Audio Archive: Rob Stevens

Special thanks to Paul Hicks, Matthew Cocker and Cary Anning at Abbey Road Studios

Lenono Film Archive: Simon Hilton

Studio One: Helen Barden, Sibyl Bender and Bob Deeb

Legal: Jonas Herbsman

Design: Daniel Streat at Visual Fields

Final retouching and post-production work: Sinisa Savic

Map and plans: Planet Illustration, Phoebe Lindsley and Olivia McShane

Initial photo restoration, panoramas and Photoshop work: Simon Hilton,
Sam Gannon and Beth Walsh

Additional research: Sam Gannon, Beth Walsh, Pamela Esterson and Olivia McShane

Imagine film and footage remastering team:
Director/Producer: Yoko Ono
Restoration Editor, Digital Remaster, Eyematch and Conform: Simon Hilton.
Mastergrade: Simona Cristea, Nic Knowland, Mireille Antoine and Joce Capper
at Rushes London. Digital Restoration: Venancio David, Brett Bono, Miguel Algora,
Kate Warburton, Madeleine Shenai, Gary and Georgina Brown at Munky. Transfers:
Dave Northrop, Bruce W Goldstein, Scott Delaney, Jack Serrani, Stephen Walsh,
Rob DeSaro, Beth Simon, Elle Crowley and André Macaluso at Deluxe Northvale.
Production: Simon Hilton, James Chads, Hannah Arcaro, Thom Hill, Paulina
Anderson, Adam Farrington, Benjamin Baker, Lee Merricks, Sam Gannon,
Beth Walsh, Olivia McShane and Alex Miles

Special thanks:
Robert S. Bader, Aaron Bremner, Catherine Camiolo, Scott Cardinal, Murray Chalmers,
Jonathan Clyde, Alexander Crowe, Steven Danenberg, Martin Darvill, Paul Davie,
Robert Dimery, Pamela Esterson, David and Delphine Frearson, Fiona Gillott, Bob
and Elizabeth Gruen, Peter Guralnick, Olivia Harrison, Guy Hayden, Mike Heatley,
Jon Hendricks, Jonas Herbsman, Amelie Hilton, Anabelle Hilton, Diana Hilton,
Amanda Keeley, Red Kelly, Jody Klein, Svanhildur Konráðsdóttir, Nick Kostas, Dorcas
Lynn, Sebastian Mekas, Jeff and Shari Michels, Elliot Mintz, Barbara Moore, Anna
Mostyn-Williams, Tom Olcott, Mark Pattenden, Ian Pickavance, Lucienne Powell, Peter
and Jenny Powell, Allan Rouse, Teresa Rudge, Roy Simonds, Gabryel Smith, Lester
Smith, Noreen Springstead, Lisa Troland, Phil Turner, Anthony Wall and Gigi White

index

Following page: John Lennon & Yoko
Ono – *War Is Over! If You Want It
Love and Peace from John & Yoko*,
1969/1971; offset lithograph,
76 × 50.8 cm.

Front and back cover: photos by
Yoko Ono © Yoko Ono Lennon.